Organizational Ethics and the Good Life

THE RUFFIN SERIES IN BUSINESS ETHICS
R. Edward Freeman, *Editor*

THOMAS J. DONALDSON
The Ethics of International Business

JAMES W. KUHN AND DONALD W. SHRIVER, JR.
Beyond Success: Corporations and Their Critics in the 1990s

R. EDWARD FREEMAN, EDITOR
Business Ethics: The State of the Art

NORMAN E. BOWIE AND R. EDWARD FREEMAN, EDITORS
Ethics and Agency Theory: An Introduction

ROBERT C. SOLOMON
Ethics and Excellence: Cooperation and Integrity in Business

DANIEL R. GILBERT JR.
*The Twilight of Corporate Strategy:
A Comparative Ethical Critique*

THOMAS J. DONALDSON AND R. EDWARD FREEMAN, EDITORS
Business as a Humanity

ALLEN KAUFMAN, LAWRENCE ZACHARIAS, MARVIN KARSON
*Managers Vs. Owners
The Struggle for Corporate Control in American Democracy*

WILLIAM C. FREDERICK
Values, Nature, and Culture in the American Corporation

EDWIN HARTMAN
Organizational Ethics and the Good Life

FORTHCOMING TITLES TO BE ANNOUNCED

Organizational Ethics and the Good Life

EDWIN HARTMAN

New York   Oxford
OXFORD UNIVERSITY PRESS
1996

Oxford University Press

Oxford   New York
Athens   Auckland   Bangkok   Bombay
Calcutta   Cape Town   Dar es Salaam   Delhi
Florence   Hong Kong   Istanbul   Karachi
Kuala Lumpur   Madras   Madrid   Melbourne
Mexico City   Nairobi   Paris   Singapore
Taipei   Tokyo   Toronto

and associated companies in
Berlin   Ibadan

Copyright © 1996 by Oxford University Press, Inc.

Published by Oxford University Press, Inc.,
198 Madison Avenue New York, New York 10016

Oxford is a registered trademark of Oxford University Press

Library of Congress Cataloging-in-Publication Data
Hartman, Edwin, 1941–
Organizational ethics and the good life / Edwin Hartman.
p.   cm. — (Ruffin series in business ethics)
Includes bibliographical references and index.
ISBN 0-19-509678-9
1. Business ethics.   2. Corporate culture.   3. Ethics.   I. Title.
II. Series.
HF5387.H374   1996
302.3'5—dc20   95-5495

987654321

Printed in the United States of America
on acid-free paper

FOR M. S. H.

Acknowledgments

Three events contributed to this book. The first was the appearance of Bob Solomon's *Ethics and Excellence*, which showed that Aristotle had even more to say about issues of interest to me than I had realized, although I had long thought of myself as an Aristotelian. The second was a seminar taught by Jim Livingston, a history professor at Rutgers, who brought together under the auspices of the Center for the Critical Analysis of Contemporary Culture a truly interdisciplinary group of colleagues and preached the gospel of pragmatism to us. The third was the long-awaited arrival of John Rawls's *Political Liberalism*, which Robert Baum suggested I read and my colleague Doug Husak helped me understand. Later, Doug read this entire manuscript and made a number of valuable observations.

As always, Ed Freeman was a source of insight and encouragement, like Socrates and yet not: a successful midwife of others' ideas, but by no means barren himself.

Pat Werhane criticized some of my central ideas in a civil but useful way and recruited Bob Solomon to do the same. They will probably think that I should have taken their strictures even more seriously than I have, and they may be right.

I have profited from the advice and the example of Michael Rohr, one of a vanishing breed of polymaths who can with equal fluency critically analyze Aristotle's *Metaphysics* Z.6 and Federal Reserve policy under Greenspan.

Candace Hetzner and Wayne Eastman, the most civilized of neighbors down the hall, were acute and good-natured sounding boards, although we probably agreed too often. Barbara Stern and Carter Daniel did what they could to make my prose style more serviceable. I learned a great deal from a conversation with Alan Ryan and a letter from David Braybrooke.

Some thoughts that appear here were first presented to faculty and graduate students at the Katz Graduate School of Business at the University of Pittsburgh and to members of the University College Philosophy Club at Rutgers-New Brunswick, the Applied Ethics Group at Rutgers-Newark and the New Jersey Institute of Technology, and the

Society for Business Ethics. Thanks to the participants for helpful comments.

In addition to those already mentioned, I learned from and thank Robbin Derry, Tom Donaldson, Tom Dunfee, Bob Frank, George Gordon, Elizabeth Hodge, Eric Katz, Don McCabe, and Nick Sturgeon.

Parts of this essay appeared as articles in *Business Ethics Quarterly* and *Business and Professional Ethics Journal.* I thank the editors for their generosity with the copyrights.

A house other than Oxford University Press decided that an earlier version of this essay did not serve its pedagogical purposes, but in doing so it provided me with the helpful and encouraging comments of Robert Baum, Tony Buono, Jane Ives, David Palmer, and one additional and still anonymous reviewer. Joanne Ciulla, Oxford's reviewer, provided a useful critique of a later draft.

At Oxford University Press, Herb Addison, Marya Ripperger, Paul Schlotthauer, Ellen Fuchs, and Jeri Famighetti were highly professional and, no less important, pleasant to work with. I am in their debt, and so is everyone who reads this book.

Rutgers University gave me a leave to get this work started and never afterward demanded to know why it was taking so long.

As always, Mary S. Hartman and Sam Hartman were supportive even as they were demonstrating how much more there is to the good life than writing a book about it.

Contents

FOREWORD BY R. EDWARD FREEMAN, XI

INTRODUCTION, 3

1. What Morality is About, 11

    Reasons for being moral, 11
    The interests of others as reason for action, 13
    Morality and one's best interests: a start, 16
    Relativism, 18
    Interpretation and the limits of morality, 20
    The Ik, 23
    Prospects, 25

2. Utilitarianism and its Difficulties, 34

    Versions of happiness, 35
    Rights and the good life, 39
    Justice and rule utilitarianism, 44
    Moral principles and administrative rules, 47
    Utility and discrimination, 49
    Intimate matters, 51
    The attractions of justice, 55
    Interpreting alien communities, 57
    Prospects, 60

3. Morality and Communities: Collective Action, 68

    Moral communities and social contracts, 69
    The commons problem, 74
    The commons and being better off, 78
    Character and motivation, 80
    Toward the good community, 83
    Prospects, 85

4. Business, Ethics, and Business Ethics, 90

    Against business ethics, 91

The purpose of the organization, 95
Contractarian views and applied ethics, 97
Contexts and consequences, 98
Criticizing communities: relativism again, 100
The principles of morality, 101
Against theoretical ethics, 103
Tacit ideology, 105
Principles for good organizations: A Rawlsian proposal, 107
Some modest remarks on justice and rights, 110
Prospects, 111

5. Morality and Autonomy, 121

Persons, 122
Pleasure and action: the utilitarian self, 125
Autonomy, 128
Choosing one's desires, 134
Emotion, 135
Prospects, 137

6. Problems of Corporate Culture, 143

The rational as social, 144
Two experiments, 146
The nature of culture, 149
Culture as a way of managing, 151
Culture and a theory of motivation, 154
Japanese culture, 155
The perils of culture, 157
Culture and the commons, 157
Culture, roles, self, 160
Prospects, 161

7. The Good Community and the Good Organization, 166

Exit, loyalty, and voice, 169
Exit, 170
Loyalty, 171
Voice, 174
Dealing with many voices, 177
The good life and the good community, 182

BIBLIOGRAPHY, 189

INDEX, 197

Foreword

Business ethics has undergone some major changes in the last few years. No longer do ethicists and business people always talk at cross purposes. The discourse of business and the discourse of ethics are being connected in important ways. Edwin Hartman's book will be a milestone in the development of business ethics, ethics, and the business disciplines, for one cannot separate out its contribution to all three areas.

First, Hartman shows how business ethics can adopt a rather thoroughgoing pragmatism and thereby speak to the issues that are on executives' minds: What is the good life and how do corporations play a role in leading the good life? Hartman's answer is that organizations are communities and that the central question of business ethics must be: What are the right kinds of communities?

Second, he demonstrates why the most important controversies in ethics are being played out in medical schools, business schools and places other than departments of philosophy. Hartman's knowledge of the business world reflects his experiences as a businessperson as well as a scholar. This combination allows him to take tedious philosophical argument and breathe life into it. A similar process is taking place in professional schools around the world.

Finally, Hartman has much to say to executives. While his mode of writing is often philosophical, the consequences of what he has to say are important for those executives trying to build their organizations on a foundation of ethics and values. With Hartman's book we can picture a theory of organizations and theories of other business disciplines that make full use of his pragmatism.

Organizational Ethics and the Good Life gives us a glimpse of what we so badly need: a vision of society and political life that takes the reality of modern organizations into account. In Hartman's view, capitalism and other modes of organizing are not epiphenomena growing out of individualism; rather, they are constitutive of modern political life and they have ethical concepts and ideas built into them rather than imposed on them from the outside.

The purpose of the Ruffin Series on Business Ethics is to publish the best thinking about the role of ethics in business. In a world in which there are daily reports of questionable business practices, from financial scandals to environmental disasters, we need to step back from the fray and understand the large issues of how business and ethics are and ought to be connected. The books in this series are aimed at three audiences: management scholars, ethicists, and business executives. There is a growing consensus among these groups that business and ethics must be integrated as a vital part of the teaching and practice of management.

Ed Hartman has given us a rare treat, one that we can savor for some time. It is thus a privilege to publish this book in the Ruffin Series.

R. EDWARD FREEMAN

Organizational Ethics and the Good Life

Introduction

The field of business ethics divides roughly into those who are at home in business—some in organization theory or organizational behavior, some in economics—and those who are philosophers first of all. Apart from the past or current commitment to religion found among many practitioners on both sides, their orientation is significantly different. I grew up within the second group and am a convert to the first, but, like an ex-Catholic Baptist who no longer worries about transubstantiation but still prefers Gregorian chants to gospel hymns, I am incompletely made over.

I hope this essay will engage both groups, not least organization theorists. I do say some things that will be familiar to one group but perhaps not to the other. To some readers the text will seem at times to move from the obvious to the obscure. I trust, however, that neither side will find any of it impossible to follow and that both sides will find something new to them even in what I have to say about their part of the field. There is perhaps more here than will interest some management scholars about the nature and status of business ethics as a discipline. These scholars will at least be gratified to see that I regard an understanding of business as a necessary condition of competent work in business ethics.

I am opposed to certain individualist views and their ethical implications; I do not regard the Hobbesian approach as definitive; I am opposed to a certain common type of utilitarianism. But I am going to begin with some individualistic and Hobbesian and utilitarian assumptions, many of which have found favor among organization theorists as well as among economists, and shall pull out their implications to show that they cannot stand without significant revision.

Much of what I have to say appears to ignore, or to make arguable assumptions about, current technical issues in moral philosophy; I cannot discuss everything that is worth discussing. I do not think the current inconclusive state of some technical arguments prevents my making any sound claims about the nature of ethics. Consider, for example, the issue of the similarity of science and ethics. This is a locus of intense controversy among today's ethical theorists, who argue not only about the objectivity of ethics but about the subjectivity of science. Even if I could settle that argument, as I surely cannot, this essay would not be the place to do it. What I can do is to indicate that ethics and science are more alike than some readers are likely to think and that one should abjure facile despair about reaching rational agreement in ethics and should avoid talking loosely about its subjectivity. The point is emphatically not to show that science, because it falls short of being straightforwardly objective in all the ways one might expect, is in grave epistemological difficulty. On the contrary, that it is not should reassure those who have noted some problems about objectivity in moral theory. Something can then be made of that. The significant question is, How do we make moral progress in the meantime, in the midst of our uncertainty about these matters?

Philosophically I am a pragmatist, neither a skeptic nor a Platonist, on most subjects. So, for example, I do not believe that we ought to try to discover any self-evidently true foundational principles on which all scientific truth rests or that describe how it can be discovered. In this I take natural science to be similar to ethics, although I acknowledge many differences between them. It is characteristic of pragmatists to say not that we are approaching truth but that there is no truth worth discussing beyond the best available theory—best available, that is, for some purpose. A pragmatist might hold that the closest we can get to truth is not to state the characteristics of the best possible theory but to create the best possible environment for doing science, or the best possible for people to live together. A pragmatist can believe that theoretical progress is possible in both natural science and moral philosophy; that does not imply that there is something to which progress is bringing us ever closer and beyond which no progress is possible, still less that scientists and moral philosophers know in advance where progress will take them. They can know after the fact that progress has been made, but sometimes it is progress according to criteria that are themselves new and improved and that will not likely stand them in good stead forever.

A pragmatist will be skeptical of the claim that there is some true but as yet unknown theory that brings together our now relatively inchoate beliefs about utility and justice and rights; the important point is that there is movement in the right direction, or rather in some right directions. A relativist will say that there is no such theory but only a series of poorly understood and worse enforced agreements. A constructivist will offer a theory of how rational people will arrange things in a certain sort of community. Whether or not that is all there is, I do not think there can be an ethical theory that does anything like the most we might ever want an ethical theory to do. I am a pragmatic sort of pragmatist, however; rather than claim, perhaps self-defeatingly, that there is no such theory, I prefer to say that for the moment we might best spend our time gathering information about where certain ethical principles do not work—that in itself is quite valuable—and some insights about how to make moral progress possible. Whether moral philosophers, or scientists for that matter, are converging on the truth is immaterial to me. I do not care whether in describing a good kind of environment I am describing the best means to achieving moral (or scientific) truth or saying as much as could ever be said on the subject of moral (or scientific) truth. The important thing is to identify and describe the good environment.

My approach is hospitable to pluralism but not to any interesting form of relativism. We have good reason to explore a variety of conceptions of the good life and their implications for morality, but we do so within limits. There are certain kinds of life that we cannot imagine any sane person desiring, and certain views of what one ought to do that we can have no reason for calling moral. Our ability to communicate with each other, to converse and argue about moral issues or anything else for that matter, requires that we largely agree on some essential matters.

In a previous essay (Hartman, 1988) I offered the notion of theoretical satisficing, a parallel to Simon's device for explaining the behavior of managers, who, contrary to the usual sort of standard myth, do not in fact maximize stockholders' wealth or anything else. As Winter (1964, 1971, 1975) pointed out, in passages that I think apply to my subsequent view better than to Simon's previous one, it could hardly be otherwise. There comes a point at which just finding out whether additional information is worth the additional cost may itself turn out to cost more than the value of the information; to try to determine whether it is entails a further cost, which . . . and so on to infinity. All this applies to moral questions. It applies in practice quite clearly: we simply cannot solve the problems about the extent to which (for example) rights trump utility considerations by the time we have to make actual organizational decisions. But it applies in theory as well: we simply cannot solve those problems at all.

It was Aristotle who first and most famously argued that politics is the culmination of ethics. I have come around to a similar point of view: I would broaden the claim and say that ethics is finally about communities, whether they be political entities or organizations. I mean by this to suggest that ethical theorists should concentrate first on the nature of the good community, rather than begin by trying to combine utility and justice and rights to make a theory that can guide action. Those theories simply do not combine; even if they did, their use would complicate and otherwise subvert moral attitudes and institutions. In the end, the best we can do is to build communities that encourage people—it would not do to force them, even if it were possible—to adopt appropriate preferences, institutions, and contracts and to be loyal to them, although critically rather than slavishly. I shall argue for the inference that there isn't much point, even for philosophers, in studying just pure ethics: we should concern ourselves with business ethics and politics and similar activities.

It is worth noting how this view reconciles opponents. Gilbert Harman, an ethical relativist, and John Rawls, a constructivist but no relativist, both argue that ethical questions are finally political ones. Harman claims that there is no ethics, only politics; Rawls claims that justice is a political conception rather than a metaphysical one. Even some ethical realists, whose view of ethical theory is the opposite of relativism, sound like constructivists when they embrace a dialectical device like the Rawlsian one of reflective equilibrium as the best way of getting as close to the truth as possible. These are matters for which I need to argue, rather than assumptions with which to begin. I begin instead with some views that most people on various sides of the major controversies should be able to accept.

Chapter 1 takes the view that it is an essential purpose of ethics to make people better off. The argument for that view incorporates a move that I shall make in several versions as we go along: if an institution has standards that do not have anything to do with being better off, then we have no reason to call it a moral institution or to use the word *moral* to translate an alien culture's word that applies to such an institution. So we deny certain extreme forms of relativism. On the same grounds we restrict the notion of being better off to states that we can imagine ourselves desiring. It is crucial to my overall argument that we can thus define the nature and subject matter of ethics without finding any foundational moral principles that tell us why we ought to be moral.

Chapter 2 argues that, contrary to what one might expect, nothing in Chapter 1 implies that some form of utilitarianism is correct. If morality is about making people better off, then it is about promoting the good life. That is not necessarily all it is about, however; in any case, the good life may encompass not only happiness in a straightforward sense but also a great many other desirable things, including the sort of respect for others that relates to both justice and rights. These matters cannot be adequately addressed just by the use of principles, so we must introduce such things as character and virtue.

The nature of the good life is an issue essential to morality, and it comes forward with particular force as we consider life in the organization and whether that life can be a good life. There is an extraordinary variety of states that might be part of the good life, and we do not seem to be in any position to designate any one conception of the good as the right one, so we have reason to be skeptical about the usefulness of utilitarianism. And if, as seems plausible, any life that could reasonably be considered good has something to do with the autonomous exercise of one's powers and enjoyment of one's goods as one wishes—which is not necessarily the same thing as just doing what one wants all the time— then autonomy is a primary issue for morality, and a particularly interesting issue in an organizational context, where some people get to tell others what to do. So is justice, since morality seems to have something essential to do with taking others' interests as equal in importance to one's own. But organizations in a capitalist economy operate on a notion of justice that incorporates deserving, based on productivity, rather than equality. How do we adjudicate between systems that take such different views of justice? And—to raise a question that recurs in later chapters—how can these indefinite notions of rights and justice, or anything else for that matter, serve as a foundation for morality? The answer is that they cannot: there is no unified theory, utilitarian or otherwise, that tells us what it is to be moral. Here for the first time I suggest that we infer that morality has to do with the basic structure of a community and not only with (say) measuring aggregate happiness, which can be neither measured nor aggregated. In business ethics in particular the basic structure is extraordinarily important.

Chapter 3 considers a contractarian way of dealing with the diverging strands of morality. In discussing the contractual relationships implicit in organizations, I offer the metaphor of the organization as a commons, which it is a central purpose of morality to preserve, in the interests of all participants. While we can profit from discussions of collective action issues, we do not want to accept all the usual assumptions of the Prisoner's Dilemma and the commons argument. The least acceptable ones portray one's interests as unvarying and narrowly selfish, and it is only by rejecting these assumptions that we can contemplate the good life as a place where well-being and morality overlap. The life of a person who is disposed to contribute in such cases if others do, rather than be a free rider, can reasonably be considered a good life. And what sort of community best supports the person of good character? One that is organized according to the famous Rawlsian procedure.

Chapter 4 moves beyond the metaphor of the commons but does not abandon it: I suggest that an organization resembles a community more than it does either a market or a system defined by its owners' objectives. It is therefore the sort of aggregation to which a Rawlsian approach proves to be better applicable than is a more traditional contractarian one; the latter is a tempting but flawed way to describe the status of business ethics. Communities clearly raise a great many moral issues, and if we attend to the relationship between communities and morality we can see through the facile distinction between theoretical and applied ethics that relegates business ethics to a secondary and parasitic status it does not deserve and on a Rawlsian account does not have.

Business ethics is about creating the right kind of community, whether it is an organization or a community that comprises organizations. Today we live in political communities and also, although less than in the past, in communities created around extended families, neighborhoods, churches, and fraternal organizations. But the community with which many of us identify most closely is constituted by the people who work in the organization that employs us. The reasons Aristotle gave for saying that politics is the culmination of ethics are today reasons for saying that business ethics is the culmination of ethics. So when we think about creating the good life, in which well-being and morality overlap in the individual, we might well think first not of the politician but of the manager, and we might well use the tools and insights of business ethics.

Central to this discussion is the idea of the good life—it may or may not be a moral life—which it is a purpose of moral agency to promote. Chapter 2 takes issue with a facile utilitarianism that regards the good life as unproblematically related to the fulfillment of the individual's desires. As one's desires and one's view of the nature of the good life may be affected by one's community, and as it is possible that the good life for some person has something to do with the happiness of another, there might be a community whose influence is such that the good life for an individual in it will depend on others enjoying the good life as well. An organization might be such a community.

I shall argue that the good life must be, whatever else it is, one that is lived in a good community; hence it is particularly important to determine what a good community is. Communities characteristically have much to do with determining their participants' shared view of the good life, and community agreements, rules, and practices determine to a great extent what is right or wrong. In making a moral assessment of a community or someone in it, therefore, it is an important first step to understand the agreements, rules, and practices that shape the locally shared sense of right and wrong. That understanding, however, leaves a question unanswered: if a community significantly determines people's view of the good life, then what could possibly distinguish a good community from a bad one? And what is wrong with coercion by socialization? The question requires that we think about what if anything a good life might be apart from the opinions and preferences of those living it. We ask the question in Chapters 5 and 6 and argue for some elements of an answer in Chapter 7.

Discussion of the good life and of its susceptibility to social determination and perhaps even brainwashing, along with concern about autonomy, leads to discussion of the nature of the person, for the most part in Chapter 5. The person is characteristically a reflective being, with the ability to deliberate by considering not only alternative courses of action but also alternative values and forms of the good life, to some degree determining one's principles and behavior accordingly. At the same time, the person is a social being, rather than one whose character and values are formed in isolation. A sound account of the good life must take these essential features into account and must allow for autonomy in the sense Chapter 5 sets out. My aim is to defend views about the good life that are incompatible with any interesting form of relativism—as opposed to pluralism, which advocates that we encourage the expression of a range of views, including some about the nature of the good life, but not that we suppose they are all true. I aim also to maintain a distinction between a community that accommodates our nature and one that brainwashes us. I attack the Humean view—still alive in the literature of management—of the nature of reason as purely a matter of effective means to any old end. And I argue for a view of reason as not naturally opposed to emotion. These last two arguments are Aristotelian, altogether compatible with the Aristotelian view that virtue is central to morality and that it is a matter of being made happy by the right things. If that view is true, then the standard psychological egoism assumed by many economists and game theorists is false, with the result that there is one less difficulty in the way of showing that the moral life can be a good life.

Chapter 5 discusses autonomy; Chapter 6 discusses how corporate culture may threaten it or support it but in the end defends the view that a strong culture of the right kind is the best means of preserving the commons in a way that is compatible with the participants' autonomy, even if it operates in part by appeal to the emotions. These discussions make clear that in considering whether morality is in our best interests, we ought to think about what we might reasonably want our interests to be. While I think it a mistake to assume that people always act rationally in their own best interests, I mean to argue something not altogether different: that being a morally good person is a matter of taking the right sort of thing to be in one's best interests.

A morally good organization, of the sort that Rawlsian founders might organize, is one that is hospitable to such a person. Chapter 7 argues that we have good reason to want to be contributing members in an effective organization that permits the disaffected to leave by participating in a free labor market, earns the commons-preserving loyalty of participants, and encourages reflection and discussion about issues of ethical importance, including the nature of the good life. The closest we can get to defining the principles of morality that are of greatest concern to organizational ethics is to describe such an organization and the sort of person who would thrive in it.

From my emphasis on the good life, even from my opening with the question "Why should I be moral?", it should be clear that I want to consider how much sense it makes to say that morality is about the kind of person one is as well as about the kind of act one performs. I can hardly settle that issue, but I do argue that any good community, any good organization, requires not only good rules but also people of civic virtue. I have to say that moral persons are at the very least necessary for good organizations but also that a good organization helps make people moral. In so doing it benefits them, for it causes the virtuous life and the good life to coincide.

It would be fair to regard my views as communitarian and to say that I view the self as socially constructed; fair or not, however, it would be unhelpfully vague. It is difficult to see how anybody could wholly reject communitarianism or claim that the self is in no sense socially constructed, and easy to take part of my argument as a *reductio* of certain individualist views. What is perhaps more helpful is to give one's views on specific issues; I shall do that and let others decide the rather boring question whether those views make me a communitarian.

In any case, it is important that we not just baldly assume or claim that certain communitarian propositions are true. I undertake instead to begin with views that are not conspicuously communitarian and note how I find myself pushed in a communitarian direction on certain issues. So, for example, one of the problems about the Prisoner's Dilemma and related puzzles is that they presuppose that everyone's motivation is always narrowly selfish. Not only is that presupposition false, it is very important that it is false. But the initial point I want to make in using these puzzles is that even when people are reasoning selfishly, they can see the point of acting communally. Then I can begin to make the point that there is (seemingly paradoxically) something to be said from one's own point of view for not reasoning selfishly.

The influence of Aristotle on this essay has been even stronger than I expected at the outset it would be. There have turned out to be some difficulties with principles, and the notion of a virtue has some promise. Let virtue ethicists take some comfort in that if they care to. But I am no essentialist; in particular, I think Aristotle's essentialism dooms his ethical views to an unacceptable parochialism.

Those who take a postmodern approach to business ethics (a band of them have taken over the third number of the third volume of *Business Ethics Quarterly*) will likely believe I have given them some aid and comfort. I do believe, for example, that foundationalist views that we have reason to blame on Descartes have infected our conversations about ethics, hence about business ethics. In particular, I say the foundational principles of morality have almost no content in the absence of some context. But relativism does not follow. Nor, although I think there is some necessary connection between what is rational and what I can understand, do I think rationality is subjective in any important sense. I should like to avoid the language of postmodernist criticism, and its methodological assumptions. Let them emerge naturally, if they will, from my relatively modest pragmatism. Depending on your orientation and your generosity, you may attribute my caution to my just beginning to understand the issues; or, as I prefer, you may see me as undertaking to create clear arguments rather than great pronouncements about science, objectivity, and so on. In any case, I am surely not a relativist. I do not claim to be able to find a language that deserves universal privileges, but I can state why some languages are bad. My views are surely more modern than post: they are closest to those of John Rawls, the paradigmatic liberal, and of Richard Rorty, who flaunts his bourgeois liberalism. But the greatest influence on what I say here or anywhere else is Aristotle, the defender and refiner of common sense, the greatest philosopher of them all.

1

What Morality Is About

It seems obvious that the institution of morality is supposed to make people better off than they would otherwise be.[1] When we try to say how we know that is true or what it means or what follows from it, however, the claim may begin to seem both dubious and trivial. A certain sort of relativist might question whether morality necessarily has anything to do with making people better off, or with any sort of outcome, on the grounds that what is morally right is at least in part a matter of what people in a community agree on, and people in a community might not agree to take one another's well-being seriously. One might also deny that there are rights other than those granted by community agreements, or justice aside from adherence to community rules. I claim that morality does indeed characteristically make people better off, but not that being better off is a simple state or an individual matter, rather than one affected by one's community, even one's organization.[2]

The enterprise of business itself, quite aside from ethics, is supposed to make us better off than we would be without the fruits of the production it organizes.[3] And so it normally does, occasionally in ways economists have not noticed. Sometimes, however, it surely does not, and that some business practice makes people worse off gives reason to believe that it is an immoral practice. Insofar as any institution makes people better off it is *prima facie* moral.[4]

REASONS FOR BEING MORAL

Why should I be moral? The question, raised by philosophers for millennia, is raised today with skeptical emphasis on the pronoun by some businesspeople and many MBA students. (One hears a typical student say, "Well, I suppose we could all be nice little altruists. . . .") The usual way to interpret the question is, How is it in my best interests to be moral?[5] Some famous philosophers have argued that the moral person is indeed better off in some way for being moral. Plato's *Republic* develops a profound and influential account of human well-being and virtue according to which each requires the other. Aristotle makes virtue a necessary

condition of genuine happiness.[6] Religious writers promise heavenly rewards but in so doing suggest that morality in itself is an investment that merits a return. Some early utilitarians argued that when we treat other people morally we achieve happiness in accommodating our natural feelings of sympathy. Adam Smith, for example, whom we associate with the view that unrestrained selfishness creates the best outcome for all in a free market, argues in *A Theory of Moral Sentiments* (1966) that people just naturally care about one another's interests.

Yet being moral is at least sometimes costly, especially in business: it can require self-restraint and occasionally self-sacrifice, and a clever but selfish person will have reasons to behave immorally.[7] Poe and Dostoevsky describe phenomena with which a few of us are familiar, but where is the evidence that the likes of Ivan Boesky are truly unhappy before they are caught? Cannot larcenous behavior be a source of sly satisfaction, which one likes to share with one's friends?

If immoral deeds do not make their agents unhappy, then questions arise about why one should bother teaching business ethics, quite aside from whether one can. The standard reason for teaching management, finance, accounting, and marketing seems to be that one learns principles and practices useful by virtue of their contribution to the effectiveness of one's employer organization, hence indirectly to one's own interests. But it is not clear that moral behavior benefits an employer, particularly one engaged in effective but immoral practices. Employees' moral behavior may be of greatest benefit to the organization that is willing to take advantage of its employees, who themselves therefore do not profit from their own moral goodness. Teaching ethics may be futile or worse from the point of view of the organization, and still more so from the point of view of the employee.[8] Who exactly, then, benefits from the teaching of business ethics or the propagation of morality among individuals engaged in business? One could make a case that any profession by its nature requires an ethical code, but how does that requirement help the individual?[9]

To the questionable optimism about the happiness of the moral person there is a parallel for the case of corporations: that ethics is good business. Not content to state as a matter of common sense that corporate morality or immorality will eventually be discovered and rewarded or punished, James Burke (1985), then chief executive of Johnson and Johnson, provided actual evidence that companies with ethical credos are more profitable than others. What remains undemonstrated is whether companies with ethical credos are truly ethical companies,[10] whether their success is a result of their morality rather than of the clarity of their mission as a whole, whether morality is a cause of success rather than a luxury that only well-managed companies can afford, and whether the operative factor is really morality rather than a reputation for it.[11]

In the literature on organizational behavior, recent versions of the human relations approach—job enrichment, Theory Y management, Ex-

cellence, and certain accounts of corporate culture, for example—suggest that treating employees well and encouraging them to develop according to their potential is a good way to stimulate productivity. Leaving aside the question whether there is something particularly good about this approach from a moral point of view, would it not be equally effective simply to make employees believe that their interests are being looked after?

THE INTERESTS OF OTHERS AS REASON FOR ACTION

The discussion to this point raises the question whether I can have a reason to be moral unless being moral is in my best interests. That is an important question, since moral considerations would be of little importance if they generated no reasons for acting. The answer is affirmative, although it does not follow that any reasonable person is thereby moral. The point is only that the moral quality of some possible act can be a reason for doing it.

The standard economist's view, widely espoused among businesspeople who have considered the matter, is that the ultimate reason for action is always one's own perceived best interests; that view implies a negative response to this question—a mistaken embrace of psychological egoism, as I shall begin to argue later in this chapter. It is true that if someone asks me why I want something to be the case, it is normally an adequate answer to indicate how that outcome will improve my situation, and it would be pointless to ask why I want to improve my situation. Although I can act intentionally against my own best interests, our standard pattern of explanation and justification of intentional action, reflected in the way we habitually talk about people, presupposes that we normally do what we think best for ourselves. Many of our standard explanations presuppose that there is a range of things that we agree are nearly always in one's best interests: eating when hungry, avoiding pain, and so on. Explanations that do not invoke this standard pattern are often regarded as referring to causes but not reasons. Although self-interested behavior is necessarily the norm, however, given what counts as evidence for what we take to be in our interests, it is not universal.

Nor is it true that one's best interests always constitute a satisfactory explanation for one's behavior. Consider: "You're telling me you didn't rescue a drowning man just because you didn't want to risk catching a cold?" Surely that sort of response is more appropriate than this: "You're telling me you rescued a drowning man just because it was the right thing to do?" The usual pattern of explanation does not show that the involvement of my own best interests is a necessary, any more than sufficient, condition of explaining anything I do, nor does it show that I always act in my own perceived best interests.

To put the point another way, there is no one kind of reason that serves as the foundational explanation of human action. Economists for the most part hold that people are rational and that rationality is a matter of acting effectively in pursuit of one's objectives, hence in one's own interests. They do not actually argue that moral behavior is self-interested or that the enlightened self-interest of senior executives will create the same sort of behavior in the organizations they manage; they therefore have no reason to assume that a self-interested senior executive is necessarily good for the organization. If so, good policy from the point of view of the organization's stockholders requires the eternal vigilance of the board of directors, a sound compensation system, and the possibility of a hostile takeover.

Gauthier (1986) and others have argued that to act rationally is to act morally, hence that morality is in one's best interests in the long run; a subtle economist might thus come to see the point of being moral. That argument, of which some versions have been associated with Hobbes, seeks to get from the proposition that utterly selfish behavior in a community is collectively self-defeating—in itself an important point, which I shall discuss further in Chapter 3—to the proposition that it is individually self-defeating.[12] But rationality is not necessarily a matter of self-interest alone if one can have reason for acting against one's interests.

And one can. Even when my moral duty is incompatible with my inclinations and my self-interest, even when I have no actual motive to do some good act, there may still be reason for me to do it: namely, that it is the right thing to do. I emphasize that this is not primarily a point about motivation: an evil person may well have no motive to perform a good act that will not benefit its agent. An amoral one may understand the nature of moral obligation and even its application to the case at hand but simply not care.[13] An improvident person may not even have a motivation to take his or her long-term interests into account. What all these people do have is a reason for doing the right thing.

Hume takes a different view with his famous claim that reasonableness is a matter of efficiency of means to end and that an end is not the sort of thing that can be reasonable or unreasonable except insofar as it is also a means to some further end. He thus implies that moral duty itself provides no reason to do anything, that reason does not favor saving the drowning man at the risk of catching cold. Few economists or social scientists would take issue with Hume on this point; Weber in particular consistently holds that rationality is a matter of the appropriateness of means to ends, and not of ends. Economists typically hold that an explanation of behavior succeeds—that is, it identifies both the reason and the motivation behind the behavior—insofar as it shows how the behavior serves the agent's interests. Self-interest is the foundation of action, on this account, which thus incorporates psychological egoism. But success in explanation is not a matter of whether the explainer can adduce some foundation of self-evident knowledge on which the explanation rests; it is a matter of whether someone understands.

In fact, however, one's ends can be incoherent, or different in some way from what one believes them to be, or unexpectedly expensive, or just stupid things to desire. It is surely odd, too, to say that if Jones doesn't care about his health it follows that he has no reason not to smoke, particularly if he might later wish he had not smoked.[14] It is possible for Jones to have reason for doing something he does not want to do and denies having reason for doing, although I do not see how it is possible for him to want to do something (that is, have a motivation for doing something) that he has no reason to do.[15] Surely health is a reasonable end, one of those things that Aristotle identified as valuable whether or not they are valued.[16] We can argue about whether friendship is something a rational person would want—a necessary component of the good life—apart from its consequences.[17]

There is a great deal at stake here. If you think that only means can be considered rational, you will probably[18] take related positions that are highly questionable in spite of their long history—for example, that pleasure is the one good end for the rational agent, hence the end of any rational means; that all rational people are motivated by the prospect of pleasure, which is the consequence of pleasant activities; that we always desire what is desirable; that we can rank activities on a single scale, such as according to how much pleasure they cause for the agent; that utilitarianism is straightforward as well as attractive. I shall argue against all these views in this and the next several chapters.

Whether something is a reason for acting is closely connected to whether it can be put forward as part of a familiar and acceptable sort of explanation. When Jones explains something he did, Smith[19] will accept the explanation as giving a reason for action if she can see something attractive about his act, or the outcome Jones reasonably expects it to have. The action need not be attractive from a selfish point of view; it may be attractive because it is admirable, or helpful to someone else. Most people will not find the possibility of being two minutes late for a board meeting an adequate explanation for refusing to take the time to keep a stray toddler from running out into traffic. More broadly, our reason-giving explanations presuppose that we share certain views about what is good and important and what is not. If Jones and Smith radically disagree about what is good and important, then they cannot explain their behavior to each other by invoking reasons; but such cases are nearly unheard of, since people talk mostly with those who do not radically disagree with them on such matters.

It is a primary characteristic of a moral point of view that to adopt it is to take others' interests as well as one's own as reasons for action.[20] That morality is supposed to do more than just make a single agent better off[21] is suggested by Kant's famous dictum that one is required to treat people as ends in themselves rather than only as means to one's own ends. If I explain some action of mine by saying that it helped Smith, then one might want to ask me, So why is that a reason for *you* to do it? But questions of that form are seldom asked, for almost any person's advantage is a reason—although certainly not always a decisive one or the only one—for doing something; in that sense, although not only in that sense, every person is to be considered an end.

As an essential purpose of moral behavior is to contribute to the ends, hence (ordinarily) the well-being, of people other than just the agent,[22] we should not consider moral any sort or system of behavior in which consideration of the interests of someone other than the agent plays no part. The notion of that sort of morality makes no more sense than the notion of a pleasant sound that no hearers like to hear.

A *prima facie* criterion for assessing the morality of an act[23] is its ultimate contribution to the well-being of people. I am morally obligated to take others' interests as a reason for action. Of course it does not follow that the moral thing for me to do in every individual case is to try to make as many people as possible as well off as possible, especially if I am a businessperson working in a highly competitive market. All the same, one can see why some philosophers would adopt a utilitarian position, and why economics would be of great interest to some who do.

MORALITY AND ONE'S BEST INTERESTS: A START

Many ancient philosophers would have hesitated to say that morality is primarily about attending to the well-being of others. For them the primary question was about virtue, and the question was "How I shall live?" That was a broad question, whose answer required reference to prudence and courage and honor and other virtues not all essentially other-regarding, in some cases even harmful to others' interests. As I indicated earlier, Plato saw an issue to be addressed in the relationship between virtue and self-interest and was unwilling to dismiss it by saying, in effect, "Well, so what if doing good is sometimes incompatible with doing well? We should do the right thing anyway." My view is that, although doing good might disadvantage the moral agent, the moral life and the good life can and should be made to overlap.

In discussing self-interest, economists and psychological egoists often make two assumptions that are distinct as well as questionable: first, that people always act according to what they take to be their own best interests, and, second, that people are narrowly selfish in the sense that their own best interests do not embrace the well-being of other people.[24] If these assumptions are true, then the idea that morality is the, or even a, way to the agent's happiness is problematic. If either is false, then we may reasonably hope that one might be made happy by one's own moral behavior or its consequences. A situation in which your moral behavior has consequences that please you is desirable; it is therefore desirable that those who create a community of any kind, including an organization, bring about that sort of situation.

One way to meet this objective would be for a community to reward good behavior and punish bad. While there are some organizations capable of doing that—it is harder than it looks—we might well be reluctant to cede to governments the authority to do it extensively in larger communities. In any case, a certain kind of moral purist might argue that people ought to be moral without regard to the prospective reward. It is necessarily and even trivially true that people have a moral obligation to be moral, but it is surely better that people act as moral people act because they are rewarded for it than that they act immorally. The supply of saints being thin, we need to find some useful way of encouraging the sinners.

The first of the two questionable assumptions implies that we are all sinners, or at least selfish. But while that appears to be a cynical and false view, we have reason to suspect it is devoid of content: it surely is if any proposed counterexample is analyzed as a case of a do-gooder motivated by the pleasure derived from thinking of oneself as virtuous, or something of the sort. In that case nothing whatever could count as evidence against the view, and we cannot imagine what it would be like for it to be false. If what is in one's own perceived best interests is in effect stipulated to be identical with what one does intentionally, then it is quite trivially true that every intentional act is a selfish one.[25]

For the second of the two assumptions—that one's own best interests do not embrace the well-being of other people—I know of no justification. Most people who are not sociopaths take pleasure in the well-being of family members and others, such as neighbors. There is no good reason to hold that my being given a dime is in my interests but my seeing my friend recover her health is not, particularly if I am always willing to spend more than a dime on my friend's health. I can take more than momentary pleasure in a great variety of things. If I am a morally good person, I take pleasure in doing things that are morally good. That is a familiar Aristotelian position, and one surely more realistic than the view of the person as a field of battle between morality and pleasure.[26]

This morally good person who enjoys a good life is, according to Aristotle, a good citizen of a good state. From an Aristotelian point of view, the best practically achievable situation is the community in which all flourish because all are acting to make everyone better off. (That is my description of the community, not Aristotle's.) It is possible to extrapolate the Aristotelian view to our time: the contemporary Aristotelian could take the salient community to be the organization and hold that the one who leads the excellent life is a good employee of a good organization. As Aristotle would give the statesman primary responsibility for propagating morality, we now have similar reasons for assigning that responsibility to the manager.[27]

Ideally the manager would fulfill that responsibility by seeing to it that the organization hires people who are made happy by virtuous conduct. But that is neither easy nor sufficient. No matter how good the screening process, not all the people in (much less around) an organization will be virtuous, or see much to gain in being so. How then does virtue survive? That is a great question for us, and the appropriate management of rewards and punishments is only part of the answer.[28]

RELATIVISM

By this point in the argument, a cultural relativist will be prepared to object that I have given no basis for my view that morality has something to do with making people better off.[29] My claim is that this is necessarily true, as a matter of linguistic convention, what Arrington (1989, p. 275) calls moral grammar. As with many conventions, this one is of substantive import and cannot be changed arbitrarily. The crucial question is this: what basis could there be for calling any other sort of institution a morality?

This will sound parochial to the relativist, who will point out that it is conceivable that an act might be morally obligatory in some remote culture while being immoral if you or I did it in our culture; that is indeed not only conceivable but true. In fact, we should be careful about saying "did *it*," for the bodily and other movements involved might not constitute the same sort of act when they occur in a significantly different culture. Circumstances, cultural or not, may make certain events an insult, or the closing of a deal, or the third out of the inning, or, if there turn out to be bullets in Jones's gun, a homicide. Depending in part upon socialization, what makes people happy varies from one culture to another. But what is not conceivable is that (other things being equal) an act might be morally legitimate in some culture because it directly or indirectly brings upon the affected parties pain, destruction, unhappiness, and loathing for its agent.

In a roughly similar way, it is conceivable that a person you and I find ugly might be considered beautiful by people in some remote culture (among teenagers, for example), but it is not conceivable that this person could be considered beautiful by the people in that culture if they cannot bear to look at him, if they have an urge to flee from his presence. This is not to say that beauty is purely a function of whether people want to look, or that well-being is purely a function of whether people want to be in the state in question.

The difficulty of reaching a legitimate agreement about what is morally good is real, but not fatal to moral discourse. A thoroughgoing moral subjectivism has no more basis than does a subjectivism that argues that it cannot be shown that Thomas Watson Jr. was a better (or worse) manager than Henry Ford II. The defender of the claim of superiority will argue that what makes one manager better than another is greater contribution to the organization's long-term growth and profitability and that, therefore, Watson's contribution clearly exceeded Ford's. Now it is arguable that growth and profitability are functions less of managerial ability than of environmental factors—say, the kind identified by PIMS reports and evaluated by the GE-McKinsey matrix—and that there are problems about defining concepts like profitability precisely and satisfactorily.[30] Our disagreements about the criteria for good management, however, and about just what is involved in organizational effectiveness do not prevent our using the term *good manager* to communicate adequately for most purposes and to make true or false statements; nor do they thwart reasoned discussion of various candidate criteria for good management. As Quine (1961) and others have persuasively argued, a disagreement about definition may turn out to be a substantive disagreement. It does not follow that dictionaries are useless, or wholly indistinguishable from encyclopedias.

We do not need to define morality in very great detail; any competent attempt to give an account of morality must leave broad scope for moral disagreement, for example about the nature of the good life, lest we find ourselves trying to settle moral issues just by bringing definitions to bear. But we cannot argue about moral issues at all unless we have some widespread agreement on the subject under discussion. Kuhn (1971) shows how definitions of crucial terms shift along with scientific theories and how agreed definitions are necessary for science but sometimes act as barriers to scientific progress. The same sort of thing applies in morality: moral progress may render obsolete a vocabulary once essential to moral discourse. Readers of Kuhn do not always grasp the feature of his work that rescues it from subjectivism: he does believe that there has been and will be scientific progress. In due course I shall argue the same for moral progress.[31]

That we may not be able to agree on whether Thomas Watson Sr. was a better manager than Henry Ford I does not disable all judgments of comparative managerial quality; nor does it make it impossible for us to argue rationally over Watson Sr. versus Ford I, let alone Ford II. Try to find a baseball fan who agrees that, because we cannot finally show that Willie Mays was better than Joe DiMaggio or vice versa, there can be no basis for saying that Willie Mays was better than Frankie Baumholtz. No one, except possibly a student in an introductory philosophy class, has ever seriously asked, "Who's to say whether hitting, fielding, and running the bases have anything to do with being a good baseball player?" Even in a business ethics class you are unlikely to hear anybody ask, "Who's to say whether long-term profit and growth and contribution to the economy have anything to do with being a successful manager?" But we do have serious arguments about the criteria and their priority: they give life to scholarly journals.[32]

Yet there are communities in which people have values and agree on rules that are not our values or rules; couldn't there be an alien culture with a morality radically different from ours? The point of the following section is that there could not be: any institution of the aliens that differed in a truly radical way from our conception of morality could give us no reason to call that institution a form of morality.

Notice that we can state what morality is supposed to do and broadly define it without having found any basic principles on which we have reason to believe it is founded. I have not even shown that there are such principles, nor shall I. And while there is good reason to say that common sense about morality cannot be wholly wrong, it is not my point that by great good fortune common sense has roughly identified what morality is about. What we necessarily have, at the very least, is a rough understanding of what we mean when we talk about morality. In Chapter 4, particularly, I shall argue that the time-honored moral principles give us little more than that.

It is conceivable that we might someday decide just to stop talking about morality, as scientists decided to stop talking about phlogiston. That would presumably happen if our situation or our motivations changed so radically that we no longer paid any attention to others' welfare. As things are, it is almost impossible for us to imagine what it would be like to be in that situation. And as things are, no set of practices can count as morality that does not comport in some measure with our views of the nature of morality.

INTERPRETATION AND THE LIMITS OF MORALITY

One might object that people in an alien society could have a moral code whose purposes did not include the general welfare. But then one must be prepared to answer the question, What reason would there be for calling such a thing a *moral* code?[33] If it required treating like cases alike, there would be reason for calling it a code, but it might be a legal or even an aesthetic code. Suppose it were taken so seriously as to give one reason for action independent of or even in opposition to one's own interests. It would still not be a moral code unless it were others' interests that were capable of overriding one's own. If the aliens used the word *gavai* to describe behavior forbidden under the code, what would we accept as a reason for translating the word *gavai* as *immoral*, rather than as (say) *taboo* or *disgusting*? Surely not the mere existence of a reason to act.

There might be an alien culture in which torture was regarded as legitimate on some occasions; that could be consistent with a moral code. But suppose an alien were to call cruel some practice whose victims clearly did not dislike it, regret it, or wish to avoid it; or suppose the alien speaker refused to acknowledge that pointless infliction of great pain was cruel. In either case we would have more reason to doubt the alien's command of English than to believe that the alien culture had a very different conception of cruelty. If an alien spoke an alien language and an interpreter translated one of the alien's remarks as "We acknowledge that some acts are cruel, but we emphatically deny that it is cruel to torture little children purely for amusement," then we would have reason to question the accuracy of the interpreter's translation. It is as though the translators had the aliens regularly and apparently seriously saying the equivalent of "It's raining" during dry and sunny weather. To understand a language different from one's own, one has to assume that at least most of what its speakers say is true. And if the alien described a local institution that was intended to foster pain and suffering as "our moral code," then one would surely have reason to question the very use of that term. It is as if the aliens were to say "This is how we play baseball" in reference to an activity without teams, bats, balls, or bases.[34]

It is easy to underestimate the difficulty of even contemplating a radically alien moral system or belief system of any kind. People whose beliefs on certain subjects are utterly different from our own would be people whose language we could understand poorly at best. If the differences were truly radical, we would have no basis for ascribing any beliefs or even any language to them.

People with values radically different from ours would be equally difficult to fathom. Part of the function of interpretation is to determine the point of some practice, hence its direct or indirect benefit to the agents. The interpreter may reasonably consider an alien practice stupid or worse—think of clitoridectomy—and yet identify some purpose that it is thought to serve. But the notion of aliens' values and desires radically different from ours is no sounder than the notion of radically different beliefs; at some point it would make more sense to infer that the interpretation was not succeeding than to believe that the aliens desired a certain thing.

It is tempting to speculate about conceptual schemes so different from our own that we cannot understand them at all, but what reason could we ever have for believing that there is any such conceptual scheme? By the hypothesis under consideration, we would have no basis for identifying any such thing as a conceptual scheme. One might as well say that trees speak to each other but that their beliefs and desires are profoundly different from ours.[35] The same goes for systems of moral value.

It follows that considering whether a code is a *moral* code cannot be separated from considering whether it is in some respect or other a *morally adequate* code from our point of view. In a similar way, while there is no contradiction in the notion of a bad scientific theory, if some body of statements is utterly hopeless from the point of view of evidence and methodology and coherence, then we have good reason to deny that it is a scientific theory at all.

At what point do we say that the code does not qualify as moral? At the very least, we ought to deny that people in a certain culture could consider it *moral* to obey the apparently whimsical and brutal commands of some god. If Abraham decides to sacrifice Isaac purely because God has told him to, then the act is not characteristically moral, but only obedient.

If, on the other hand, we attribute to Abraham the view that it is moral to do what God wants done, then we must take Abraham to be assuming that there is some further reason for obedience to God; if Abraham is to have a chance of being right, that reason must have something to do with the good life for someone. To adapt an argument from Plato's *Euthyphro*, if an act is pious simply because the gods love it—if piety is not a property that is logically independent of the gods' fondness for it—then piety is not a moral category.[36]

Our judgments on and even our descriptions of the actions, rules, institutions, and language in alien cultures will be problematical when they differ from us with respect to "thick concepts," which is what Geertz (1983) calls concepts that one can understand only by seeing how they are embedded in a culture's complex practices, which may incorporate moral or factual presuppositions. In baseball, double play is a thick concept; in business, profit; in a political community, representation; in an organization, controller, dotted-line reporting; in a religious community, blasphemy; in a moral community, dishonesty, courage, honor, rights. A first step in understanding an alien culture, a precondition of assessing its institutions from a moral point of view, is understanding its thick concepts, particularly those that do not map readily onto ours. In due course we may come to understand a thick concept and (not a separate enterprise) the aliens' actions only after investigating an unfamiliar network of connections among concepts and identifying certain assumptions and values that seem to some degree reasonable to us, even though we may not accept them.

To ask questions like "What is Latin for *yuppie*?" or "What is the atheist's term for *blasphemy*?" is to show that one has underestimated the difficulty of understanding. To say that the Greek for *chutzpah* is *hubris* betrays a similar problem in a less severe form. To agree straightforwardly that it would have been dishonorable for Hamilton to refuse Burr's challenge to a duel is to take honor to be a thick concept, which is all right, since in my view virtues are thick moral concepts, but it is a mistake, for it entails accepting an unacceptably parochial version of the concept of honor. An atheist says there are no cases of blasphemy. You and I ought to agree that there is such a thing as honor, but we ought to deny that dueling is honorable. Honor has something to do with living a good life and, arguably secondarily, something to do with contributing to the good life for others. To argue that dueling is not honorable requires that one oppose the notion that a good man [*sic*] is willing to kill or die to avenge a slight.

We can imagine people claiming moral allegiance to a code that mandates acting according to standards of honor and nobility and manliness [*sic*] that have little to do with anyone's welfare. We can imagine people being praised for recklessness and called dishonorable for showing rational prudence; that constitutes moral criticism, even if there is no implication that anyone's interests are harmed.

Even in these odd cases, however, the virtue that is being violated does rest on others' interests in that it normally affects or once affected or is thought to affect others' interests, to make some direct or indirect contribution to what is generally considered the good life. Lying, for example, would not be dishonorable or immoral if it never had negative consequences.[37] Where there is no such reference to a contribution to the good life, and in some instances in which there is, it is just not the case that one has any sort of moral obligation, as for example to agree to a duel. People in that society who held that view were wrong, as people in the Mafia are wrong about what honor requires. If honor is a moral concept, then, contrary to what people once believed, it is not dishonorable to refuse a challenge to a duel.[38] Honor characteristically receives praise and admiration, but not all praise or admiration of human traits is moral praise or admiration. Some businesspeople are praised for their unscrupulousness, and proud of it. That they boast of rapacity but not of cowardice suggests there are some admired character traits, such as manliness, that are not virtues because they involve no sort of contribution to the good life, even indirectly, though some of them once did. They may even embody prejudice.

Moral philosophers and anthropologists try to explain such concepts, particularly the ones we use in discussing morality; some undertake to assess them by reference to substantive moral principles.[39] Practitioners of business ethics ought to analyze and assess the thick concepts associated with corporate cultures and with the culture of business as a whole. It will turn out that criticizing the concepts and their associated moral views from outside is a difficult task. (Nor is it easy from inside.)

THE IK

In arguing for limits on what we can reasonably call a moral code, I have conceded that there is some looseness in the limits, but limits there are. To test whether the world can contain radically different moral codes, consider now the obnoxious Ik, who treat one another and especially their children and elders with apparently gratuitous cruelty and take delight in causing pain.[40] They appear to have some sort of code of behavior, but is it a moral one?

Suppose the Ik use the term *gavai* to describe how they traditionally undertake to treat each other: a gavai person is then one who causes suffering but does not suffer. Suppose they carefully raise their children to be gavai. Suppose the most gavai people in each community, the ones who most persistently and creatively terrorize children and other weak people in particular, are admired. Suppose the Ik are stoical about taking it but genuinely enjoy dishing it out. Should we not then translate the word *gavai* as *moral*?

I think not. The system is utterly inadequate from a moral point of view because it does not promote even the Ik's conception of happiness or well-being. We may suppose that an Ik will normally treat other Ik in the traditional way in part because there is nothing to be gained and something to be lost in not doing so: if we are both Ik and I fail to abuse you or make it clear that I suffer greatly from your abuse of me, you will abuse me all the more because I have shown weakness. In a particular case the individual Ik follows the code and is gavai in part to avoid suffering further abuse from other Ik being gavai; following the code is to the individual's advantage. But in the aggregate the code generates for most people just the sort of abuse that the individual wishes to dispense but not receive; in that sense it gives people in the aggregate what they do not want. Hence the code is so morally inferior that it leaves us with no reason to consider it a moral code at all.

The Ik code is incoherent, in the sense that if everyone in the society undertakes to be gavai, then a great many will fail. One could say of it, following La Rochefoucauld, "Success is not enough; others must fail."[41] It is a decisive criticism of gavai as a moral concept that everyone's being gavai hurts everyone's or almost everyone's interests, and that it would be better for everyone or almost everyone if nobody were gavai.

One of the tasks of a manager who would be ethical is to see what practices within organizations benefit the people in them. That is normally a necessary condition of the morality of the practices, but not a sufficient one. Consider *omerta*, an essential component of the code of honor in organized crime. On a particular occasion it may benefit a criminal to confess to a crime and implicate others in exchange for a reduced sentence, although those implicated will pay heavily. In the long run, however, the practice of refusing to confess will reduce sentences in the aggregate so long as every criminal in the brotherhood has confidence that everyone else will keep silent and resist the temptation to implicate him. In this situation, then, it is reasonable that *omerta* be obligatory, that strong punitive measures be taken against even apparent infractions, and that the issue not be subject to extensive critical discussion. In this way an organized crime community solves the so-called Prisoner's Dilemma for all its members.[42]

We can interpret the institution of *omerta*, as we can interpret certain other institutions, by saying what the point of it is: it solves the Prisoner's Dilemma and in other ways maintains a solidarity that has many beneficial effects from the point of view of those who participate in the institution within which it operates. As with certain practices in an organization or business community, we can explain it but may all the same be able to criticize it from a moral point of view.

Suppose gavainess did make the Ik better off, in the sense that the Ik liked taking it as well as dishing it out. Could we not then apply the notion of morality to them even though their values differed greatly from our own? Surely we would need only to find some basis for saying that the system gave them something like what they wanted, bizarre as that might be. But there is a problem about that: what we normally consider bizarre desires will not provide us with a very satisfactory explanation of their behavior. We would not be satisfied with an explanation such as, "He ordered that the entire inventory be liquidated at a huge loss because one of his salespeople had an annoying laugh." In the absence of a great deal of explanatory background, we may reasonably doubt that the best explanation of their behavior invokes such desires, unless we hypothesize that they have some false beliefs—say, about the effects of human sacrifice. I argued earlier in this chapter that if these beliefs are wildly false we must question whether it is reasonable to infer (from their actions and words) that they have them. The same is true, I argued, if what the aliens desire is truly bizarre. To explain the behavior of people in an alien community by reference to intentions, hence desires and beliefs,[43] requires answering the question, What is the point of their doing that? The less coherent and attractive the answer to that question, the less satisfactorily it explains their behavior.[44] The less satisfactorily the local conception of what is good explains to us the behavior characteristic of some community, the less reason we have for regarding the moral standards of that community as satisfactory. And if the putative moral standards of a community are utterly unsatisfactory from our point of view, we have no reason for regarding them as moral standards at all.

The poignant moral problem here is that for the individual Ik, the only way to survive is to be gavai; we can easily think of situations in our own experience, particularly in business, in which that is so. A community that creates that sort of situation and makes a standard practice of it can destroy morality. It is not necessarily characteristic of business to create such communities, but there are such communities in business. When that is the case, what is to be done? One of the central themes of this essay is that the good community or organization is one in which it is rationally self-interested, in ways I have begun to discuss, to be moral. A crucial question for us, and a practical question, is this: How can an organization be that sort of community? Another is this: What should the individual do when the organization is not that sort of community?[45]

PROSPECTS

As my argument proceeds, I shall say more about justice and rights and add still further qualifications to this first chapter's claims. One point that needs to be emphasized here and now is that the notion of being better off does not provide a foundation—still less *the* foundation—for morality. In two senses it fails to do so. First, as I have argued in this chapter, it does not answer the question, Why should I be moral? by showing how behaving morally is always in one's best interests, for that is not the case. Second, as I shall argue in Chapter 2, it does not answer the question, What must I do to behave morally? because the notion of being better off itself lacks the certainty characteristic of a foundational answer to that question. Among other things, it is just not true that whatever makes people better off on balance is morally good. In any case, the very idea of the good life, implicit in that of being better off, is itself subject to change and dispute; that feature of it imparts to ethics some of the looseness we associate with relativism. It is at least possible that leading the good life is a function of being moral, in which case we are going to have a hard time defining the latter by reference to the former.[46]

Yet I have already begun to attack the view that just any kind of life might qualify as a good life. In particular, I have suggested that, whatever else we think of ethics, we cannot imagine it being altogether different from our current conception of it. Nor can we imagine other people acting on reasons that make no sense at all to us or entertaining a great many beliefs for which we can see no basis at all. We cannot but be parochial in those respects. We therefore have reason to begin our theorizing with the assumption that what we believe about ethics is mostly true.[47] But a starting point—particularly that one—is not a foundation.

NOTES

1. I shall have a great deal to say about what being better off amounts to, especially in Ch. 2. Happy people are better off than unhappy ones, other things being equal, but it does not follow that being better off is identical with happiness. That it characteristically makes people better off on the whole is not an adequate definition of morality, nor do I claim that that characteristic is *the* point of morality.

2. Arrington (1989) displays the great variety of forms that relativism has taken. He denies that morality can be defined by reference to anyone's being better off or by reference to any goal outside morality. He claims that being better off is insufficient as well as unnecessary for morality, since it is compatible with lying's not being *prima facie* wrong. That lying is wrong is a matter of moral grammar, he claims; see his Ch. 6, esp. pp. 285ff. But surely we can give reasons for saying that lying is *prima facie* wrong. Arrington also claims, rightly I think, that a system that does not give an essential role to respect for others is not really a moral system. See his pp. 241f., and n. 31, below.

3. In Ch. 4 we discuss who the primary beneficiaries of an organization should be. Even those who argue, with Friedman (1984 and elsewhere), that the first responsibility of a company's management is to create long-term wealth for the stockholders defend their view in part by reference to the long-term social consequences of such a system.

Having now used the terms *morality* and *ethics* as though they were synonymous, I should say explicitly that I do not accept the view of Williams (1985) that they are different and that the former is a characteristically modern and flawed conception that makes false and crippling claims about the possibility of theories of morality. Ch. 4 deals further with the possibility of moral theory.

4. In Ch. 4 we consider the extent to which the beneficial effects of business constitute a moral justification for behavior within business.

5. There are those, most prominently Kant, who do not believe morality needs to justify itself by its results—least of all just those that affect the moral

agent—or define itself that way either. From Kant's point of view, acting morally is a special case of acting rationally. In the space available to me I shall not thoroughly scrutinize the idea that to act reasonably is to act morally, although I shall have occasion both to profit from and to criticize Gauthier's (1986) version of that view. I hold that morality is best characterized and justified by its relationship to the good life. My position is more Hobbesian than Kantian, and in some ways more Aristotelian than Hobbesian.

6. Plato and Aristotle could not easily have done otherwise, since the ancient Greek notion of virtue encompassed more than just moral excellence and suggested a generally admirable and successful life. It would have sounded paradoxical to say that a certain virtuous person is miserable. Cooper (1986), for example, in translating Aristotle renders *eudaimonia* as "flourishing" and points out (p. 89) that Aristotle holds that the fate of one's children after one's death affects one's *eudaimonia* (*Nicomachean Ethics* I.10 1100a22ff.). He does not thereby offer an absurd conception of the good life.

Readers of the *Gorgias*, for example, can see Plato and the sophists struggling to make sense of a question that we now find easier to pose, if not to answer. Williams (1985), esp. Ch. 3, demands sympathetic consideration of the ancient Greek view of virtue as being first of all personal excellence. That view does not assume that one's virtue is necessarily related to others' interests. For Aristotle, at any rate, it turns out that way, since his view is that the individual is happy who is a good citizen, since humans are essentially civilized creatures. This seems to me an attractive position, as will become clear, but I see no justification for making it a premise in my argument.

7. There is an air of incredulity in Stark's (1993, p. 40) citation of DeGeorge's words: "'If in some instance it turns out that what is ethical leads to a company's demise,' then 'so be it.'" What's wrong with that? It is necessarily true that we have a moral obligation to do what is morally right, even if it has bad consequences for us. Of course, the manager who is truly a morally good person can compare one moral principle with another and set priorities and take the consequences of any contemplated actions and the interests of a variety of stakeholders into account. Hence, it is not necessarily immoral to manufacture a car in which it is possible to have a fatal accident, or to dump some amount of pollutants into some river. These issues come up again in Ch. 4.

8. Nothing is implied in this argument about whether we can speak literally of the interests or the moral obligations of the organization. I cannot show that we must, but it does turn out that some morally unsatisfactory states and events are the result of the structural features of an organization rather than of anyone's intention. See further French (1984), who comes as close as anyone to giving a clear sense to the notion that an organization, as opposed to its people, acts and can be morally praised or blamed, if not actually kicked or damned.

9. Bowie (1991, 1991a) argues that an ethical code is characteristic of a profession. Both articles, which attack psychological egoism, have contributed to what I say on that subject in this chapter and elsewhere. The same is true of Derry (1991).

10. This is partly a moral question, not simply an empirical one, for to identify any company as a moral company is to make a commitment to some ethical view, at least implicitly. That is not necessarily a problem, but one must be aware of doing it when one is making that commitment as part of what one might otherwise consider empirical research. The last thing we want to do is try to create an

operational definition of morality or a definition that has what organization theorists call construct validity. Donaldson and Dunfee (1994) worry about this issue, as do several of the authors contributing to vol. 2, no. 2, and vol. 4, no. 2, of *Business Ethics Quarterly*.

11. For a fairly typical skeptical view see Vogel (1992).

12. The Kantian view that anyone who has a genuine reason to act has a universalizable reason, hence a genuine reason to act morally, I do not care to defend. Nagel (1970) argues convincingly for the possibility of altruism but not for its necessity. Gauthier's argument is not so pure, resting as it does on the notion of rational self-interest. But that argument requires such an agent to have a nearly unattainable level of rationality and knowledge.

Talk of individual and collective self-defeat is the invention of Parfit (1984), according to Darwall, Gibbard, and Railton (1992, p. 133), to whom I am much indebted.

13. Brink (1989, esp. Ch. 2) defines amorality along these lines. He surveys the voluminous discussion of the question whether it is necessarily true that one has a motive—as opposed to a reason—to do what one considers morally obligatory, and decides not. I agree, in spite of the venerable tradition to the contrary.

14. Brink would agree; Williams (1981) would not. Doesn't it make sense to say that *there is reason for Jones* not to smoke as well as that it is in Jones's interests not to smoke? It seems at most a small further step to say that Jones *has reason* not to smoke. But that is, of course, not the same as saying that Jones is motivated not to smoke, as he may well not be. Might not Jones simply be wrong in saying that he has no reason to do action A?

15. The reason can be very thin, however. I may want to pour a can of oil over my head just to find out how it would feel.

16. I am not suggesting an analogy between morality and health. The point is only that one can have a reason without having a motivation.

In Ch. 5 I shall argue that autonomy has something to do with being able to act according to a desire based on reasons for action, rather than just according to one's immediate desire. One may have a reason for action but not want to act, but in such a case one may wish one did want to act if one knows one has a reason to do so. One may want to perform some unhealthy act whether or not one wishes one did not have the desire to do it. In either case, one has a reason for not performing such an act. So the concept of motivation in play in that argument is fairly complex.

17. For the Aristotelian view of this and related matters, see Nussbaum (1990, esp. p. 62), who generally agrees with Aristotle.

18. I speak of probability here because these positions do in fact tend to occur together, even though the logical relations among them are not very tight at every point.

19. In my examples Jones is always a man, Smith always a woman.

20. We can put the matter less simply and shall eventually do so. In a passage we shall discuss in other contexts, Scanlon (1982, p. 111) claims that "the desire to find and agree on principles which no one who had this desire could reasonably reject" is not unusual and is characteristic of morality.

21. The unselfishness characteristic of the moral person is essentially related to the justice that is also necessary to morality and without which no institution can be a morality, although moral codes may differ over what counts as and jus-

tifies differential treatment. That one's own interests do not have any natural priority over others' is just a special case of the proposition that nobody's interests have any natural priority over anybody else's.

22. Such writers as Gerald Dworkin (1988) and Arrington (1989) would reject the notion that morality has any essential purposes, in this sense, at all. On their account, Why be moral? has no answer. Indeed, we must state this or any purpose of morality very broadly. But I know of no good argument that morality is in some essential sense pointless, even though I have no universally satisfactory answer to the question, What is the purpose of caring about others' interests? If Dworkin and Arrington are suggesting that there is no self-evident bedrock on which morality rests and from which moral principles follow, my agreement with them on that point will become increasingly obvious.

23. We defer for the moment the question whether acts or their consequences or intentions or persons are the primarily moral items. Some of what I say will imply that persons are, in some ways not always properly appreciated, the focus of morality.

24. Sen (1987, pp. 79ff.) emphasizes the important distinction between these two assumptions; in addition, he notes that standard economic theory pays insufficient attention to the interdependence of people's goals. Adam Smith might have made the first assumption, but he would surely have rejected the second. In subsequent chapters I shall make much of a point similar to Sen's but broader: being better off—having what is in one's interest—is a state that may differ greatly from one person to another and for one person from one time to another. In particular, I shall consider the implications of Aristotle's view that one's character is a matter of the sort of thing that gives one pleasure. Morality and happiness are compatible insofar as the morally good person is the person whose character is such that he or she is made happy by what is moral.

25. A great deal has been written about psychological egoism, which has been attacked by some and taken for granted by others but seldom actually defended by anyone. It might well be defensible as a useful assumption for some areas of economic theory, but in conversation about ethics it is a disaster. Etzioni (1988) attacks psychological egoism as an empirical thesis and considers the consequences of its being proved false. For an account of the shreds of truth that a generous interpretation might find in psychological egoism, see LaFollette (1989, esp. pp. 502–507).

In defending the first of the two distinct assumptions, the psychological egoist raises questions about the second by broadening the notion of the sort of state that might be considered felicific.

26. According to Aristotle, a virtuous person characteristically has appropriate emotions along with dispositions to act (see *Nicomachean Ethics* II.3 1104b13–16, and other passages in Book II). Virtue is therefore a matter of being made happy by the right sort of thing. A defender of the two assumptions I have been attacking might argue that in acting morally the agent is motivated by the prospect of a feeling of pleasure (perhaps self-satisfaction) that is caused by the moral act and is independent of it. Apart from the question of evidence for this view, the notion of pleasure as a feeling identifiably distinct from the pleasureable act is based on an untenable Cartesian psychology.

The notion of the good person as one who fights off the temptations of the flesh we associate with Puritan Christianity. But in the Gospels there is evidence that one of the distinguishing features of the Christian message is that one's dispositions as well as one's actions must be of the right sort. See, for example, Matt. 5:21–31.

27. The analogy of state and organization plays a large role in this essay, especially in Ch. 4. Libertarians like Friedman do not find it congenial.

Aristotle holds that we can learn a great deal about what is moral by looking at the nature and purpose of the human being. In my view, one of the characteristic features of the human being is the possibility of variety and change in nature and purpose. But I shall argue in Chs. 5 and 7 that Aristotle's characterization of the human being as a rational and political animal contains some elements of a sound argument that the good life and the moral life may coincide in the right sort of community.

28. Stark (1993, pp. 40, 43) criticizes the view that moral behavior must be driven purely by altruistic motives so that, as he puts it, "ethics has to hurt." He appears to attribute to some of his opponents the assumption that concern for others and self-interest must be separate motives for people of good moral character. This assumption is the second of the questionable ones that Sen rightly rejects. In any case, Stark himself would probably agree that someone who behaves as moral people do only to get the consequent reward is not a reliably good person.

29. Not only relativists—those who believe there is no such thing as right and wrong apart from local opinion on the matter—will have trouble with what I say in this section. Kant, for example, would deny that making people better off is the most important characteristic of morality.

30. Ethicists' arguments about the nature of morality bear some resemblance to accountants' arguments about exactly how to define profit. Is ROA more important than ROE? What is the significance of the frequency with which companies show large profits year after year while bleeding cash? Morality and profit admit of both easy cases and controversial ones; the trick in both fields is to find a theory that reduces the controversy. As a practical matter, the definition of profit in a typical investment bank that gives bonuses on the basis of each individual's contribution to profits is a huge political issue. It is not trivially true, because it is not true at all, that businesspeople always take profit seriously or that people in general always take morality, or even their own interests, seriously.

Nothing I say here is meant to propose profit as very similar to morality. For reasons we shall discuss at some length, the two are different in a number of significant ways.

31. I shall not assimilate science and ethics any further than is necessary to make the necessary claims about ethics. One effect of the works of Quine and Kuhn has been to suggest that some of the reasons for subjectivism about ethics are also reasons for subjectivism about science. This is good news for those, like Rorty (1979, 1989, 1991), who are in some respects subjectivists about science as well as those, like most of the contributors to Sayre-McCord (1988), who are objectivists about ethics. Ch. 4 deals further with this cluster of issues.

32. So also in baseball. Sabermetricians have demonstrated to the satisfaction of attentive fans some facts that had not been widely understood before: for example, that Steve Garvey was not a very productive hitter and that Bobby Grich was a great player.

33. My position here is similar to that of Foot (1979, *passim*), although her immediate target is the view that moral judgments are first of all prescriptive and only secondarily descriptive. On that issue, too, I am closer to her than to her an-

tagonists, including my admirable teacher Hare. I do not deny that judgments of moral goodness and other kinds have a normative element, and I certainly do not advocate anything like an operational definition of any moral term; nevertheless, in due course I shall cash out the idea of a good life in what one might call a partly Aristotelian way. My own agenda does not require me to give an account of the meaning of an evaluative term and the relationship of its meaning to the criteria for its application.

I believe I also have the support of Arrington (1989, pp. 241f.), despite our disagreement mentioned in n. 22. He argues that when we talk of an alternative moral system we may not be using the word *moral* in a literal way; strictly speaking, we mean "an alternative form of social structure and control," rather than a genuine moral system. He would deny the name of morality to any system that does not at least entail respect for others and for their rights and in that way might seem to have an even more demanding notion of morality than I do; in the end, however, it is not at all clear that he does, for my account eventually includes being respected as an essential component of the good life, and it is the notion of the good life that gives content to the notion of being better off.

34. Of course, the Martian might refer to some activity as "our baseball" and mean that it is the traditional Martian sport. That would be a reasonable thing to say, but of no importance to the point I am making. The African-American comedian Franklin Ajaye says of basketball, "That's our golf," and audiences have no trouble grasping his meaning.

35. My argument here resembles Davidson's (1984), which in turn is much influenced by Quine's (esp. 1960). For an application of the argument to morality see Rorty (1991, esp. vol. I, pp. 27–30). In this brief space I cannot do justice to the magnitude and complexity of the controversy over this issue. Quine is famously skeptical about the standard distinction between analytic and synthetic; Davidson likes to disparage the easy distinction between scheme and content. I am not certain that either of them would accept my application of their views.

36. My own view is that we have reason to take divine commands to be moral imperatives only if we have reason to believe that God is good, and evaluating God is both difficult and presumptuous.

37. It is perfectly true that lying does not always have any negative consequences and that it can be wrong even when it does not. The concept of lying would have no application, no meaning remotely like ours, in a world in which lies seldom or never had negative consequences. But that is no reason for saying that lying is wrong only by definition or as a matter of moral grammar, as Arrington (1989, p. 275) does.

38. It is true that dueling was legal, because the laws were different. But that just shows one of the differences between law and morality. We have made moral progress: we have learned something about honor, as we have about fairness and decency, since the days when people wrongly thought fighting duels had something to do with honor and owning slaves had something to do with property rights. Only if the whole notion of honor had become inoperative by now could one argue that dueling was honorable, as an atheist who does not accept the concept of heresy as viable might argue that one person accused by the Inquisition really was a heretic but another was not.

As honor is related to one's observance of local tacit moral agreements, what is honorable may differ from one locale to another. For example, in our society I am not dishonored if another man hugs my wife; but that act has a very different meaning in some other cultures, and for that reason an American visitor ought to be circumspect. But it does not follow that it is honorable to observe a certain local tacit moral agreement if it is a morally bad one, as the institution of dueling is.

39. Moral realists, including Brink, think that there are principles like that, as respectable as principles related to science. For me the interesting question is the status of such principles. We discuss the pertinent issues primarily in Ch. 4.

40. I do not claim to be trying to describe the Ik accurately, as does Turnbull (1972). I offer a thought experiment designed to make a point about limits on what might count as morality.

41. One might argue, although I shall not, that the same is true of capitalism because failure in the marketplace is essential to it. One great difference is that while organizations must fail, people need not do so, at least not in the long term. Another is that successful competitors in the market need not get actual enjoyment from the loser's loss, but there is an Ik-like problem where they do, as is alleged to be the case among investment bankers and elsewhere. Lewis (1989) describes an organization in which that is the case.

42. There is a description of the Prisoner's Dilemma in every textbook on game theory, and elsewhere, too. The dilemma in question is the one that faces an alleged perpetrator whom the police are pressuring to confess to a crime he and his partner have committed, although the police can't prove it. Each is told that if he confesses and implicates his partner and his partner remains silent, he will get (let us say) one year and his partner five. If both confess, each will get three. He knows that if he neither confesses nor is implicated they will both be found guilty only of a lesser charge and sentenced to two years. In the aggregate the two are best off if neither confesses, as *omerta* dictates. But each can reason that whether his partner confesses or not, he will be better off confessing and implicating his partner. Each can reason as follows: if he does not confess, then by confessing I'll get one year rather than two; and if he does confess, then by confessing I'll get three rather than five; so either way I'm better off confessing. So if each acts in a rational and self-interested way, each will confess, and each will get three years. A way of ensuring that they cooperatively refrain from confessing would be something both could freely and rationally embrace.

43. Since an intention presupposes a desire and a belief, it is difficult if possible at all to infer either a desire or a belief from an action, even if we know it is an intentional one; we have to know the belief before we can infer the desire, or the desire before we can know the belief. But if we cannot think of any combination of remotely plausible desire and remotely plausible belief that might account for a certain intentional action, then we have no reason to assign an intention.

44. There are individual differences here, and these questions can be raised about individuals as well as communities, but it is normally possible to explain individual behavior in part by reference to community values and beliefs. One of the characteristics in virtue of which a number of people constitute a community is that they share a language and therefore certain beliefs and the ability to understand each other's behavior and to communicate because they share those beliefs and certain preferences as well. On several later occasions, particularly in Ch. 6, I shall discuss the implications of the ways in which the individual's desires and therefore his notions of what counts as happiness and therefore his conception of the good life may be socialized. The point of the current discussion is that

there are limits to what can count as a conception of the good life, whatever its origin.

Explaining any thick concept seems to require saying what the point of some practice is. A practice may not have a point that is very attractive to us, but it cannot be wholly repugnant to us in every respect if we are to give an exegesis of it.

45. Turnbull (1972) shows that at least a few of the Ik's terrible traits have some survival value in the desperate circumstances of their lives. If gavainess creates tough, resourceful people who can survive in the Ik world but will expire without much fuss if they become a drag on the community, then it bears some similarities to *omerta* and other highly unpleasant practices that are the basis of honor in primitive or criminal societies; hence, it is a moral concept but a deficient one, as are a number of concepts associated with ancient notions of honor. If, however, individual Ik are motivated neither by others' interests nor by any conception of obligation that rests on an institution that serves a community purpose—if they just enjoy being mean—then gavainess is not part of even a bad moral code. To make that case requires some considerations that appear in Ch. 2.

46. The notion of foundation is more common in epistemology than in ethics. The view that in order to justify a claim to know anything one must infer it from some self-justifying kind of knowledge is an old and superficially plausible one. My arguments against foundationalism in ethical theory (mostly in Ch. 4) bear some similarities to that theory's epistemological counterpart. Egoism as a foundational reason to be moral and utilitarianism as a foundational account of the nature of morality have some of the allure and the disappointments of sense data as the foundation of knowledge. Our knowledge about our sense data depends, for example, on what we have learned in conversation with others in our community; similarly, our interests are determined to a large extent in interaction with others in our community. But just as it still makes sense to advert to experience when we test certain knowledge claims, it still makes sense to advert to the question whether people will be better off when we test certain claims that some act or institution is morally acceptable.

47. Readers who need an argument here may consider the following. It can never be reasonable to interpret another person as seriously denying nearly everything we believe, since in any purported case it will always be more reasonable to assume that we have misinterpreted the person's words or that the person is misspeaking or joking; hence, it is not conceivable that we are wrong in nearly all we believe. By a similar argument, it can never be reasonable to attribute intentionality to someone by taking that person to be aiming at some objective that in our opinion has nothing whatever to be said for it; it is always more reasonable to assume that that person is acting involuntarily or is aiming at some other objective thus far unknown. Hence, it is not conceivable that all the things we desire are undesirable. Similarly, it can never be reasonable to interpret another person as seriously morally condemning nearly everything we morally praise (for example, by putting forward a radically different view of what is as desirable, hence what counts as being better off), since no matter what the person says it will always be more reasonable to assume that we have misinterpreted the person's words or that the person is misspeaking or joking. Hence, it is not conceivable that we are wrong in nearly all we morally praise or that nearly all of what we consider morally good is morally bad.

2

Utilitarianism and Its Difficulties

If morality is supposed to make people better off, one might think that what is moral is whatever maximizes being well off in the aggregate. If the morality of an act is determined by whether it generates more goodness than does any possible alternative, and if goodness is a matter of the amount of well-being of one or more people, one might infer that the individual always has a moral obligation to try to maximize happiness for everyone.

This is not a sound argument. For one thing, it is not clear that any old happiness can be the objective of moral activity, since some forms of happiness are not obviously good. Is it good to be happy because you believe something false? That hardly seems to count as being better off. More generally, traditional utilitarian theories give no adequate account of what is involved in well-being, or of the good life. Standard economic theory, which has been thought to be the realization of utilitarianism, makes some questionable presuppositions about the good life, in particular about its connection with the fulfillment of desire. This problem about utilitarianism is of particular interest to business ethicists because one of the criticisms of the culture of business is precisely that it socializes people to prefer and be content with a life inferior to what they might otherwise have lived.

Utilitarianism has a special attraction for economists, which is what most of the original utilitarians were; economics has seemed to promise a way to quantify desires and their satisfaction, as for example by way of Pareto optimality, and cost-benefit analysis has dealt with a range of problems in public policy and elsewhere.[1] According to the agency theory normally associated with economics, individuals are rational maximizers of their own interests, which are an individual matter, affected by others' well-being only indirectly. As people may be assumed to have the information necessary to act appropriately on their desires, their uncoerced actions are a reliable guide to their intentions,[2] and their freedom to act will result in happiness for them. But this theory is flawed throughout, and its flaws generate issues to discuss in this chapter and elsewhere, particularly in Chapter 5. In any case, it is far from clear that being better off is amenable to definition by way of Pareto optimality or cost-benefit analysis.[3]

Utilitarianism is a more plausible answer to the question, How shall *we* live? than to, How shall *I* live? and does better at explaining why *we* are better off if *we* are moral than why *I* am better off if *I* am moral. This helps explain its appeal to legislators and managers. Managers who operate by creating rules rather than by monitoring individual actions owe more attention to the utilitarian consequences of principles than to those of acts. But managers not only make rules, they create attitudes, even virtues. It does not follow that there is anything wrong with utilitarianism; what does follow is that even if utilitarianism is right, moral deliberation may yet not be straightforwardly utilitarian.

The nature of the good life, by reference to which utility surely ought to be defined, is a challenging issue. Whatever its nature, the good life is widely agreed to have something to do with autonomy, which is neither identical with well-being nor only a means to it. Talk of autonomy raises issues about rights, which may have something to do with the good life even when they have nothing to do with happiness. Justice too creates problems for utilitarianism, because it gives reasons to believe there are some acts that contribute to the good life more than do alternatives that are nevertheless morally superior. To begin with, then, we need a better account of the good life than standard utilitarianism gives.[4] The widespread feeling that organizations do not always support the good life adds a certain interest to this issue.

VERSIONS OF HAPPINESS

The most alluring claim of standard utilitarianism is that one can readily measure the comparative morality of various possible actions according to whether they maximize utility, as though utility were like profit.[5] Utilitarianism has traditionally encouraged us to think about quantities of pleasure and pain. From that point of view, nothing else is supposed to be morally important, not even the individual's life, except insofar as it is pleasureable on balance.

Critics of utilitarianism claim that one cannot quantify utility and calculate in the way Bentham seems to suggest,[6] but Benthamite utilitarianism is not the only possible kind. It is one thing to say that the purpose of morality is to create a world in which there is the greatest possible well-being (subject, one might add, to the constraints of justice or similar factors), and quite another to say, what is clearly not the case, that the individual ought always to try to calculate and decide what to do on the basis of what seems likely to generate the most happiness.[7] Any manager will see the point immediately. Even if it is the purpose of a certain organization to maximize profit, it does not follow that the individual employee should on every occasion do what he or she thinks will maximize profit. That would be a bad way to generate profit; similarly, utilitarian calculation would be a poor way to maximize happiness.[8]

At its crudest, as in the form of the unargued assumptions of economists, utilitarianism takes the view that well-being is a matter of the fulfillment of one's desires. The standard implausible assumptions of rationality, perfect information, and consistency of desires are supposed to preempt the objection that one might turn out to be unhappy as a result of getting what one wants, but in fact one might. In that obvious sense, although not only in that sense, one's preferences are not stable. What the good life requires at a minimum is the satisfaction of desires that are rational in some way.[9] It follows from the standard economist's view that such desirable things as friendship are of value only as means to the fulfillment of one's desires, hence of happiness—that is, they are not of value in themselves.

In any case, utilitarianism overrates happiness. It is of particular interest to business ethics that some kinds of happiness are not good, not reasonable, broadly speaking. I mentioned earlier that happiness based on false beliefs seems unattractive. So does happiness based on other kinds of failure of understanding. Social pressure may foist a poor sort of happiness upon a person by lowering expectations or otherwise causing one to adopt an inferior view of what counts as happiness. Consider this famous passage from *Brave New World* (Huxley [1932], pp. 58f.):

> Before Bernard could answer, the lift came to a standstill.
> "Roof!" called a creaking voice.
> The liftman was a small simian creature, dressed in the black tunic of an Epsilon-Minus Semi-Moron.
> "Roof!"
> He flung open the gates. The warm glory of afternoon sunlight made him start and blink his eyes. "Oh, roof!" he repeated in a voice of rapture. He was as though suddenly and joyfully awakened from a dark annihilating stupor. "Roof!"
> He smiled up with a kind of doggily expectant adoration into the faces of his passengers.

One is inclined to say that this happy but pathetic elevator operator is being treated as a means to corporate and community ends rather than as a rational and autonomous human being with ends of his own. But he likes it; and whether or not happiness is identical with the satisfaction of desire, he meets the utilitarian standard. That he desires and is fulfilled raises the question of what to say about people who are content with those worldly pleasures for which privation or socialization has caused them gladly to settle, without the courage or knowledge to desire anything further.[10] We are reluctant to say that a community that makes people willing to be useful morons is doing them any favors. If utilitarianism takes the point of morality to be the fulfillment of desire, and if a strong corporate culture can determine what one desires, then utilitarianism is surely problematical.[11]

Huxley is attacking the standard utilitarian equation of happiness with the good and the associated refusal to countenance any reason for saying that one kind of good is superior to others. On that theory, there is no reason to say that the pleasure of listening to Mozart is superior to that of listening to the rapper M. C. Hammer, even if the Hammer listener has never heard Mozart.[12] Nor does the theory permit any basis for saying that a life of going up and down in an elevator is less happy than one that includes enjoyment of all kinds of high culture or adventure. Nor can the theory devalue drug-induced euphoria, so long as there is no problem about getting drugs. If we believe, as Huxley clearly does, that there is something stunted and sad about the elevator man, that he is in a state that it is not the purpose of morality to promote, standard utilitarianism does not give us any support for our belief, or vice versa.

Huxley notes not only the poverty of happiness but also the community's effect on what counts as happiness for its people. There are certain natural limits to human desires, for there are certain things no sane person could ever be happy with: physical pain, for example.[13] But one's notion of happiness is malleable. The very pleasures and desires that are characteristically human, such as the ones associated with states at the upper end of Maslow's (1970) hierarchy, are dependent on one's community because they are dependent on others' opinion: honor, prestige, being a winner.

Why, after all, did Michael Milken, the junk bond purveyor, seek happiness in making enormous amounts of money? To purchase desirable items that he would otherwise be without? Why did he argue ferociously with his boss over $15,000 (Stewart [1991], pp. 208f.)? Within Drexel Burnham Lambert and elsewhere among investment bankers there was a clear shared sense of what counted as success, the basis of esteem and self-esteem. The same is true of any organization or business with a distinctive culture; investment banking is a marvelous example.

It is inevitable that one's happiness is related to others' opinions; there is nothing wrong with that. In extreme cases, however, one must raise questions—for example, about whether workaholism and unscrupulousness in the pursuit of eight-figure financial rewards have anything to do with the good life. Some of my students not only understand but share the conception of the good life that animates the Milkens or at least the Henry Kravises of the world.

But what can we say about them? That they are wrong and Thoreau right? To pity them for their view of the good life may seem a little like being glad you don't like broccoli because if you liked it you'd eat it, which would be bad, because you hate it. That a conception of success is socially constructed does not necessarily make it a bad basis for an individual's happiness: There is no reason to believe that the only real happiness is the lone wolf kind. So it becomes important to be able to characterize the right kind of socialization by the right kind of community or, at the very least, some wrong kinds. We want to be able to rule out Huxley's dystopia and critically assess—just for example—the culture of high-stakes investment banking.

We do have some ways of criticizing communities; I now mention one that can serve to start us discussing some issues that will concern us throughout this essay. The milieu in which the Henry Kravises find happiness is wrong from a moral point of view insofar as it resembles that of the Ik—that is, insofar as the happiness of a few depends on the failure and consequent unhappiness of most. For reasons given in Chapter 1, it is something close to a necessary truth that morality is about the happiness of more than a few in the community. In a community in which most people hold to La Rochefoucauld's notion of the good life, as may be the case in the world of acquisitions and mergers, only a few can achieve happiness. To recall a term used in Chapter 1, the Kravis notion of the good life is collectively self-defeating.

At this point we may feel inclined toward Aristotle, who does not believe that pleasure or the fulfillment of desire makes one happy in Aristotle's sense of the term (in Greek, *eudaimon*), which connotes at the very least not only thinking one is better off but actually being so. The vignette of the elevator operator he would take as illustrating his view that happiness has something to do with the fulfillment of one's nature as a human being, not just the fulfillment of any old desire. This is further than I care to go, but Aristotle's emphasis on rationality and sociability as human characteristics is worth mentioning and remembering for later discussion. There is in it the implication that the right kind of happiness is one that a viable community supports, one that is in at least that sense not self-defeating.

The restriction that a morality-supporting conception of the good life must be promotable throughout a community leaves considerable leeway for differing views of the nature of the good life. It does not, for example, favor enjoying Mozart more than rap music or tell us what is wrong with the society depicted in *Brave New World*, which persuades that neither happiness nor desire-fulfillment can be all there is to the sort of life that morality is supposed to promote.

Even if it can adequately characterize the good life, however, utilitarianism still falls short of encompassing morality, for the good life may be created and spread by means that are unjust or that violate someone's rights. We must therefore consider rights and justice, criteria of morality that supplement and possibly modify utility. In the end I shall argue that it is difficult to define and defend them independently of utilitarian considerations, or vice versa; the three criteria turn out to be significantly interdependent, and none proves to be a solid foundation for morality.

RIGHTS AND THE GOOD LIFE

If the good life has something to do with fulfilling one's potential, as Huxley suggests, then any adequate moral theory must treat a person as a human being capable of acting autonomously.[14] Ethics is applicable only to beings that deliberate and choose, to those for whom the question of the good life and how to plan for it can arise; it is not possible that ethics is indifferent to the matter of freedom to deliberate and choose. Autonomy is of particular interest in an organizational context, where some people get to tell others what to do and thus appear to infringe upon their autonomy. That the good life has some essential connection to acting autonomously is one reason to claim that considerations of rights overlap with utilitarian considerations. Another reason is that issues about the kind and degree of autonomy people ought to have may be settled in part by reference to broadly utilitarian and even political considerations. My argument is that knowing what kind of community supports the good life, which includes a measure of autonomy, is a necessary but not sufficient condition of being able to decide what rights people have.

From Plato to Bentham and beyond, some philosophers have doubted that there is any moral obligation to grant people the right to autonomous action apart from the probability that they will act in their own best interests, or in someone's, at any rate. Advocates of rights hold that not to acknowledge the essential importance of free choice is to traduce the essence of morality. Libertarians like Friedman (1982) argue that capitalism is the most productive possible system but that its protection of rights is a distinct and essential point in its moral favor.

That autonomy is roughly a matter of the satisfaction of rational (as opposed to any old) desires[15] does not imply that one's community has an obligation to permit only those acts that are truly autonomous and may forbid any act that the agent irrationally wants to do. Even a utilitarian who does not take rights seriously as separate from utilitarian considerations could argue that on practical grounds we must grant people the right to certain irrational acts; empowering any politician or manager to regulate behavior so closely will lead to bad consequences, including depriving people of the leeway they need to create and act on their own values.

Even most utilitarians would probably agree that a community that provides a good life for its participants may be one that requires them all to respect certain claims made by others on the basis of contracts, implicit or explicit, made in the community. These claims might have a justification in utility, in which case rights could still be proof against immediate utilitarian considerations in the way contract-keeping is, for some of the same long-term utilitarian reasons having to do with probable social consequences.

Hence, for example, in a good community I have a right to property according to the laws that express the just consent of the governed. If I have more money than I need and you are a bit short, have I a right not to give you any of my money? The transfer would decrease my happiness slightly and increase yours greatly, hence seems the utilitarian thing to do. But without an institution of property largely immune to such considerations there would be chaos; people would be required constantly to defend their accumulated goods against attack and would have no incentive for accumulating goods by work, and possibly no way to do so. Commerce and other institutions critical to civilization would not survive if we brought utilitarian considerations to bear directly and decisively against every claim based on property rights.[16]

Consider the rights of employees against their employers.[17] In discussing the issue of the employee's right to a job we take into account the possible effects of the employment-at-will doctrine on fired employees' fortunes, on workplace morale, on person-job fit, and so on. We also factor in the ease of leaving a job, relative to the ease of (say) leaving one's country. What is required—not sufficient—is a clear understanding of the long-term local and institutional consequences of granting or withholding certain liberties to employees. It is hard to see how one could do this without knowing a great deal about organizations, about psychology, about a good many other topics.

At the very least, however, we must understand that there are certain rights that are not reducible to utilitarian considerations in the sense that they should not be for sale. So, for example, we now have something close to a consensus that it is wrong for a female employee to be faced with a trade-off between higher pay and freedom from harassment. There are indeed utilitarian considerations against permitting the practice: productivity is enhanced in the aggregate where stockholders can be confident that all managers will focus on growth and profitability and so will not discourage able employees. Beyond that, however, our consensus holds that women have a presumptive right to be treated with respect.

The extent to which we can base rights on utilitarian considerations is a controversial issue; fortunately, I need not settle it, nor would much be accomplished if one could prove the affirmative. (It will become clear that I believe one cannot.) But it seems clear that a good life is an autonomous life, that autonomy is valuable if anything is. If just that much is true, then to add considerations of rights to utilitarianism hardly changes it radically.[18]

We can go further. A certain reflectiveness is characteristic of intellectually mature people; they can not only decide what to do but also decide what to value. In effect, then, the good life for them includes a significant amount of freedom to decide what they will take to be good, to define the good life for themselves, within limits. In so doing, they may even decide what is in their interests—that is, what their interests are—and cultivate desires for what will create a good life for them. If this is so, then the kind of psychological egoism characteristic of standard economics cannot be a remotely adequate view.[19]

Rawls (1993, especially Lecture VIII) argues that a good political entity preserves above all else the right of each citizen to embrace his or her own conception of the good, so long as others retain the same right. Rawls doubts that there can be a conception of the good that everyone has good reason to embrace (see especially 1993, Lecture II, section 2, pp. 54ff.), but argues that in any case it is no business of the state to enforce any such conception. (He does not seem to doubt that there could be bad ones, and I shall argue that there are.) I would go further in two respects. First, I would extend the point to organizations; managers are no better than politicians at fixing on a conception of the good. And while it is appropriate for people in an organization to share certain values, it does not follow that all of their values ought to be essentially identical or that management should police values. In fact, not even the managers' and employees' reasons for being in the organization are all identical; even if they are, neither profit nor any other objective that people in the organization may share should always override individuals' interests. Second, I can see no reason at all for believing that some conception of the good could ever be shown to be superior to all others; it seems altogether implausible. This is not to deny that some conceptions of the good might be incoherent or self-defeating or pathetically unimaginative or (as Rawls indicates at p. 304 and elsewhere) unfair, while others are not; hence, in some cases, we have reason to argue for one conception (likely our own) against another, as for example on the grounds that the latter is incoherent, or is based on almost no experience of life, or is Ik-like. What we cannot do, and what states and organizations should not try to do on behalf of their citizens or employees, is rank them all and make rules accordingly.

Rawls seems to accept the Aristotelian view that not all of the good things in the world are good for the same reason—for example, that they create happiness. Some things, such as friendship, are good in themselves and not on account of their consequences. There is no common scale on which all good things can be measured and ranked (so Rawls suggests at p. 303 and p. 312, for example). If this is true—and our inability to find such a scale argues in favor of our acting as though it is true—then utilitarianism is in serious difficulty. Not only that; it is hard to see how we could find any principles that permit us to make rational decisions on a utilitarian basis. (If we add other kinds of basis that tend in other directions, the rational decision process becomes still more problematical.)

If Plato, for example, were right in holding that one can give a detailed account of the nature of the good life and that that life is good independently of whether the person who lives it has chosen it unimpeded and uncoerced, then there would be no reason to permit people to try to make decisions about how to conceive of the good. But Plato is wrong about this, and Rawls is right. As we cannot identify in detail any sort of life that is better for everyone than any other sort, no individual or state has reason to demand that any person have one sort of preference rather than another, so long as his or her preferences are compatible with others having a like freedom to have and act on their own preferences; there is no justification for restricting this sort of freedom in the Platonic way. We must face the fact of pluralism and not try to legislate it out of existence.[20]

Ronald Dworkin (1985 and elsewhere) agrees. He sees civil liberties as justified not by their probable effectiveness as guarantors of virtue but by their ability to protect people from a government that might yield to the temptation to impose its "external preferences" on citizens—that is, the preferences some citizens have concerning what other citizens should value. The point is that governments—and, for that matter, other individuals—should not be permitted to interfere with people's right to decide for themselves what is important in their lives. Dworkin claims that that right follows from the purpose of politics, which according to him is the fulfillment of as many of people's goals for their own lives as possible: "The [liberal] theory of equality supposes that political decisions must be, so far as is possible, independent of any particular conception of the good life, or of what gives value to life" (1985, p. 191).

Once we acknowledge a plurality of incommensurable goods, standard utilitarianism is thrown into question and considerations of justice and rights come to the fore. For insofar as there is no basis for ranking certain conceptions of the good ahead of certain others, we (or the government or management) are faced with a number of conceptions of the good that we ought to treat with equal respect—legally, at any rate—and that people ought to be allowed to pursue unimpeded; in that sense we should follow principles of justice and autonomy, at least in talking about conceptions of the good.

I do not argue that it is the purpose of a company to fulfill its employees' own goals, although something of that sort seems to be precisely the purpose for which a social system supports commerce, in particular corporations with limited liability.[21] All the same, it is hard to see the justification for an employer's imposing any external preferences on an employee. But what counts as imposition? In a free labor market the employee can leave the company for a better deal elsewhere far more readily than a citizen can leave the country of which he or she is a citizen, so one always has the obvious recourse. The company has more power to impose in certain labor markets, but it does not follow that an employee has the same claims against it that a citizen has against the government. There are some legitimate powers that management has that government does not; there are others that government has that management does not. It is hard to see how one could sort these out—as we shall begin to do in Chapters 6 and 7—entirely without regard to utilitarian considerations.

It is worth repeating that justifying certain employee rights by reference to utilitarian considerations gives Benthamites no comfort. We find no good reason to believe that a manager is justified in using utilitarian calculation to decide how to treat an employee in some questionable situation; in particular, there is no general license here for managers to override rights on utilitarian grounds. The notion of utility in use here is a very broad one. In fact, insofar as rights are goal-based, the goal on which they are based is in some cases so open-ended as to be hardly a real goal at all; it is precisely that people have the right to set their own goals unimpeded. We are neither justifying rights by reference to goals nor justifying goals by reference to rights. Neither is fundamental relative to the other.

What I mean to suggest here, and to argue further in due course, is that a good organization, like a good society, is one that is hospitable to the autonomous search for worthy goals and values. Moral progress is possible, and in fact has been made to some degree,[22] although it does not follow that an autonomous search will lead to the final truth, whether about values or anything else, or that there is any other identifiable goal underlying and justifying these rights.

To say that persons have a right to free choice raises the question, What sort of thing has one a right to choose to do? The answer traditional since Mill—a utilitarian answer, as one would expect of Mill—is that if one is a grown-up in possession of one's faculties, one may do whatever one likes if it does not harm others. The problem is that, particularly in business, where one is normally surrounded by highly sensitive stakeholders, almost anything one does and much of what one refrains from doing affects others, potentially negatively. To invoke protection from external preferences does not advance matters very much.

A libertarian will say that an adequately self-regarding action respects others' negative rights, which are essentially rights to be left alone.[23] The libertarian position is intended to protect people from control by the passionate intensity of the majority, whose tendency is to include others' preferences in its scope, for example by claiming to be harmed by any of the wide range of states and events that make them feel bad. So Robert Bork (1971) argued concerning the case of *Griswold* v. *Connecticut* that there is no principled basis for claiming that a married couple's right to use contraceptives in the privacy of their home overrides the majority's right to be spared the anguish they would experience in contemplating this practice, unimpeded by a permissive government.[24] Dworkin would respond that this is a matter of the majority's imposing external preferences on people. Conservative opponents can make one or both of two replies: they can claim that they are themselves harmed by the licentious practice in question, or they can claim that civic virtue requires that we police bedrooms and in other ways go after external preferences whether liberals like it or not.

A broadly utilitarian account of rights, which implies that what rights one grants the individual depends greatly upon one's view of the rules and practices characteristic of a good community, can handle Bork's problem. Its answer to his defense of the state's intrusion into sexual relationships is that a good community is one that permits people to feel safe from that kind of interference in certain matters between consenting adults, much as a rule against punishing the innocent permits people to feel safe and plan their lives with confidence so long as they abide by the law, as it is extraordinarily important for people to be able to make and implement plans for their lives. Autonomy is consistent with certain constraints, but not with unknown and random governmental constraints or with constraints on private matters. Whether or not this is what philosophers mean when they talk about a goal-based view of rights, it is surely not a crass utilitarian view; we can still hold that the notion of utility requires that of autonomy at least as much as the other way around.

Respecting rights does not always make everyone or even anyone happy, but a community that countenances certain rights is the kind that supports the good life. Can we say the same sort of thing about acting justly?

JUSTICE AND RULE UTILITARIANISM

In Chapter 1 I argued that it is characteristic of the moral point of view that one takes others' interests as reason for action; that others' welfare matters to the moral agent; that the moral point of view involves not only taking others' interests into account but also regarding their interests as equal in importance to one's own. That much impartiality seems to be implicit in the idea that morality is about others' interests and not just the agent's. Dworkin and Rawls explicate the notion of rights by making the free *and equal* person the central figure in morality, thus suggesting that equality is essential to morality. Rawls stipulates further that only those rights may be granted to any citizen that can be granted to all. In that way he would reduce unwarranted interference with autonomy and at the same time introduce a form of justice as equality with respect to basic rights.[25]

It is legitimate for me to take special care of my own interests—that is part of a reasonable division of labor in a good society—but in paying attention to my own interests I have a moral obligation to grant others a like attention to theirs. It follows that moral principles make no exception for me, except insofar as I have some attribute that others might have as well. And by parity of reasoning, moral principles make no such exception for anyone but require that there be some reason for unequal distribution of goods and burdens. From that point of view, impartiality is not so much a variance to be required of utilitarianism as an essential part of it; everyone's welfare deserves equal respect in the absence of any basis for overriding anyone's—as, for example, criminal behavior or special rights or duties, which themselves may be compelling on grounds of reciprocity, which is itself a form of fairness, or on other utilitarian grounds.

Yet justice, like rights, trumps utility in some cases. As an act that is acceptable from a strict utilitarian point of view may violate someone's rights, so may it raise problems about justice. Consider the manager who discovers that accidental use of a certain medication has caused Smith, the unit's outstanding employee, unwittingly to make an enormously expensive mistake. Suppose the manager sees that it is possible to suppress the damning evidence and frame the CEO's useless brother-in-law, who doesn't need his job anyway; then the utilitarian course of action is to frame the brother-in-law and preserve people's respect for due process by telling no one what has really happened. Our intuition that this would be unfair and thus morally wrong indicates that a straightforward utilitarianism is not self-evidently correct. Generating good is essential to morality; but even if we cannot derive much of morality from the notion of reason as Kant claims can be done, we can demand some good reason for treating like cases differently and not find it here. Our intuition that suffering ought to be administered fairly, hence only to those who deserve it, is also strong and makes the utilitarian approach to this manager's problem repugnant.

The standard utilitarian response to this story is the doctrine of rule utilitarianism: one should not do what creates the most happiness but instead follow the rule that, if followed generally, will create the most happiness. A rule that permits one to persecute a scapegoat would undermine confidence in the law or in management's fidelity to fair principles; a rule that one ought to keep one's promises if and only if doing so is better for all concerned would ruin the valuable institution of promising. On that account one sometimes has an obligation to do something other than what would do the most good under the circumstances. The point of the criticism "What if everybody did that?" is to invoke a rule that has utility even though some acts performed according to it do not. Thus, the soldier's duty is to stand fast according to orders even if others are likely to turn and run, even if he cannot hold the line all by himself. In that and similar cases, such as contracts and promises, the adoption of rule utilitarianism would serve the further utilitarian purpose of supporting people's confidence in one another.

This is not a good way to deal with the problem. The rule that will create most happiness here—what rule utilitarianism requires—is that one should frame innocent people if it will promote the general welfare and will not be discovered—and that is not fair. (An influential argument

along these lines is made by Lyons [1965].) It is always possible to construct a rule that mentions those crucial conditions that are necessary if
such actions are to generate the appropriate useful results; rule utilitarianism seems not to be an improvement on act utilitarianism. On the
contrary, where it does differ from act utilitarianism, it may impose an
obligation to do something futile because, although the result of everyone's doing it would be good, not everyone will, and the good result will
not happen. It may require doing something that will help the organization only under certain circumstances that do not hold and will hurt it
where they do not. Suppose your department can get an important proposal out before the deadline if and only if ten people stay at the office
and work on it late into the night, and suppose everybody but you goes
home at five o'clock. Surely you have no moral obligation to the organization to work alone all night if you know your effort will be futile.[26]

A straightforwardly utilitarian rule consistently applied may violate
people's rights. Consider a rule that licenses discrimination against the
handicapped and thus saves all the money that would be spent in accommodating them. There is no evident algorithm for trading off rights
and utility insofar as they are distinct,[27] not least because there is no
reason to suppose they are commensurable (see note 6). Normally we
bring intuitions to bear, but by themselves they are not conclusive, and
even a single person may have inconsistent ones.[28]

Apart from problems about fairness and rights and futility, standard
rule utilitarianism is no improvement on ordinary utilitarianism; they
are self-defeating in the same way. The determination always to perform
whatever act, or even whatever sort of act, maximizes happiness will have
unhappy consequences, not least as a result of the breakdown of rules
and institutions that enable people to trust one another.[29] Now we want
to ask, And what rules and institutions are those? If morality is about
making people better off, then it must attend to the rules and institutions that are required for the task. "Are required," that is; not "would be
required" under assumptions that never hold. This is an important point,
for it suggests that managers need to take care in designing rules and institutions with a view to the facts of the matter.

Contrary to what Plato's *Republic* suggests, there is no reason to believe
that ethics—any more than economics or management—is about how to
organize a community of perfectly rational and omniscient maximizers,
or about any other sort of situation that never arises.[30] Nor is ethics about
situations in which everyone else does whatever the deliberating agent
does. Insofar as we distinguish theoretical from applied ethics by saying
that the former generates propositions that are true under circumstances
that never hold, we raise the question why anyone should be interested
in theoretical ethics. Why should anyone, even a philosopher, care what
a classically rational and self-interested person will do if everybody else is
the same, since there are few if any people like that? If business ethics is
a form of applied ethics—and that is not obvious, as I shall argue in

Chapter 4—surely it should not apply principles that in practice damage people rather than make them better off.[31]

Scientists do theorize about ideal objects, and their theories are useful for many purposes. Economists make benignly false assumptions that sometimes help them make predictions that are approximately true, but assuming that people are rational in the way economists assume they are leads to excesses when the subject is ethics. We see these excesses in libertarian ethical theories, for example, and in the facile use of game theory to address moral problems. Libertarians, game theorists, and contract theorists have something to say to us, and I shall be giving them a platform in this essay, but we must watch their little falsehoods carefully.

The question why anyone should care about purely hypothetical people and situations leads us to consider a number of issues, of which two are particularly important. The first, explored in the next section and in Chapter 3, is how management might create a situation in which people need not decline to act morally out of fear that others will not act morally and thereby put them at a disadvantage. The second issue, explored in Chapter 4, is the relationship between theoretical and applied ethics. The least we can say for the moment is that that relationship is not like the relationship between theoretical and applied science and that the latter relationship is itself not quite what it seems to be.

MORAL PRINCIPLES AND ADMINISTRATIVE RULES

Managers and legislators have the task of creating actual rules and institutions that make their world safe for morality. Those who take both morality and management seriously will want to know which rules and institutions, assuming that they are publicly announced and that members of the community can reasonably expect them to be upheld most of the time, will generate the most well-being. That criterion disqualifies not only principles that make false assumptions—for example, that everyone is a rational maximizer—but also intuitively unsatisfying rules that include such locutions as "if no one will find out about it," for no manager could ever administer such a rule. It also disqualifies certain rules that one would have an obligation to follow even when following them would do no good because they are not generally followed; recall the illustration about futilely staying late at the office. Rules of the right kind usually depend for their appropriateness on wide acceptance and so must be framed with an eye to its probability. A good rule not only provides an escape clause in certain clear cases of futility but also increases the probability that others will follow the rule.

Yet surely one may sometimes have an obligation to act in a way that under the circumstances will be futile, as for example by keeping a promise to a dying parent or holding the line when others probably will not, despite one's good example. One may have the intuition that there is something illegitimate about placing so much weight on the distinction between principles that can be publicly and effectively agreed to and those that cannot. Although futility is unappealing, we may hesitate to make morality too much a matter of what does or does not work. Among other things, we want to avoid placing too much reliance on the individual's possibly self-serving judgments about consequences. ("Well, he'll never miss it," one says, or, "She'll be better off if she doesn't know.")

Why, then, does a good principle obligate one to keep a promise or do anything else when it will do no good? There is a possible response that reminds us of a critical feature of morality. It is important not only to encourage useful behavior but to encourage attitudes and emotions and traits of character that support behavior that is useful most of the time. It is a good thing that most of us are not usually inclined to break promises or lie and feel a sense of repugnance when we do. Since inclinations of this sort are the result of much training and cultivation, people are often unable and more often unwilling to distinguish between (say) useful and useless promise keeping. If they regularly tried to do so and to act on the distinction in the name of utility, then promises would not have much credibility. The success of morality depends on most of us wanting to be and succeeding to some degree in being a certain sort of person, a person with certain inclinations, a person of good character. This fact militates in favor of simple principles, since an inclination of the right sort, a component of a character of the right sort, will likely be rather a blunt instrument, not the sort of thing that readily adjusts to the subtle features of every situation.[32]

In advancing this line of thought, I suggest, as I shall again, that morality is not merely about the quality of certain acts but about character—that is, about being the kind of person who is motivated not only to follow certain principles that usually have utilitarian consequences and contribute to social solidarity but also to treat others in the community with appropriate respect, quite apart from rules. I suggest too that managers can support moral behavior not only by making rules—which are more easily enforced the simpler they are, other things being equal—but by affecting employees' inclinations and even their values.[33]

How do we distinguish between acts which, because they are futile or worse if undertaken in isolation or without support, are not obligatory and those that, although pointless, are still required? Why do I have an obligation to tell the truth uselessly but not futilely to stay and work on the proposal if it will take ten people to complete and there is no one else around?

Part of the answer to this question is that there is a general agreement and unspoken expectation, a sort of implicit social contract with some utilitarian support, that one will tell the truth. That there is something like an agreement creates the presumption of an obligation. Hence, there is reason to expect that others who have signed on will abide by it rather than take advantage of one's truthfulness or honesty or other moral behavior, and they are more likely to do so if they are so inclined. If people did take advantage regularly, then the practice would expire, and so eventually would the obligation to support it. The very concept of honesty would expire, too, and probably the word as well. In that sense there would be no more lies.[34]

Philosophers' ingenious attempts to propound a satisfactory global utilitarianism based on commensurable goods will surely never succeed. Managers must create rules and institutions that, while they cannot be counted on to cause moral behavior every time, at least create an environment in which people are encouraged to be moral and to consider what being moral entails. One can never know that one has done this as well as possible, even after the fact, but the same is true of any managerial task.

The principles that any community has good reason to propagate are ones that create the good life for those who have a stake in the community. Such principles should not be self-defeating; they should be able to be widely propagated; they should not often lead to futile efforts or pointless sacrifices or false expectations that people will always act rationally or cooperatively. They must be realistic, so as not to encourage defection and thus make adherents worse off to no good purpose. And those who live with these principles must be satisfied on the whole that they are not unfair and do not violate individuals' rights; hence, among other things, they should not specify in detail what the good life is.

Where do we get such principles? I essay an answer in Chapters 3 and 4, along these lines: the best we can do in designing principles of utility, justice, and rights is to find out what the likely prevailing principles would be in a community populated by and satisfactory to people who are like us but who also want to establish and act on principles that can form the basis for acceptable moral justifications among them. This is not wholly unrealistic; contrary to crude psychological egoism, most of us have what Scanlon (1982, p. 111) calls "the desire to find and agree on principles which no one who had this desire could reasonably reject," and we have an obligation to act accordingly.

UTILITY AND DISCRIMINATION

That equality has something important to do with morality does not imply, nor is it true, that everyone ought always to be treated the same. The great issue for justice is this: what justifies unequal treatment?

Not all discrimination is wrong, and utility is in some cases a possible basis for morally acceptable discrimination. An organization with legitimate aims might discriminate in favor of people with characteristics that contribute to achieving corporate objectives—for example, ability to operate a lathe efficiently. Race and sex would not normally justify discrimination, but a casting director might legitimately discriminate against a white actor auditioning for the role of Othello.

The pertinence of these considerations to affirmative action is clear. One of the arguments for what is sometimes called reverse discrimination is that it assists in achieving an integrated society, which is a just and efficient objective and not at all a racist one. But there remains the objection that it is simply not fair to discriminate against people on the basis of race unless race is pertinent to the job. That objection rules out discrimination justified by long-term, socially oriented, partly utilitarian considerations but permits discrimination and differential reward based on such business-related factors as ability to run a lathe or portray Othello plausibly. Yet the latter kind of discrimination also rests on a utilitarian justification insofar as it presupposes that the efficiency of a society's business system may justify discrimination on the basis of personal characteristics such as intelligence. Why should we countenance discrimination based on business necessity, which itself is morally important primarily because business plays a certain useful role in society, while opposing discrimination based more directly on social usefulness?[35]

One possible reply is that discrimination on the basis of talent is simply fair, because talent deserves to be rewarded. Most people would claim that those who are, say, smarter or physically stronger than others deserve the reward they receive in proportion to the contribution that their native gifts enable them to make; the arrangement is fair, a kind of equal exchange. To say that a person who is lucky enough to be extremely talented deserves to make millions is surely less compelling than to say that a morally good person deserves a reward and not a punishment. It appears that we reward talent on a theory of desert based largely on utilitarian reasons for providing incentives for people to develop and apply their talents. These reasons are morally compelling to a capitalist's intuitions, but probably not to those of a socialist. They are not self-justifying in any case; nor are the more egalitarian intuitions of the socialist. Invoking fairness does not obviously favor either over the other.

The notion that talent deserves to be rewarded, like the notion that property should be respected, has a strong hold on our intuitions. Although we find plausible the claim that good character deserves to be rewarded—or at least that innocence deserves not to be punished—we may nonetheless wonder why someone fortunate enough to be able to play baseball very well is deserving in the same sense. The San Francisco Giants pay Barry Bonds $7 million per year because the owner believes that Bonds is worth at least that much to the team and that some other team would have hired him if the Giants had offered him significantly less. It is not clear how considerations of fairness add anything. Yet fairness does seem to be at issue in rewarding virtue, as opposed to talent. But so do utilitarian considerations; turnabout is effective as well as fair. That these intuitions about fairness have some utilitarian basis does not make them trivial or crass—they are related to ideas of reciprocity, loyalty, and self-respect that may bind individuals into a stable community—but we should recognize that basis for what it is; if we hold out against utilitarian arguments for affirmative action, we should do so because they are bad arguments, if they are, and not just because it is a case of utilitarian arguments being balanced against considerations of fairness.[36]

The intuition that there is fairness as well as utility at stake when we reward talent resembles the intuition that one should not lie; that too has a utilitarian basis, and it too may admit of exceptions, as when the consequences of telling the truth are catastrophic. But the rules for rewarding talent and against lying are so important and exceptions are so easy to rationalize that one ought not to override them except on overwhelming grounds, and then only after careful consideration and with reluctance and even a feeling of repugnance. What creates a problem in the case of affirmative action is that the same can be said of using race as a basis for discrimination, even of a benign sort.

In spite of the advantages of simple rules, however, one can always legitimately raise the question, Is this a situation in which the rule applies? When are we justified in setting aside a certain moral rule? If a further rule is invoked to answer that question, there will arise a further question: When are we justified in setting aside the second-order rule? An infinite regress looms, and we must acknowledge that we shall not find airtight moral rules.[37] Where rules fail to settle the case—and if goods are incommensurable, as I claimed earlier, that will sometimes happen—there had better be a measure of wise intuition and good will to take up the slack, along with a willingness to abide by moral rules as normally interpreted even when it is not clear that to do so will have desirable consequences. Hence the importance of the inclination to be the right sort of person, of emotions like repugnance and admiration, of virtues like loyalty. Hence also the importance of a certain moral intelligence not reducible to knowledge of a list of rules.

Anyone well acquainted with business will acknowledge that one of the differences between effective and ineffective managers is that the former know how to be guided by the rules that ineffective managers also know but cannot use. Long experience seems to be a necessary but not sufficient condition of this ability, which typically cannot be articulated. One difference between managerial and moral practical wisdom is that it is easier to use results to gauge the former.

INTIMATE MATTERS

Utilitarian principles are least adequate where people care most. They are rarely brought to bear in intimate and important situations, where people must understand and rely on each other—in matters of sex, family, and religion, for example. There the rules of the family or of the community, which may be an organization, are normally clearer and more specific than the standard broad-gauged principles of utility or anything else (a point argued by Hampshire [1982]). Even if they are not the only ones or in all ways the best ones that might have been promulgated, they probably are ones that reflect the locals' feelings on what is most important about themselves and that match their expectations. Here too it helps if people have a sense of honor that leads them to feel a repugnance at breaking these rules and a desire to be the kind of person who does not want to break them.

In matters of this sort our confidence in each other is so important and the consequent need for adherence to the rules so great that we shrink from acting on utilitarian grounds and even from evaluating these rules from a utilitarian point of view, or from that of justice and rights. In fact, these local rules greatly influence our shared view of what is valuable, of what contributes to the good life, of what is fair, of what people ought to be permitted to do without interference. People in a community may well have similar emotions and intuitions and likely share similar conceptions of the good; that makes life smoother for most of them, but not for all.

Hampshire uses the analogy of language to clarify the status of local personal practices relative to univeral principles. The vocabulary, syntax, and other features of a language distinguish it from other languages, but we can assess languages according to certain standards of coherence and perspicuity.[38] Perhaps Hampshire is too optimistic, however, for the assessment of a language will reflect assumptions that are implicit in the language in which the assessment is expressed, and those assumptions may be questionable from the point of view of some other language. There are no languages wholly free of such assumptions, no standards self-evidently correct from the point of view of all languages. The standards we do use to assess languages are not available a priori but derive from our discoveries about which characteristics of language let us perform which tasks most effectively. We find that a number of languages do about equally well by those standards and that others have problems; so far as we know, any might be improved. Whether the same is true is of moral standards is a matter worth considering. We shall find reason to doubt that broad principles of utility, justice, and rights can be known a priori and to doubt as well that it would do much good if they could be.

None of this is leading up to an argument for some form of relativism. I have not implied that an English speaker cannot really make a grammatical mistake because grammar is relative to a language.[39] Nor is it true that having an extramarital affair is morally all right because in some societies it is not frowned on or that ridiculing a colleague is all right in any organization because it is accepted in some. Still less is there reason to say that it is morally acceptable for a man to beat his wife for talking to a stranger or to lie about a colleague where it is socially acceptable for him to do so. It is morally irresponsible to drive on the left on an American highway; not so in Britain. But driving eighty miles per hour in dense traffic is unsafe in both countries. No agreement, no expectation can make the one good or the other safe. The mere prevalence or acceptance of some practice or other in business or in a particular organization does not justify it.[40]

Even if we do not believe that there could be an ideal language, we can reject certain languages as incoherent or otherwise inadequate, and we can deny that we have any reason to say that certain noises or marks constitute a language if they cannot be interpreted as being sufficiently in agreement with our own. And so it is, as I argued in Chapter 1, with moral principles and institutions. At the very least, you ought to be able to understand an alien moral code to the extent of being able to imagine that if you were an alien and one of your family did that to you, you would be aggrieved. In this way the limits of our empathy help define the limits of what we shall consider a possible moral system. Here is evidence that the norms, and the emotions as well, that we learn in intimate situations have an importance that transcends those situations.

Williams (1981, pp. 17f.), campaigning against principles-based morality, argues that the importance we place on acting appropriately in intimate situations reveals problems with utilitarianism and with impartiality as well, since considerations of utility and fairness are often overridden by such facts as that the beneficiary is after all one's wife. He argues that a husband does the right thing in choosing to rescue his wife rather than some other equally deserving person and that the intimate relationship on which the decision is based is the kind of thing that gives life meaning. We might wish to call this situation just an instance of responding to a special duty of the sort that utilitarianism usually countenances, but there is nothing here like the lawyer-client relationship. The point is that we share certain convictions and intense feelings about how to act, and in particular about how to treat one another, without which morality would be weakened and life in our communities would be impoverished.

This is not to say that acts of this sort are beyond criticism on grounds of utility and justice. One ought to rescue one's spouse, and the law ought not to compel one to testify against one's spouse. In contrast, to side with a friend or a family member who one knows has committed a serious wrong is the sort of thing a *mafioso* would do. Any community with which we are familiar requires institutions of family or at least friendship held together by norms and feelings that can override utility and impartiality. In a good community, those norms and feelings confer a limited license, and the limits are set by reference to broadly utilitarian considerations. Setting these limits requires recognizing that we are all attached to various groups more or less closely. There are appropriate ways to deal with family members, with neighbors, with fellow citizens of a town or of a country, and so on.

Good societies need this sort of partiality. Bennett (1993) uses traditional sources in making the case that it is in just these intimate relations that we develop feelings that are crucial to morality, feelings that undergird compassion and respect and generally the habit of regarding the other person's interests as part of one's own.[41] If, as I argued in Chapter 1, morality is not self-recommending, the cause of justice requires that we develop these feelings, in families first of all. They cannot be intensely experienced outside a fairly narrow circle of friends and family, but we experience some trace of them more broadly and would likely not otherwise become motivated to take moral principles seriously. With good reason we permit and even encourage others to feel that way about their own circles, and we bring up our children accordingly. There is nothing paradoxical about the claim that these feelings and the actions they cause are good in themselves and at the same time have broad utilitarian consequences.

Aristotle, whom Bennett follows, does not think of the moral person as one who spurns pleasure in favor of doing the right thing. Recall from Chapter 1, note 26, that he claims that the truly good person is one who takes pleasure in doing the right thing, for one's character is indicated by what gives one pleasure; it is characteristic of the virtuous person to have appropriate emotions along with dispositions to act. People in organizations too may be intimately related. It is appropriate for an employee to be loyal to a company and attached by affection and trust to co-workers in ways that go beyond the language of the contract. Particularly when, as is now often the case, the workplace performs some of the functions once served by churches and civic organizations, these attachments give meaning to the employees' lives.[42] Here, too, while utilitarian calculation should not control personal relations, it is appropriate to assess the local practices from the point of view of utility, and justice as well. There can be excessive loyalty, and one's identification with one's organization can facilitate exploitation; that cannot go uncriticized. The story of the elevator operator in *Brave New World* shows the futility of happiness as a criterion for assessing communities. We give that community low marks because, to put it crudely, the wrong things make people happy, and that they do helps show that happiness isn't everything. The same is true in many organizations.

In part because respect is so widely valued, there is always something to be said for deference to local norms. So, for example, if a community takes certain sexual mores very seriously, a facile utilitarian attitude towards sex is not only inappropriate but anti-utilitarian. If we all firmly believe that extramarital sex is a betrayal of one's spouse, the belief is self-fulfilling. In those circumstances the act is a sign of disrespect for one's spouse, a kind of attack on his or her integrity. It can inflict the deepest sort of pain, and so is reproachable on utilitarian grounds, although not only on those grounds. But that is because of the attitude we in the community share towards it—not, be it noted, just because of the attitude of the individuals involved. The community's attitude is part of what makes it an act of humiliation, somewhat as rules of linguistic appropriateness make a certain statement an insult. That is part of the reason we say it is not so much that some act is right because it creates happiness as that it creates happiness because it is right. Another part of the reason is that such an act shows respect for a person and in that sense is in that person's interests, as Sen and Maslow would surely agree. A significant function of moral education is developing a similarity of intuitions—for example, concerning what respect for another person requires—sufficient to make people in a community not only understand but trust one other.

Many of the claims of the previous paragraph apply to violating the norms of one's organization, which, even if they are not rationally defensible against alternatives, may be taken very seriously and ignored at one's peril and that of others. People who move from one organization to another may find that what was wit in the old organization is impudence in the new one, what was fawning is respect, what was honest confrontation is mutiny. And they may find that what was a concern for honesty in one organization is disloyalty in another. Not to honor local practice is to raise questions about one's respect for the locals. But to repeat, out of caution: it does not follow that local practices are always worth honoring.

Utility does not, then, clearly serve as a foundation of everything one must take morally seriously. What we do may create happiness because it is right, rather than vice versa. This can happen where our lives are guided by certain ideals that unite people in our family or community. I may aspire to be courageous or a good father or dignified irrespective of whether it will fulfill most of my desires or make me particularly happy. Of course these things may make me happy; if they do not, I may wish they did.[43] In a very similar way, what is right can create happiness because it is just.

THE ATTRACTIONS OF JUSTICE

There is experimental evidence (see Frank [1988, Chapter 6]; he follows Kahneman, Knetsch, and Thaler [1986] and Thaler [1985]) that justice is desirable in itself: people want rewards that are not only big but fair relative to others' rewards for their contributions, and those who are treated unfairly will punish cheaters even when it is against their own immediate interests to do so. If Smith and Jones lie thirsting on a hot beach, and Jones fetches two bottles of cold beer, the amount Smith is willing to pay for her beer will be affected by how much Jones paid. If Jones got it for $3 per bottle at the hotel bar, Smith will pay $3, but she will not (so it turns out, in many cases) pay $3 if he bought the two beers for $1 each. Any compensation manager can testify to the great concern people have about whether their pay is equitable relative to that of others in the organization and will find this scenario unsurprising. Smith's position can be expensive in the short run, but it can pay off as would-be cheaters and exploiters come to see what they must to do ensure her cooperation. (For a similar but more detailed position see Schmidtz [1992] on reciprocity. His discussion will come up again in Chapter 3.)

Justice is an important motivator to most of us. We try to justify our behavior to others by reference to reasons acceptable to them and us. There is hypocrisy abroad, certainly, but it is parasitic on the genuine "desire to find and agree on principles which no one who had this desire could reasonably reject," as Scanlon (1982, p. 111) writes; and the desire to justify one's own actions by reference to principles like that is essentially the same as the demand that others do the same.

The fairness that people like Smith demand is the kind I have claimed is characteristic of capitalism: it has something to do with deserving, which in turn has something to do with being rewarded according to the value of one's contribution, whether or not one has earned the personal endowments that make that possible. That notion of fairness has a utilitarian component. So too, to a point, does the notion of honor in organized crime. It is useful that one's enemies know that one's honor demands vengeance at any cost. In that respect, a sense of honor may have utilitarian consequences, but that is not all that can be said for it.

I have suggested that utility and fairness overlap in part because our views about what can count as morally adequate grounds for discrimination—desert, for example—will have some utilitarian support. But they overlap for another reason: the former is about the good life, and the latter contributes to the protection of the good life in a community and in any case seems to most of us a component of the good life. The respect for others that fairness demands is for most of us a significant part of a reasonable conception of the good life, something that most of us clearly desire strongly enough to be prepared to sacrifice ephemeral goods for it (with the result, if Frank and those he cites are right, that we get certain longer-term goods). Think again of what Maslow (1970) considers the forms of happiness characteristic of those who need not concern themselves with such basics as food and shelter. They involve others' respect; at a still higher level, they involve self-respect, of which, according to Maslow, the respect of others is a necessary condition.

Victims of condescension, contempt, and dishonor suffer more than loss of income: they are injured just by virtue of others' attitudes. If you do not treat me fairly, you are not only depriving me of something I want but also treating me as being less than you and less than I am entitled to be treated as being. I suggested earlier that an act—for example, an act that shows respect for another person—may cause pleasure because it is good, rather than the other way around. It may also cause pain because it does not conform to the way people who respect one another treat one another. In the story about the beer, Smith believes that Jones is exploiting her, and she simply refuses to be treated that way. To call Smith foolish is to fail to see what motivates her: a sense of self-respect, which is surely a component of the good life and which must be reflected in others' respectful treatment of her.

Elster (1989, pp. 110f.) tells a story of a man who offers a boy $10 to mow his lawn; the boy demands $11; the man refuses and mows it himself. A neighbor offers the man $20 to mow a lawn no larger than his own; the man refuses. It is not clear that the man is being irrational. Elster's diagnosis is that he does not consider himself the kind of person who would hire himself out to mow someone else's lawn. It is incompatible with his self-respect. Like Smith, he will not let himself be ripped off. This suggests, as do some of our views about sexual morality and other intimate matters, that certain basic desiderata are part of the very notion of one's self-interest, perhaps even of oneself, and so not subject to questions of the form, Why do you want that?[44]

This is not to say that one's sense of self excuses all excesses. We can probably explain Ivan Boesky's decision to break the law in pursuit of great riches, even after he already had great riches, by reference to his view of what constituted self-respect, but that view is a pathological one for a number of reasons, one of which is that it so nearly follows La Rochefoucauld's view as to undermine any possible community.[45]

It is worth repeating that I do not argue that all moral considerations lead finally to utilitarian ones. It goes both ways: the right sort of utilitarian view turns out when analyzed to include an aspect of fairness, and while it is a basis for deciding what rights one has, it is equally true that one takes it as basic to one's interests that one is treated with respect for one's rights. We may reasonably infer that no one kind of consideration—utility, justice, or rights—provides a foundation for morality.[46] In particular, we might have hoped that some form of utilitarianism suitably modified by justice and rights would give us algorithms for moral judgment, but it is not so. For we must give a partly utilitarian account of justice and rights, and there is no definitive account of happiness or of the good life on which utilitarianism can be firmly based. If there were, justice and rights would be involved in that account, and in part for that reason it would be antithetical rather than helpful to calculation and aggregation. It does not follow, nor is it true, that moral progress is impossible: in particular, we can come to see that certain conceptions of the good life are impoverished. In fact, to anticipate some arguments that are to come, we might say that we do not find what is good so much as create it.

I trust it is clear by now that the absence of a firm foundation for morality in utility or anything else does not imply any interesting form of relativism. What follows is some further argument against foundationalism and relativism both.

INTERPRETING ALIEN COMMUNITIES

Utilitarianism is supposed to transcend community boundaries, to provide a way of assessing moral standards that may differ from one community to another. But happiness, which is supposed to be the common currency, is itself affected, even to some degree determined, by one's community. In intimate matters especially, but elsewhere too, communities have not only their own rules but also typically widely shared conceptions of the good life, hence widely shared agreement on what constitutes good reasons for action. Agree as we may that the purpose of morality is to make people better off, we must acknowledge that there are widely different views about what counts as being better off, particularly across community lines, and even different ways of being genuinely better off. Can we put any limits on what some community might regard as the good life?

We can. Even as we look across cultural boundaries, we encounter limits to relativism, to what we can think of as a moral practice or a moral system. The argument to that effect parallels the one made in Chapter 1 and in this chapter.

A critical evaluation of another culture—say, Japanese society—requires some interpretation: we must understand the *point* of what goes on in that other culture in order to be able to say, Yes, under those circumstances it does make some sense to do things that way; I can see why some people would want to live that way—even if one would not oneself. In a pedestrian way, one can see why it makes sense for Marines to owe their superior officers a level of obedience that professors do not grant their department chairs. Our understanding of morality in some exotic society that employs concepts unfamiliar to us presents a deeper and more complex but not essentially different problem of seeing why people act the way they do.

My argument here relates to a question discussed in Chapter 1— whether morality gives us any reason to act. The answer seems to be a clear affirmative. For we do understand people who say they did something because it was the morally right thing to do. We often understand them more fully than we do people who say something like this: "I could have called an ambulance and saved that child's life, but the call would have cost me twenty cents."

The act of interpretation that explains strangers' behavior is not so different from the act of interpretation that justifies it. The former answers the question, "Why should anybody want to do that?"; the latter suggests an answer to the question, "Why should anybody want that done to him or her?" In either case we could say, "I certainly wouldn't want to do that" or "I certainly wouldn't want that done to me." In such a case, the best explanation or justification the outsider can find may not be satisfactory. It may indicate that the aliens' view of the good life rests on incoherence or reasoning in a small circle or factual inaccuracy or ignorance of consequences or failure to consider all the possible ways in which life can be good. In some cases, one may be able to say only that that is just how the people in that community want to live. Discussing the issue with people in the community may or may not aid our understanding or their moral progress.

Discussion does not always aid moral progress because the values that matter most to people are least subject to examination (or even awareness) and evaluation from a utilitarian point of view or any other. The values that animate the man who refuses to hire himself out to mow a neighbor's lawn or the spouse who takes marriage vows altogether seriously are part of the self in the sense that one would not feel oneself to be the same person if they changed.

Just asking the question, "What is the point of that?", where "that" refers to some practice or rule that we do not have in our community, indicates that there is a significant difference in the ways the communities judge certain acts, with the result that the purpose or principle of some act is not obvious. The question also presupposes that there is some point, some interest comprehensible to the questioner to be served by the practice or rule. In order for us to recognize a different morality as a morality at all, we need to share it to the extent that we can state the point of its central practices clearly enough so as not to invite endless perplexed repetition of the question: "Yes, but then what's the point of *that*?" Granted, in the other community people may be socialized to a different conception of happiness, but there is a limit to how different it can be. If it is recognizable as happiness, if someone in our community can say, "Yes, I can see how that state could count as happiness, although it does not appeal to me," then the alien community and ours have something significant in common, and there is some principle that can be used to help assess both its practices and ours. And if we cannot at all recognize the alien community's state of happiness or see how the aliens can be pursuing anything that could remotely be called the good life, then we have no basis for asserting that they have a moral point of view at all.

This entire discussion presupposes that people are intenders and thinkers. We might look for good reasons not to take rights seriously if they were not, but the very idea of people like us—enough like us for us to understand one another's intentions and thoughts—having good *reason* not to consider one another intenders and thinkers (hence reasoners) is self-defeating. We attribute intentions to people of whose opinions and desires we can make sense, hence to people whom we can take to be at least minimally rational. It follows that we cannot altogether separate our judgment that they are acting intentionally from our judgment that they are acting so as to make themselves better off. From that it follows that we cannot altogether separate utilitarianism from concerns about autonomy. But it is also true that in attributing autonomy to people we acknowledge that they may not all come to the same views about what is desirable.[47]

Consider again the elevator operator in *Brave New World*. I cannot demonstrate that he is living a bad life or that he is being treated immorally. The most I can say is that we cannot imagine ourselves being satisfied with the life of an Epsilon-Minus Semi-Moron, in part because the question of being satisfied with a certain sort of life cannot arise for an Epsilon-Minus Semi-Moron. What I can do is describe the requirements for a moral community of people capable of reflective thought and intentional action and therefore concerned about autonomy. That is important to us because we are like that.

While there are limits to what we can call the good life, however, we surely have little reason to believe that utilitarian considerations can be of much help in adjudicating among communities that cleave to significantly different conceptions of what is good.

PROSPECTS

Utilitarianism will seem an attractive theory to anyone who believes that it can unify ethics by capitalizing on the essential importance of being better off; to one who thinks that economists can readily tell us what it is to be better off, utilitarianism will be almost irresistible. The message of this chapter is that these hopes are to be disappointed because of three great problems with utilitarianism.

First, in practice it is self-defeating to try to cause managers and others to calculate and act in utilitarian ways: the result will not be one that utilitarians would prize. This is especially true in matters of great personal interest to us, but not only there. If instead we advise managers to do whatever will result in what utilitarians prize, we shall be giving them no remotely useful advice, much as if we were to advise them to increase the real long-term wealth of the stockholders or tell scientists that they should save the phenomena but not multiply entities beyond necessity.

As a practical matter, then, moral advice that is to guide action must refer to virtues, rules, agreements, and institutions—less about the good effects of individual acts than about the structure of our community. But what characteristics do the virtues, rules, institutions, and agreements have? Particularly in an organization, they ought to be productive; hence, they need to organize people so that through cooperation they produce a surplus of goods relative to what they could produce individually.[48] We therefore find ourselves talking in ways that apply to business ethics, since the production of surplus is an essential feature of good organizations and other communities (we shall pursue this point in Chapter 3), but second-order utilitarianism is inadequate for a further reason that applies to any sort of utilitarianism.

The second great shortcoming of utilitarianism is that it does not fully encompass justice and rights. Morality has to do not only with producing that surplus but with distributing it: the institutions and structure of a good community must ensure that the distribution of goods is fair and adequately respectful of people's rights.[49] Utilitarians may point to the need to bring utilitarian considerations to bear in giving an account of justice or rights, but there is an equal need to refer to justice and rights in giving an account of the good life. It follows that utility is not the foundation of morality. But what should be set equal to what, and what rights deserve protection? Utilitarians may point to the need to bring utilitarian considerations to bear in giving an account of justice or rights, but there is an equal need to refer to justice and rights in giving an account of the good life. It follows that utility is not the foundation of morality.

The third problem is that there are different and incommensurable goods, in part because there are different conceptions of the good life, and it is not at all clear which one is best. The problem is not that our knowledge of what is good is inadequate but that it is characteristic of us that we decide what the good life is rather than discover it. (How we do this is a subject of Chapter 5.) For that reason utilitarianism fails, at some genuinely important points, to provide a basis for evaluation and comparison and so cannot get off the ground. And it is a good thing that utilitarianism cannot get off the ground. It is a good thing that we, and most particularly our political and economic institutions, respect a variety of conceptions of the good and a variety of kinds of life, rather than imposing a single one on all within the community. We rightly grant people autonomy in that sense.

At the beginning of this chapter I noted that some forms of happiness are not obviously good and that one of the problems about business is that it sometimes socializes people to settle for an inferior sort. Now I am arguing that it is good for us to be open to a variety of conceptions of the good. Later on I shall discuss and accept Rawls's view that a good community permits its citizens to pursue any form of happiness that is compatible with others having a like freedom to pursue their preferred form. But Rawls does not argue, nor do I believe, that all conceptions of the good are equally good. La Rochefoucauld's view of the good life is one that we could all embrace without contradiction, but that would make life pretty grim for many of us. I shall argue that there are conceptions of the good life that do support good communities and that managers have a right and good reason to encourage these conceptions.

Utilitarianism finally does not give us a unified theory of ethics. Philosophers as different as Plato and Bentham hold that a good community is one that grants happiness to those who live there. What else these have in common is no coincidence: neither thinks rights are important, and both believe it possible to give an unproblematic account of happiness. If we deny that possibility in view of the inevitable plurality of incommensurable conceptions of the good, including some that encompass justice and autonomy, then the best we can expect a community to do is to grant space impartially to a variety of (but not all possible) conceptions of the good. The extent to which this argument applies to organizations, which typically bring together people whose conceptions of the good are fairly similar, is something we shall discuss further.

Because conceptions of the good differ, and because those pursuing them are capable of both cooperating and interfering with one another, and because cooperation is to be encouraged and its burdens and fruits are to be distributed appropriately, it makes great sense for us to address as crucial to morality the structure and systems of the community that must orchestrate this cooperation while impartially protecting everyone's right to the pursuit of happiness. Rawls's famous formula applies to business ethics as to political theory: the basic structure is the subject.

In the two following chapters I shall argue that fairness and rights are best defined by structures and institutions that would be created by those motivated by "the desire to find and agree on principles [and institutions] which no one who had this desire could reasonably reject," as Scanlon puts it. These structures and institutions will create appropriate equality and rights by granting people liberty compatible with like liberty for all people. Chapter 3 explores the possibility that some sort of contract theory meets our needs—the conclusion is a disappointing one—and raises questions about how we might distinguish a good contract from a bad one. Chapter 4 addresses that question and suggests a Rawlsian procedure for arriving at a description of the productive, fair community that respects rights.

NOTES

1. Posner (1983) and Buchanan (1985) push economics as far as it can go in ethics, and then some. Schelling (1984) uses economic arguments to show that certain plausible moral positions have unexpected anti-utilitarian consequences.

2. The most stubborn objection to behaviorism is that, because an intention is based on a desire and a belief, one can infer the desire from an intentional action only if one knows the belief, and one can infer the belief from the action only if one knows the desire. (See Ch. 1, n. 43.) One way to deal with the problem would be to assume, as economists normally do, that the agent's belief is always true. By the argument in Ch. 1, it is reasonable to assume that the agent's beliefs are mostly true, but that does not get us to behaviorism.

3. Sen and Williams (1982), to whom I am indebted, collect attacks on utilitarianism and summarize them in an astute introduction. Sen (1987) demolishes some standard economic assumptions. Griffin (1991) is a helpful retrospective on utilitarianism. Brink (1989) formulates a utilitarian theory that avoids many of the objections gathered by Sen and Williams. Sen (1989) attacks the most optimistic claims for Pareto optimality, in particular that it deals adequately with fairness. He also holds that Pareto optimality is inconsistent with individual rights that most people take seriously: in brief, some people have strong preferences concerning what other people do, and satisfying them will violate the other people's right to act autonomously.

4. Contemporary utilitarian philosophers avoid some of the pitfalls I shall note in this chapter, and I do not claim that in so doing they lose their right to call themselves utilitarians. My primary target is the ideological basis of most economic theory with which we are familiar, although my strictures will apply as well to other forms of overconfidence in our ability to solve moral problems by utilitarian means.

5. In one way it clearly is not, according to standard economic theory: one person's utility cannot be measured against another's. But are we really never able to know that Jones is happier at this moment than Smith? It is a mistake to suppose that what cannot be measured in all cases must therefore be ignored in all cases.

Profit itself is not easy to define and measure, as I noted in Ch. 1. What is even more difficult to measure is a crucial matter for applied utilitarianism: the extent of various parties' contribution to a company's production with a view to deciding what distribution of profits can be justified in the name of desert and incentive. See Sen (1989, p. 539).

6. It is not clear that any theory, whether based on utility or universalizability or anything else, can create moral tests that are commensurable. We are always going to have arguments about cases in which, for example, an intense friend-

ship causes anguish—Is it in fact better to have loved and lost than never to have loved at all?—or honoring someone's rights is very expensive. Aristotle's view is that rationality does not require, nor does there exist, a single metric by which we can make or assess every decision. If this is true, utilitarianism had better moderate its pretensions. See Nussbaum (1990, pp. 55–66) for an approving discussion of Aristotle's position.

7. This roughly follows the distinction between philosophical and normative utilitarianism, as described by Scanlon (1982, p. 108). The former is an answer to the characteristically philosophical question, What is morality about? The latter is an answer to the characteristically normative question, What am I supposed to do? At various points in this essay I shall take the position that the latter is the more important question, at any rate for managers. Mine is therefore something of a pragmatist position, but an extreme pragmatist would probably argue that the first of the two questions just makes no sense.

8. It is probably true, as a number of wise people have said, that undertaking to maximize one's own happiness is a terrible way to maximize one's own happiness. It is probably also true that organizations do not maximize profit by subordinating all considerations to it. (To paraphrase Browning: "I could not love thee, Stockholder, so much, loved I not other stakeholders more.") This suggests, as Parfit (1984) and others argue, that utilitarianism is not very good at guiding action, even from a utilitarian point of view. But certain problems are more amenable to utilitarian calculation than one might suppose, as Schelling (1984) repeatedly demonstrates.

9. See Griffin (1991), esp. pp. 75–80. Talking about rational desires or about interests as opposed to desires obviously makes utilitarian calculation a great deal more difficult.

A desire can be rational enough to figure in an explanation of behavior while at the same time not being rational enough to justify attributing autonomy to the agent. An example: an addict's irrational desire for a fix would explain his robbing someone on the street. The rationality of the desires characteristic of an autonomous person is a matter we shall discuss further, especially in Ch. 5.

10. See Sen (1987, pp. 45f.)

11. By a strong culture I mean one that is pervasively and deeply influential. The notion of a strong culture is more familiar to organization theorists than to anthropologists. These and associated issues figure prominently in Chs. 5 and 6.

12. Elster (1989a, pp. 65f.) follows Solomon and Corbit (1974) in holding that the pleasure characteristic of consumption fades over time and subsequent dissatisfaction returns ever more quickly and intensively, while that characteristic of self-realization (say, building a boat or writing a book) typically increases as one continues to enjoy it over time. It is plausible that the more those who enjoy Mozart's music hear of it, the more they like it, while the same is not true without limit of rap music. So one might argue that Mozart is superior on fairly straightforward utilitarian grounds. Even if that argument is a good one as far as it goes, however, we can still argue that there is something superior about pleasures that make demands on our rationality quite aside from whether they last longer. Unless we have had a very bad day, we do not envy Huxley's elevator operator when we learn that he is regularly given large doses of the euphoria-inducing drug soma.

13. I suggested in Ch. 1 that the limits to what we can imagine desiring help set limits to what morality can be about. I shall have more to say on that issue at various points from now on.

14. If the fulfillment of desire were the essence of happiness, as economists presuppose, then utilitarianism would by its nature take adequate account of rights.

15. I shall argue the point in detail in Ch. 5. For the moment, consider whether a drug addict could be said to be autonomous.

16. Nozick (1974) tries to move still further from utilitarianism by advocating a libertarian theory that links property rights more directly to freedom of action. Indeed, it is not easy to see how there could be freedom to act without freedom to enjoy the results of one's action, particularly as it is nearly impossible to draw a sharp line separating action from result. But Nozick cannot avoid a problem about the extent to which one can ignore utility. It is not clear how all moral issues (as opposed to legal ones) about photocopying, for example, could be settled by invoking property rights without reference to utility. (See Edel et al. [1994, p. 200]).

17. One of the essential questions about employment that consideration of property rights raises is whether there are certain rights that it is morally impermissible to bargain away, hence some agreements that are illegitimate and need not be respected. Ch. 4 deals with this sort of question.

18. Rawls (1993, Lecture VIII) discusses in passing, but very subtly, the interplay between utility and rights. In so doing he suggests that different social structures and historical circumstances may call for different rights, as well as different conceptions of justice.

19. In saying this I do mean to imply that whether or not some act or institution is in one's best interests is a much less straightforward matter than people have usually supposed, and less useful in moral argument. Chs. 4 and 5 give further reasons for saying this, and sponsor a more nearly Aristotelian view of interests.

20. A sadist's preferences cannot be outlawed, but they can be discouraged, as can those of anyone who has a conception of the good life that cannot be realized generally; acting on them can of course be forbidden.

21. In Ch. 4 I argue against the view that there is any such thing as the purpose of a firm.

22. One of Ronald Dworkin's targets (in Ch. 17) is the Report of the Royal Commission on Pornography, which was largely the work of Bernard Williams. The report argues that since one does not know now what social, moral, and intellectual developments will ever be possible or which ones will be desirable, the best possible society is one that is conducive to people's making intelligent decisions about what lives are best for them, then enjoying those lives. In other words, the best society helps make people autonomous. Most restrictions on pornography defeat this purpose. This seems to me a reasonable position, although, as Dworkin notes, it is a better defense of freedom of the press than of the freedom to make use of pornography in private.

23. Businesspeople often use libertarian arguments as well as utilitarian ones against government regulation. That requires caution, for two reasons. First, that a corporation is the sort of thing that can have rights is not obvious. Second, libertarian arguments can be used in support of the kind of ecological policy many businesspeople do not like; surely, for example, a libertarian of all people would not overturn the citizen's right not to be damaged by pollution just by reference to economic utilitarian considerations, which are precisely what businesspeople are fond of adducing in calling for a "sensible" or "balanced" view of ecology.

24. Bork might be read, more charitably and more consistently with his general views, as claiming that there is nothing in the Constitution that decides the case one way or the other and that therefore the matter ought to be decided by the will of the majority. He does seem to believe, however, that it not only has not been claimed in the Bill of Rights but just cannot be shown that conjugal sexual relations ought to be exempt from majority rule in the way religious practices are. He equates the victim of the knowledge that safe sex is taking place with the victim of industrial pollution—a fine example of conservative victimology.

25. I think we can consider justice and rights to be essential to morality on the grounds on which Ch. 1 considered being better off essential. Rawls seems a bit more modest: he just has no interest in contemplating any purported moral system that does not take freedom and equality seriously. Occasionally he suggests that giving free reign to external preferences is downright dangerous, and invokes religious wars as evidence.

26. The obligation in question would not, of course, rest on purely utilitarian considerations, but I think the example still makes the desired point.

27. I trust it is clear by now that I think they are often not entirely distinct. In this case, is there not a utilitarian basis for granting that handicapped people have a right to make such contributions as they can?

28. Remember, though, that not all our intuitions can be wrong about morality.

29. Ch. 3 will give us further reason to doubt that the best way to create welfare is to have every individual try to create it, for it turns out that in certain common sorts of situation the welfare of each individual is poorly served if each individual tries to serve his or her own welfare.

30. For a vigorous argument that goes further along these lines see Braybrooke (1987). Some economists might argue that that is exactly what economics is about, but it is not in general a good idea to assume that something is the case that in fact never is. Scientists do it sometimes, but they have learned when to do it and when not to. See Cartwright (1983), who is relatively permissive about fictions, but in a way that gives little comfort to fictionalizing economists. Hollis and Nell (1975) mount a sustained attack on the claim that the assumptions of economists are false but useful in the way those of physicists are.

31. We might think of the field of organizational behavior as applied sociology, but sociology does not propound theories that assume that everyone acts rationally or believes only what is true. If it did, organizational behavior would be far more useful to it than it would be to organizational behavior.

32. Yet one of the characteristics of a truly moral person is the ability to navigate in complex situations where incompatible principles compete. That ability, which pertains to managerial as well as ethical principles, is part of what Aristotle called practical wisdom. Aristotle did not denigrate principles, but he did understand the impossibility of applying them rigidly. There is a difference, though, between violating a principle for reasons of convenience and doing so because there are other principles at stake.

33. Managers can affect employees' behavior not only through rules but through norms. The latter need not be explicit; in fact, people may be unaware of being under their influence. I shall pursue this point, which is not in all respects good news, in Chs. 5 and 6.

34. This is a sign that the concept of a lie is what Geertz (1983 and elsewhere) calls a thick concept, which usually needs to be explicated by reference to its con-

text, including other concepts. A false and deceptive statement is not a lie except in the context of our expectations about each other.

35. My likeliest opponent here is a libertarian capitalist, who might well argue that discrimination on the basis of talent or even race is the exercise of a right, while the imposition of affirmative action is the violation of one. But this argument presupposes that corporations have rights, and that is questionable; even if the argument succeeded, it would not show that racial discrimination is right but only that the government should not interfere with this form of it. The opponent of affirmative action, whether libertarian or conservative, normally holds that it is wrong insofar as it is discriminatory.

Note that the libertarian typically argues or assumes that while in the short term stern adherence to capitalist principle may cause dislocation (a euphemism common among libertarians), in the long run fairness too is served as rewards are distributed to all and only those who produce. The balancing off of the short and the long terms is not so pleasing to libertarians when liberals invoke it by arguing that consciousness of race in the short term is required if we are to have color-blindness in the long term. But most opponents of affirmative action do not believe it will lead to a fairer situation in the long run.

The libertarian might argue that it is appropriate for organizations to discriminate to achieve corporate ends—mainly profit—but that the government cannot effectively bring about socially good ends by making organizations do anything and should not try.

36. I do not mean to imply, nor do I believe, that it is possible to weigh utility against justice in any systematic way.

37. The threat of infinite regress also suggests that it will be difficult to settle arguments where competing principles seem to apply to a situation. Ch. 4 pursues that point.

38. Hampshire might have noted a further similarity between grammatical and moral rules: just as moral rules apply least straightforwardly to the most intimate matters, so grammatical rules apply least well to the words we use in our most common and most personal talking: in many languages the words for be, go, do, and so on are irregular. And is correct and appropriate speech a matter of carefully following explicit rules?

39. Edel et al. (1994, p. 71) use the language analogy in arguing against relativism: we would not call language relative, so why should the same considerations lead us to call morality relative?

40. What does justify it is to be discussed in Chs. 3 and esp. 4, as we address social contract theory. Survival value is significant but certainly not sufficient.

41. In a generally favorable review, Nussbaum (1994) agrees and cites Aristotle as the source of the idea. LaFollette (1993, pp. 330f.) makes a similar point in his contribution to Singer's anthology, in which sophisticated utilitarianism is presented favorably throughout.

42. For more about how organizations give lives meaning see the discussion of corporate culture in Ch. 6. For more about the importance of loyalty, see Ch. 7.

43. Ch. 5 deals with higher-order desires, such as the desire to have desires of a certain sort in keeping with the person one wants to be. The idea that I may deliberate about what I want my happiness to consist in is one with which utilitarianism has great difficulty.

44. Parfit (1971, 1984) has most influentially argued for a close connection between one's self and one's abiding values. It does not follow that these values are unalterable or foundational in any useful sense.

45. The notion that the world of business is a cooperative enterprise is not the whole truth, but it is more of the truth than we might suppose if we focus exclusively on the competitive aspect of business; even that aspect presupposes that most people will play by the rules.

46. In Ch. 1 I gave reasons for thinking there is no foundational answer to the question, "Why should I be moral?" In this chapter I have given reasons for thinking there is no foundational answer (in utilitarian or any other terms) to the question, "What exactly constitutes being moral?"

47. Ch. 5 has more to say about the essential relationship between rationality and autonomy.

48. The goods in question would be those that people in the organization agreed were worth pursuing. In a number of places Rawls names certain basic goods that anyone with a reasonable conception of the good would find valuable.

49. Nozick (1974) repeatedly attacks the idea that justice is a matter of how goods are distributed; distributive justice, he argues, ignores the important issues of who created the goods in the first place and whether they were transferred justly. I agree that those issues are important, but they can be addressed under the heading of rights. Under that heading, too, however, the libertarian will argue for rights because they are essential to life and not on a utilitarian basis— as though there were no connection between utility and what is essential to life.

3
Morality and Communities: Collective Action

Chapter 2 offered some reasons to believe that thinking about ethics, business ethics or otherwise, requires us to think about communities. Some of these reasons have been available since Aristotle, who claims that man is a political animal—a creature whose nature is to live in a *polis*, a city-state—and that to be a truly good man one must be a citizen of a great *polis*. On somewhat different grounds Rawls holds that the structure of the community is the primary subject of justice. The moral life requires the support of the right sort of community; that is not a truth that all moralists have embraced, but it is a truth all the same. The moral life in business thus requires the support of the right sort of organization, which is the subject of this chapter.

What makes this subject interesting is that both defining the right sort of organization and creating it are difficult. A large part of the difficulty is that organizations characteristically raise collective action problems that challenge managers' organizational skills as well as their good intentions. The problems of particular interest to business ethicists concern the contractual relationships and other agreements that create obligations among people in organizations. We have been invited to believe that one meets one's obligations by adhering to the contracts into which one has freely entered. It is not so simple: for one thing, not all contracts are good; some of them do not address the problems of collective action, and some are bad for other reasons.

Organizations do create obligations in the sense that they require their members to undertake obligations toward one another that they do not have toward people outside the organization. Some of these obligations are indeed legitimately determined by agreement, much as an individual incurs an obligation by making a promise or signing a contract or joining an association that has certain rules or by being related to someone by blood or marriage. But there are obligations other than these.

Why would anyone take on the obligations that an organization creates? A significant part of the answer, although not all of it, is this: by virtue of their structure, organizations serve people's interest by affording them the chance to get a share of the results of greater productivity. Unfortunately, it does not follow that the individual in an organization is best off who contributes most to the productivity of the whole enterprise, since it may be possible to get the benefits of the synergy created by an organization without contributing to it. As I noted in Chapter 1, utterly selfish behavior in a community is collectively self-defeating but not always individually self-defeating. It is the manager's task to give individuals in the organization reason to contribute appropriately to an enterprise that serves their interests and others'; as I have argued at several points, adequate reasons need not be narrowly self-interested ones. In that way the manager is supposed to create a moral community.

If you think that all morality is just a matter of abiding by communal contracts, you may be tempted to infer that it is not possible to criticize these contracts from some moral point of view beyond them. Then if someone asks why it is morally obligatory to meet one's contracts—a question that some social contract theorists would have profited from asking themselves—you will likely be stuck for an answer. This line of thought leads to questions about the limits to what we may legitimately agree on, about what makes our agreements legitimate, and about what, if any, obligations we have apart from them.

These are important questions for business ethics because most organizations are, as business in general is, supported by networks of explicit and tacit agreements that generate moral obligations—which, it should be emphasized, are usually honored, and must be if commerce is to go on. There is controversy over the moral importance of some of these agreements and over whether and how we can evaluate them. A certain form of cultural relativism might take the position that we cannot evaluate them, since morality is what a community agrees it is. What I have said about relativism to this point implies that, on the contrary, there are limits to what can count as any kind of morality at all. We shall not be able to define the best possible agreements, but we can at least identify some characteristics of good ones and bad ones.

One of the good things an agreement can do, as admirers of Hobbes will point out, is to save us from the consequences of our own selfish rationality. Selfish rationality is not our natural state, however, and the Hobbesian justification of agreements is not the only one available.

MORAL COMMUNITIES AND SOCIAL CONTRACTS

In Chapter 1 I claimed in effect that it is a necessary truth about morality that there is some *we* such that *we* are better off if we all behave morally. In that sense, at least, the community, the *we*, enters in an essential way into the definition of morality. The question then arises how far this well-being should extend beyond the agent's own community—who should be included in the *we*.[1] Surely one has some moral responsibility to those outside one's community: for example, it is immoral to kill even a stranger for the pleasure of it. But many of our clearest moral obligations have to do with the well-being of the people in our community, those with whom we regularly converse and transact and share institutions. We do not have the same obligations to people outside, in part because the agreements that create communities do so by creating rights and obligations for their members in the first instance. To make sense of morality one must see the community as more than just a place where people are moral or not, somewhat as a tennis court is more than just a place on which a tennis match happens to be played: certain characteristics of the court are a necessary condition of the activity being tennis, because the rules of tennis make essential reference to the features of the court. My discussion of interpretation has given some reason to believe that people in a community will share certain views about what is valuable and therefore what justifies and explains behavior.

People do not just happen to live in communities; they are political animals. Gauthier sums up the importance of communities to human life in his claim (1986, p. 19) that people depend in an essential way on "a network of social relationships"; without it, life would be radically impoverished or impossible. But Gauthier goes on to say that the "very structure" of that network lends itself to exploitation and that morality is the constraint that preserves this critical but fragile structure and the "shared ideal of sociability" it upholds. By that last I take it he means acceptance of interdependence and of the consequent need for concern for one another's interests. This is a reason for saying that an essential ingredient in any investigation of what makes an individual's behavior ethical is consideration of what makes a community good.[2] Whatever does, it is the opposite of the situation that holds in the bad community characterized in Chapter 1, in which the only way to survive is to be gavai, or at any rate narrowly selfish,[3] and in which there is no reasonable answer to the question, "Why should *we* be gavai?" If that is true, then it is essential to ethical behavior that it contributes to a community that fosters the good life for those who dwell therein. Communities, and organizations in particular, offer the temptation to cheat—to do less than one's share of the work or take more than one's share of the communal benefits—where it is impossible to divide those benefits so that the members reap only insofar as they have sown. Where that is so, moral behavior does not necessarily serve the individual's own best interests. Perhaps a contract theory will address this difficulty.

Locke is the most famous of many who have argued that there is a kind of contract between the individual and his or her community and that this contract provides the basis for individuals' rights and obligations with respect to one another. That is, the social contract obligates the parties to behave in certain ways and benefits those who comply; it permits the fruits of cooperation and of confident expectations about one another. It obligates in part because it benefits: it is hard to see how a social contract that made all parties miserable could get into the position of creating an obligation, much less an inclination, to abide by it unless failure to do so would create still further misery, possibly because others were counting on one's continued adherence.[4]

Hence a social contract has a utilitarian basis, but not only that. It respects fairness at least to the extent that it puts obligations on everyone. It respects the parties' rights at least to the extent that under the appropriate conditions the parties have freely consented to participate in the system, and the system itself then generates further rights and obligations. In view of the role that fairness and rights play in defining morality and the utilitarian importance of having people's expectations met, one is not justified in abandoning a contract simply because its results are sometimes inadequate from a utilitarian point of view. On the other hand, if one of the bases of the obligation to abide by a contract is that one has agreed to do so, then it is pertinent to ask oneself concerning a social contract whether it is one with which anybody could find any reason to comply; that is called the compliance problem. Whatever obligation one may have to abide by a bad contract, it is not reasonable to expect it to remain in effect for long.

As Dunfee (1991) has observed, contract theory, which has a long and honorable history in moral and political philosophy, has a particular appeal for business ethics.[5] We can readily think of an organization (or a well-defined market or business) as a community whose members are united by something much like a contract that generates rules that they have a presumptive obligation to follow. Keeley (1988) goes so far as to argue that an organization is essentially a network of contracts. The manager has the problem about compliance: how to make the employment contract attractive not only to the potential recruit but also to the current employee so that people sign on and stay on. Even on the unjustifiable assumption that managers can readily identify those who get the benefits of the contract without contributing their share, employee Smith can usually abandon the contract and walk the moment she believes it is no longer in her best interests to comply and cooperate. As a practical matter, then, getting compliance with the local contract does require getting people to believe that compliance serves their interests; otherwise, nonparticipation or, worse, exploitation of others' contributions will likely seem a more attractive option.

Donaldson and Dunfee (1994, 1995) argue that the immediate source of the individual's first-order moral obligation is the social contract in force in that organization or business community, provided that the social contract is legitimate. The legitimacy of local contracts is ultimately a matter of whether they are consistent with "hypernorms" that apply to all possible contracts in ways business ethicists can help us understand.[6]

Contract theory suggests that the way to create a moral organization is to solve the compliance problem by enforcing good contracts. To put it

more broadly, the manager creates a moral organization not primarily by
seeing to it that all the employees are moral people but by creating conditions under which ordinarily self-interested people have reason to act
morally. The manager ensures compliance with the local contracts by
means of rewards and punishments but also, as I shall argue in Chapters
6 and 7, through the corporate culture.[7] It is the manager's obligation to
create a community in which one need not be a hero of self-sacrifice to
do the right thing, one in which gavai behavior is not the only way to
survive.

Similarly, a manager who would create an effective organization usually does not and cannot demand simply that every employee be effective
but instead distributes accountabilities to employees in ways that create
an effective organization. Courses in organization theory teach as an el-
ementary proposition that structures and systems—and, I would add,
culture—as well as people must be appropriate to the objectives of the
organization if it is to be effective. To emphasize structures and systems
is not to embrace a slavish Taylorist reliance on organization charts and
job descriptions, for it is perfectly compatible with the true and important claim that, for example, an organization adaptive to a turbulent
environment must give people other than top managers a measure of responsibility for decisions. Much the same will be true if the issue is
morality rather than effectiveness, or if the community is not an organization. Insofar as utilitarianism places primary emphasis on well-being as
a defining result of moral action, a utilitarian has reason to consider the
moral person in a community to be, not the one who goes about trying
to perform good-producing acts independently, but instead the one who
plays a contributing role in a good-producing system.

Over and above good intentions, structure matters. It is clear, for
example, how morality in your organization will be affected if the organization chart is taken so seriously that you are discouraged from
communicating with your boss's boss or with your counterparts in other
departments: in that case it will be much more difficult for you to do anything about your boss's bad behavior. The weakness of this sort of control
on your boss may make bad behavior significantly easier. [8]

On the other hand, emphatically, structure is not everything. Much of
what the manager of morality has the employees do is itself straightforwardly moral: no lying, no stealing, keep your word, etc. There are some
kinds of rule that are moral under any circumstances, and others that are
moral only or primarily in an organizational context—for example, keep
employee records confidential. But some acts may be morally appropriate that in the absence of an organizational system are wrong.
Improbable as it seems, for example, there might be a morally legitimate
process for making corporate-level decisions about product safety; hence,
there might be a morally legitimate rule that individual engineers at a
lower level are not empowered to make decisions about safety—that is, as
Jones designs products he is supposed to be concerned not about the

consumer's safety but only about following corporate guidelines and, if necessary, taking his concerns through channels. Or Smith may participate in something she thinks is morally questionable (although not clearly evil) because a decision has been made according to due process by people she respects, and her side did not have the votes. Some obligations depend on what others are doing, since some acts that might contribute to good results in some circumstances are pointless or futile unless others do them as well; for example, nothing is gained by one person's staying late to work on a proposal if others needed for the project go home at five. For that reason alone it is a matter of moral import whether there is a contract or some sort of explicit agreement covering the case: one has a *prima facie* duty to comply with a contract independent of whether or not others do. Duties of this sort reduce futility because they increase the probability that a critical mass of people will contribute without pausing, perhaps fatally, to consider that others may not.

It does not follow from anything I have said, nor is it true, that moral issues for an employee reduce to compliance or noncompliance with employment contracts and the presumptive obligations they bring with them. For one thing, any number of problems with the terms of a contract or the conditions under which it was agreed to might make it morally illegitimate, hence not binding. The obligation it creates is *prima facie*; the contracts are only the immediate, not the ultimate, source of the obligation. Nor must one always accept the terms of the contract or abandon one's job. For another thing, not all moral obligations within an organization or anywhere else come about as a result of contracts, even implicit ones. One's status as a parent, for example, brings obligations with it whether or not one has made a deal with the child, even if becoming a parent was not intentional. One did not intend to be born in one's native community, but the absence of intention does not by itself release one from all obligations to obey that community's laws;[9] nor therefore does it permit the community to take a love-it-or-leave-it attitude on all matters. An employment relationship is voluntary, at least to some degree, but it does not follow that all the moral obligations of its parties are contractual ones.

It is one thing to claim that the contract is a useful metaphor as we discuss the employment relationship and, arguably, the citizenship relationship and others that entail moral obligations. It is quite another to say that these relationships are basically contractual ones that provide no further reason for believing there are moral obligations. It is safer to say that there is *at least* a contractual relationship in cases such as these and that there might be something more, but even that is not perfectly safe. For there might be reason to claim that there is not even a contractual relationship, or that the contractual relationship does not support any moral obligations because some condition is present or absent, or that certain conditions are far oftener absent than contract theorists believe. Indeed, the plausible claim that contracts explain many kinds of moral

obligation must be qualified by so many conditions that one might believe that we can learn more about moral obligation from attending to
the qualifying conditions than from understanding contracts. (Williams
[1985, pp. 99ff.] makes this point.)

One of the questionable assumptions of much of this talk about contracts is that self-interest of the kind sponsored in traditional economic
theory is the only or best basis for compliance with a contract. Trust and
concern for others' well-being, for example, clearly assist in community
building. If individuals in the community do not consider each other's
welfare a reason for action or do not trust each other, then each will more
likely calculate that there is nothing to be gained by behaving unselfishly;
each will consequently behave selfishly, probably to the detriment of all.
So it is with the Ik. It follows, not that Smith and Jones are morally obligated to trust each other, but that they have a *prima facie* moral obligation
to respect those institutions of the local community that build trust and
otherwise create conditions for moral behavior and the good life.

Hence, a venerable position on self-interest and community interest
may well be wrong. Adam Smith (1937, p. 423) famously wrote:

> [B]y directing that industry in such a manner that its produce may be of the
> greatest value, he intends only his own gain, and he is in this, as in many other
> cases, led by an invisible hand to promote an end which was no part of his in-
> tention. Nor is it *always* the worse for society that it was no part of it. By
> pursuing his own interest he *frequently* promotes that of the society more effectu-
> ally than when he intends to promote it. (emphasis added)

It is Adam Smith's more enthusiastic followers, not himself,[10] who have
made a dogma of the idea that self-interested economic behavior always
leads to community benefit; but the insight that that *may* happen is
already a most important one for business ethics, if only for the implication that the best way to create welfare is not necessarily to have every
individual try to create it. The generous behavior of individuals may lead
to exploitation and, in due course, to a situation that is less than ideal
from the point of view of society as a whole. If moral behavior entails creating communities that support the good life, and morality in business
entails creating organizations and other institutions that support the
good life in markets and workplaces, then facts about the consequences
of institutions and of individual behavior must become part of our reck-
oning about morality and about business ethics in particular. Not least
among these facts are the ones revealed by a family of situations in which
Adam Smith's most famous dictum does not apply because they do not
constitute the right sort of market.[11]

THE COMMONS PROBLEM

I have argued that the purpose of morality is to make people better off
but also that it does not follow that every moral act makes somebody

other than the agent better off. In fact, we know of communities and organizations and industries in which people live with compelling evidence that acting in what appears to be a moral way is futile or worse. So why should people in that sort of situation ever be moral?[12]

The answer I have to offer is that there may be reason to be moral if everyone's being moral will make people in the aggregate better off; that reason may hold even if it is not the case that everyone, or even anyone, else is being moral. The so-called commons argument gives some grounds for that answer, and it does much else besides, since it applies to organizations in an essential way.[13]

The commons argument shows how the kind of self-regarding rationality that economists standardly celebrate as leading to a robust economy beneficial to its participants may actually work to the disadvantage of all concerned, typically in the case of goods that are and must be public rather than any individual's property. It is consequently an argument against unrestrained free enterprise and in favor of regulation in certain instances, but that is only one of its applications. From my point of view, it is a critical fact that organizations create such public goods and that therefore morally good management is in effect a matter of preserving a commons.

Imagine a village with a commons, publicly owned land on which by definition any villager's sheep may safely graze.[14] If you are a villager who owns sheep, it is in your best interests to graze as many of them as you can on the commons rather than on your own land: that way your land is less depleted, and your gain is greater than your share of the common cost of one more sheep on the commons. But if all the sheep owners calculate as you do, each will graze all his or her sheep on the commons and thus overload and finally destroy or seriously damage the commons, to everyone's detriment. The problem is that it is better for all if all or most people use restraint but better for each individual not to use restraint. The solution is cooperation, but, for reasons familiar to those who know the Prisoner's Dilemma, the solution may not come to pass.

Under these circumstances, as a rational maximizer you want to get as many as possible of your sheep onto the commons. Even if you face the prospect that the grass will give out before long, you know the commons will soon be depleted even if you forbear, since the other villagers are presumably also rational maximizers and so will also quickly move their flocks to the commons; so you had better do the same. And if your fellow villagers are unselfish, your best selfish course is still to put all your sheep on the commons and get a free ride.

If all the villagers are selfish, the situation calls for a general agreement to be moderate or, if the villagers cannot trust each other, for regulation with teeth. The villagers' inclination to be trustworthy is not a sufficient condition of their believing each other to be trustworthy, nor therefore of their trusting each other, nor therefore of their acting with restraint on the assumption that the commons will be preserved: that requires that most villagers not only be but seem trustworthy, for otherwise they will likely not be trusted. Actual trustworthiness is necessary to preserve the commons if selfish action will be exposed and will undermine others' trust in the selfish agents.[15]

It is easy but not necessary to assume that the villagers have selfish, separate interests, but it is not always so, as Adam Smith himself argues in *Theory of Moral Sentiments* (a point Werhane [1993] emphasizes). The commons situation shares that assumption with the Prisoner's Dilemma: in both cases rational maximizing by each participant eventually hurts each, while the individual's cooperative behavior may be exploited by a maximizer. Clearly it is easier to preserve the commons when, out of concern for one another's welfare, people make sacrifices and are generous. Again contrary to what the commons and the Prisoner's Dilemma suggest, in actual communities people's values evolve over time: as we interact, our desires can change, becoming, for example, more selfish or less so.[16]

Today the public goods of interest are air and water, polluted by rational maximizers. Everyone must breathe and drink, but no individual maximizer much depletes his or her share of these goods in comparison to what is saved in externalizing costs by polluting. The commons-based argument for regulation is that without it everyone, even the polluters, will suffer by the destruction of these public goods. With the right sort of regulation, no one suffers a competitive disadvantage by running a clean operation.

The commons problem tells us something about professional ethics as well. If engineers agree that they will not submit to pressure to write dishonest reports and then stick with that agreement, employers will not be able to increase the pressure by saying, in effect, If you don't, I'll get somebody who will. Hence honest engineers will not be penalized. If no such agreement is in force, even an honest engineer may well consider it futile to resist the pressure and therefore not do so, for the same reason a villager who does not want to see the commons ruined will put a few extra sheep there now before it is ruined, as it will be anyway.

The logic of the commons works within many large organizations. An organization is in effect a commons under these conditions, which are necessary and jointly sufficient: (1) employees and management, whatever their distinct interests, share an interest in the organization's prosperity, with the result that (2) organizational effectiveness—that is, for present purposes, long-term stability, growth, and profit—serves employees' and managers' interests, and (3) organizational effectiveness is a function of employees' and managers' cooperative effort, and (4) it is possible to get a free ride by contributing less than one's share of the fruits of (others') cooperative toil. So a maximizer of his or her own private package of money plus leisure time may do well by exacting undue pay or being as unproductive as is possible without penalty. But if there are many such maximizers, then the common good, the aggregate value of wealth and leisure available in the organization, will be reduced and all will suffer together.[17]

The corporate commons may be fragile: to pay labor well for poor productivity, for example, or managers for performance that has no long-term payoff damages the organization, and eventually labor and management with it. A good labor climate preserves the commons. A strike damages the commons in the short run, but that a company never has a strike suggests an imbalance of power between the parties, to the eventual detriment of the commons.[18]

The standard way of preserving a village commons, if it is large enough, is to privatize it and thereby make it something other than a commons. If the villagers divide the commons into private plots, then each family will tend its small plot in its own interests. What will be shared among the villagers is support of the institution of private property. But the commons problem remains where privatization is impossible or fatally cumbersome, as in the case of the air and other goods that are arguably naturally public and as in organizations.

A laissez-faire libertarian might reject the argument that commons-preserving behavior is as characteristic of a rational person as is flatly self-interested behavior, on the grounds that a true commons situation never happens; the commons is a moral cartel, and cartels cannot last, since their members will sooner or later selfishly cheat. By itself this is not much of a refutation: the evidence that members will always cheat is just that they are rational maximizers, and that is much of what was at issue in the first place. Nor do libertarians offer any reason to deny—in fact, their view of human motivation actually seems to imply—that people in the aggregate are better off and in particular get more of what they want if there is legislation to preserve certain commons situations.[19]

The commons situation helps solve a problem we raised about rule utilitarianism in Chapter 2 and have mentioned since: it can be futile to do something that would be worth doing if everybody did it when in fact most do not do it; why make it a moral obligation to follow a utilitarian rule? It is clear that a contract, even a tacit one, can preserve the commons: in some cases it reduces the risk of futility and increases the probability that people will perform an act that in isolation would not be beneficial; since it does that, it strengthens people's obligation, and their motivation as well, to perform it themselves. In so doing it helps solve the so-called assurance problem, which arises when people are willing to do their share if others do the same but are not confident that others will in fact do their fair share. Buchanan (1994) shows how contracts and other devices help here in part by giving some determinate sense to the very notion of fair share: it is agreed to be the share each of us agreed to contribute when we signed the contract.[20]

The benefits of a widespread practice of not lying, for example, are great; lying when there are immediate utilitarian grounds for doing so will pay off handsomely once or twice, but the general practice of doing so will quickly eliminate those benefits, to everyone's cost. From lying the individual can gain certain benefits, along with the general ones that we all gain from the true assumption that people do not normally lie. In effect, the strategic individual liar is a free rider. The same cannot be said of me when I must decide whether to try to stay late to work on the proposal when no one else is staying. In not staying I am acting as a free rider only if there are enough people willing to stay and get the work done without my help. If by refusing to stay I encourage others not to, I am even worse than a free rider; so it is with the liar, whose lying may put truth tellers at a disadvantage, and so with the soldier whose flight will harm and may discourage the other soldiers assigned to hold the bridge.[21]

The Categorical Imperative seems to require that one do what if everyone did it would have the most acceptable outcome. On that interpretation it presupposes that maintaining a cooperative community requires stopping each individual from doing a utilitarian calculation with an eye on what others will likely do and concluding, "Well, what I do won't make any difference." Much the same is true of standard rule utilitarianism.

THE COMMONS AND BEING BETTER OFF

What does the commons argument show about whether moral people are better off? To begin with, *we* are better off if *we* are in a community that preserves the commons. Since the moral thing to do in a commons situation is to pull one's weight or to take only one's share, it is clear why there is reason for individuals to be moral: a generally beneficial outcome requires it. A free rider may be better off than a contributor in a commons situation, but people in the aggregate are better off if most people restrain their greed. If most people try to be free riders in a commons, then the commons will be destroyed.

I have suggested that commons considerations bear on questions of autonomy as well as well-being. The public accommodations provisions of the 1964 Civil Rights Act were criticized as compelling white merchants, restaurateurs, and innkeepers to extend their services to those with whom they did not desire to trade. In most cases, however, these businesspeople discriminated against black would-be customers less out of racist sentiment than in response to pressure: they feared that racists would boycott those who opened their doors to black people and would thereby confer a competitive advantage on those who discriminated, as each feared most others would therefore do. Although that pressure interfered in some way with their freedom of action, each behaved as a rational maximizer in discriminating, for the alternative might well have been economic ruin. The result was injustice but also, in the aggregate, economic harm to those who united to forgo black people's custom. The Civil Rights Act made it possible for well-meaning but unheroic businesspeople to act rightly and as they preferred to act, without paying a fatal competitive price, to the advantage of all who had in the aggregate harmed themselves by maintaining discrimination out of fear of a boycott and so out of self-fulfilling fear of one another's fear. In that sense, the greatest thing they had to fear was fear itself.

In an organization the commons may not be preserved if rational maximizers expend just the minimum effort and resources required for a personally satisfactory outcome, and no more. In that case the organization will tend to be unproductive, hence uncompetitive, hence unable to pay the wages that serious joint effort would have made possible. An individual who knows the possibility of this result, unfavorable for all, may calculate that one's share of the benefits net of the costs of working hard does not justify doing anything more than the minimum required to get by. The practical issue for management is to make morality and effectiveness overlap by finding ways to preserve the interests common to all contributors to the organization. Most people are not heroes of self-sacrifice; thus, motivating them to do the right thing is not a trivial task for a manager.

The privatization option is not available in most of today's complex organizations. Most managers will find it impossible to design a compensation system that directly rewards individuals for their individual performance and thus gives them incentives to be productive. Management jobs in a fluid and adaptive corporate environment cannot be defined by reference to tasks identifiable in advance whose accomplishment is a function solely of an individual's effort and skill. Effectiveness requires group effort in which the marginal utility of the individual's effort may not be measureable. The stream of unexpected problems that constitute an opportunity to manage effectively may require that new groups be constituted *ad hoc* as different talents become temporarily salient or as different people happen to be available.

The problem of the commons is a problem about getting individuals to cooperate and contribute; that is a problem of motivation, a typical managerial problem. An evident solution—not, finally, the only solution I shall propose—to the problem of getting cooperation is to have an agreement that specifies how to divide the surplus that that cooperation generates. That agreement will then be, in the way social contracts normally are, the immediate basis of moral obligations in the organization.

That an agreement can be a locally acceptable way of dividing the surplus is already an argument in its favor, from a moral point of view. It says something for an agreement that it exists, that the parties have agreed to something, although it does not say as much as some libertarians would claim. It is probable, if not certain, that the parties are better off with it than without any agreement at all, presumably because it generates a divisible surplus. Hence, the agreement has some moral status on utilitarian grounds. Insofar as the parties undertook it voluntarily, it is compatible with their rights. As a rule it will also be just, since people may reject agreements that serve their interests but that appear to be unjust, either simply because they distribute unequally or because their distribution is unequal in a way that is clearly not justified by the parties' relative contribution to the surplus or anything else. (Recall the story of the beer and the beach in Chapter 2.)

A good agreement preserves the commons. What the individual gets out of the agreement is a share of the (consequent) surplus as a reward, but the compliance problem, a version of the question why one should be moral, remains: having entered into the agreement, why—that is, on what self-interested basis—should one abide by it? Free riders get their share of the benefits without contributing; why not be one?[22] Can we do any better than to repeat that the free rider may risk undermining the commons and to urge that one take others' interests as a reason for action? Must we invoke some contract-enforcing mechanism?

Not necessarily. For being a contributor is in the interests of a person with the right interests—for example, a strong interest in finding and agreeing on principles that no one who had this desire could reasonably reject, as Scanlon puts it.

CHARACTER AND MOTIVATION

Game theorists in general and users of the commons argument in particular do not always need and should not automatically be granted the assumption that everyone's interests are narrowly selfish. Nor are everyone's interests fixed: what one's interests are may be influenced by one's environment, and one's idea of the good life may change. Becoming a party to a commons-preserving agreement may not be in one's best interests, but *being the sort of person whose interests are served by buying into the agreement* is on the whole a good thing. The life of a person who is disposed to comply and contribute in such cases if others do, rather than be a free rider, can reasonably be considered a good life, from the point of view of the person whose life it is.

One might suppose that such a person is not an individual utility maximizer, but that is far from clear: one's utility might encompass that of others, in fact usually does so in the case of people for whom things like parenthood and friendship are goods. But can a person with a disposition to cooperate be happy? Won't one then be a patsy, a loser in every game remotely like the Prisoner's Dilemma? Not necessarily; not, for example, if over time it becomes clear to others that one's disposition is to cooperate, *but only with other cooperators*. On the evidence from Rapoport and Chammah[23] about the effectiveness of the tit-for-tat strategy, a visible disposition not to be a free rider and not to permit others to ride free either will convince other players that one is a good candidate for inclusion in their cooperative ventures and a bad enemy and will therefore stand one in good competitive and moral stead.[24] It follows that a practical, commons-preserving form of rule utilitarianism or of the Kantian Categorical Imperative must be subtle enough to provide an escape for would-be cooperators faced with widespread lack of cooperation.[25]

It also follows that the great moral task of the manager, arranging matters so that morality and self-interest overlap, is not always as difficult as it may have appeared, at least for intentional agents who are reflective thinkers. If one could choose one's character and dispositions, could choose the sort of thing that would make one happy, there would be good reason to choose to be the sort of person disposed to comply and contribute but disposed also to make occasional hardball moves entailing short-term sacrifices to induce others to do the same. I argued in Chapter 1 that one can have a good reason for a choice that is not a self-interested one. The choice of what is to be in one's interests, which involves the choice of what sort of disposition to cultivate, looks to be such a choice—necessarily, since what determines one's interests can hardly be based on them. Yet it serves one's interests to choose interests that are readily achievable, rather than to aspire to the impossible and thereby guarantee frustration; if one can also choose to be in a community in which others are of the same character, so much the better.

We may be inclined to say that the difference between moral and immoral people is that the former are prepared to act against their interests sometimes. That is one of their differences: people do battle against temptation, and win some and lose some. But a more important difference, as I argued in Chapter 2, is that moral people have interests and therefore dispositions that take other people's interests into account. I shall discuss that issue and others relating to choosing one's dispositions in Chapter 5; it will come up in Chapter 7, as well. I have some explaining to do about how one can choose what will determine how one normally chooses; from the point of view of my argument, it will turn out to be crucial that it is characteristic of persons that on some occasions they are capable of deciding what to desire.

I shall indeed argue that human nature is malleable: that is, not only does the idea of the good life vary from one individual to another, but it is possible for at least some people to cultivate certain desires in preference to others. If I am right, then the operative question is, "What conception of the good life should a community promote so that self-interest and community interest overlap to the greatest extent possible?"[26] This is a question about the right virtues. A good community will value truthfulness, for example, not because truthfulness produces the most good in every case or because the rule that one should always be truthful is the best conceivable rule from a utilitarian point of view, but because the general and widely advertised inclination not only to hear the truth from others but to be the sort of person who willingly speaks it oneself will preserve the commons and otherwise support a community in which what people want and what they get will overlap to a great degree.

Of course, choosing one's own character is an extraordinarily difficult task for anyone, and not all are capable of it; choosing the characters of the others in one's community is and ought to be harder still, although a manager can try to hire people of a certain character and design a corporate culture that both favors and helps develop such people. Nor is the manager's essential job of preserving the commons an easy one. It is therefore a good thing that one can usually leave an organization and enter a more congenial one.

The question remains whether there is an obligation to be a cooperator where others never are. I argued in Chapter 2 that there is not: cooperating and then being exploited by a free rider has a bad long-term effect on the community, not just on exploitation's immediate victim, for it discourages cooperation by making it appear a foolish strategy.

Understand that I have not switched to the view that morality requires justification on the basis of self-interest. The argument of Chapter 1 implies that there can be a reason and a moral obligation not to be a free rider quite apart from whether free riders can long prosper. My point here is that not every rational person would choose to be a free rider in all circumstances. As I suggested in Chapter 2, with due respect to the importance of acting according to moral rules, we need to consider what dispositions morality needs and whether and how they are possible. It just will not do to assume that people are narrowly selfish utility maximizers and that ethics is therefore a matter of investigating the relations between morality and narrowly selfish utility maximization.

The effective and morally responsible manager had better proceed on no unjustified assumptions about what people are; that means, among other things, that there is no good reason to demand that the individual employee behave as though others were behaving as they are not in fact behaving. (Recall the argument for this point in Chapter 2, note 30.) The manager is supposed to create conditions under which moderately rational and decent people who do have interests of their own cooperate for the good of the organization. Aside from what managers have to do, however, why should even ethical theorists propound principles based on false assumptions about how people will behave?[27]

In Chapter 2 I considered the possibility of a viable utilitarianism, or a viable successor to utilitarianism. There was reason to believe that such a theory, if it could be found, would focus first not on individual acts and their immediate consequences, but on the rules and practices of a community—what Rawls calls the basic structure. If so, it is appropriate to consider the behavior, the character, the rules and practices that support that basic structure.

In this chapter I have suggested as a first approximation that good communities support the basic structure with social contracts and that these must at least preserve the commons. It is good, for example, to have a rule that one must stand and fight at the bridge, but not that one must stay late at the office if everyone else needed for the project goes home; people should be encouraged to develop a disposition in favor of reciprocity as a cardinal form of fairness.

We may be inclined to say that a good community is one in which people are happy. We complicate things, however, when we consider that one's community significantly affects what makes one happy and even what counts as serving one's interests. I have cast doubt on the standard utilitarian conception of happiness, which is of a state not directly related to others' states and not much affected by one's community. If happiness were always that way, then it would seldom be in my interests to be moral. I have undertaken to make room for the possibility that the moral life might be a preferable one for some people in some communities, that whether it is in fact preferable depends in part on the relation of one's dispositions to others' interests, and that it is a significant part of the job of managers and others in charge of communities to see that that relation develops appropriately without undue interference with people's dispositions.

I argued in Chapter 2 that the basic structure is the primary subject of business ethics and the primary concern of the manager. The crucial feature of the right structure is that it is a fair system of cooperation among people who are free and equal in the sense that their various conceptions of the good are permitted respect so long as they allow the same for others'. It appears that a necessary condition of the right sort of structure is that people be cooperative, tolerant, and disposed to support the commons, among other things. A manager cannot therefore focus on structure and be indifferent to behavior and attitudes; in that respect a Rawlsian approach does not diverge from common sense. That a decision about structure is in effect a decision about virtues is something we should keep in mind as we consider what is prior to what. We should also remember that Rawls begins with the notion, not formed in detail at first and not defended, that people are and ought to be free and equal.

It follows also that a Rawlsian liberal community cannot be entirely neutral about its citizens' conceptions of the good and, in any case, cannot fail to affect them. To limit people's right to their own notions of the good by adding the condition that these must be compatible with the same right for others is a significant move.

TOWARD THE GOOD COMMUNITY

The good community is one that encourages the good life. It does so by promoting rules, practices, and social contracts, but beyond that it encourages dispositions that are not narrowly selfish. The principles by which a good community is governed are fair and impartial. Such principles, whatever else may be true of them, are those that we can agree on and use to justify our acts to each other. They have great appeal not only to moral people but to some immoral ones, as we can infer from the phenomenon of rationalization, which, more even than hypocrisy, is the tribute vice pays to virtue. The principles we seek must be acceptable to people who wish—as many people do, contrary to the claims of psychological egoists—to engage in discourse, argument, negotiation, criticism, assessment, and justification concerning their own and others' actions, apart from whether these would serve their narrow individual interests.

It is characteristic of adequate moral principles that one could reasonably reject them only on selfish grounds; that is much of what is meant by saying they are impartial. (Recall Scanlon [1982] once more.)

Rawls (1971, 1993, and elsewhere) offers a famous way to propound or recognize principles that are impartial in that sense because they are the principles we would legislate for ourselves if we could legislate disinterestedly.[28] His view is that a morally acceptable set of rules and institutions is one that people would design for themselves in ignorance of their status and their particular interests in the community they were creating. Hence, they or their representatives would presumably write fair laws—for example, laws that permitted differential treatment only on reasonable grounds, such as the benefit accruing even to the least well off—for the same reason that if you cut a cake without knowing which piece you will get, you try to cut equal pieces. Since the people in the "original position" cannot recognize selfish reasons, they cannot reject a rule or an institutional arrangement on the basis of them. The result will be a fair system of cooperation among people who are free and equal in the sense we have been discussing and who have the desire Scanlon describes.

The founders will want to make the cake as large as possible, in the interests of everyone, and they will want to protect certain goods that they think any reasonable person would want regardless of his or her conception of the good. As maximizing the goods produced by the community in question will require some cooperation, the incentive to be cooperative is that one will get a fair share of what is produced by that cooperation, which impartiality will help generate by assuring each participant that others too will do their fair share of the work. If the reward system as a whole is to be productive for everyone and not just for those who get the most, then one who contributes more must get a greater reward. To that extent the system has a familiar utilitarian basis, but Rawls does not assume that the citizens in his Utopia will, if left to themselves, try to live off others' efforts. In any case, we can assume that the system will be designed to preserve the commons.

While mutual advantage is a desirable outcome in such a community, it is not all that justifies its basic structure. Rawls takes himself to be describing a structure on which free and equal people would agree if motivated only by reasons that all people would invoke if similarly motivated. In saying that a good society is a fair system of cooperation between free and equal persons, Rawls is not propounding a Hobbesian account, for he does not think even the most intelligent general pursuit of expediency either guarantees or ultimately justifies a good society. In that respect he seems different from Gauthier. Yet Gauthier makes a good move in arguing that the real beneficiary of a commons-preserving system is the person who is disposed to take pleasure in the happiness of others in the community—that is, the person who is not selfishly rational in the traditional economic sense.

The Rawlsian device can be applied to organizations.[29] A morally sound organization is one that would be designed by a group of people each of whom knew he or she was going to be a stakeholder of the organization but did not know which kind: an employee, a customer, a downstream neighbor, and so on. We can assume that these designers would try to design an organization that was productive but not unjustly hard on any stakeholder. Its employment contracts would have to be attractive (hence competitive) but equitable. Determining how that task is to be done—even determining what equity means in this sort of case—is nearly the crux of business ethics, as the crux of political theory is to design a polity that serves the citizens' interests without unduly interfering with their lives. It is inconceivable that the job could be done well by founders ignorant of business and of organizations, as Rawls's founders could not succeed without a knowledge of history; our founders had better be aware of how an organization can create interests as well as serve them. We cannot assume that the Rawlsian method would create an organization that would be considered good in any time and place— Rawls himself is not so bold (see especially his 1985 paper)—but it indicates how people whom we can understand to be rational and moral might go about constructing the morally best organization we can imagine, and that, for reasons I have given more than once, is a significant accomplishment.

PROSPECTS

In due course I shall argue not only that ethical behavior supports the good community, which is in many respects a commons, but also that it is essential to ethical behavior that it does so. Rawls is crucial here. A way to find the right moral principles is to ask ourselves what rules rational and impartial but not disinterested people would choose as the rules of their community, and what virtues would support such a community. If we want to know what the right ethical principles are, we must first know what the good community—not the ideal community, but the best we can think of—is like. Once we have done that, we shall have said much of what there is to be said about morality. Chapter 4 defends that view, which we associate with Aristotle in some respects, and argues that business ethics is at least as legitimate an enterprise as so-called theoretical ethics. In that chapter, thus emboldened, I return to the Rawlsian approach and suggest some of its further implications.

A difficulty with bringing Rawls to bear on business ethics is that he sets great store by the distinction between nation-states, which are his subject, and associations, such as firms. Three distinctions are particularly important to him (see for example Rawls [1993, p. 276]): (1) one does not normally choose to join a particular society, and one cannot usually leave it as one might leave a job; (2) one cannot identify one's character, personality, and values apart from one's society, whereas one's workplace does not usually have such a profound effect; and (3) a company normally has ends that unite people's efforts, whereas a society does not, or should not. But the differences are matters of degree.[30] Chapter 4 deals which whether the organization has a clear purpose. To say it does is a significant oversimplification. Chapters 5 and 6 discuss the organization's pervasive influence on one's values. Chapter 7 picks up some themes from Chapter 3 and Chapter 5 and discusses, among other things, ease of exit from an organization. The distinction between communities that serve an economic purpose and those that do not is less clean than some have supposed, with the result that much of the Rawlsian approach is indeed appropriate to business ethics. In any case, it is certainly more useful to managers than is utilitarianism.

NOTES

1. As I suggested in Ch. 2 and shall argue in Ch. 5, moral obligation will necessarily be restricted to reflective thinkers and intentional agents—whose faculties, not incidentally, seem to Aristotle essential to their being people. The same cannot obviously be said of moral rights, which arguably extend to animals. They are not entitled to vote, but they ought not to be treated cruelly.

2. Note the relevance here of Rawls's view that his subject is the basic structure.

3. The real Ik of Uganda might argue that what we call cruelty is required if their tribe is to survive, unburdened by those who cannot contribute, in impossibly difficult circumstances. They would be wrong; their moral system is not even functional for their new status as farmers. The implication that creating circumstances that are not impossibly difficult and norms that are not dysfunctional is a moral responsibility of politicians and managers is one that will occupy us throughout this essay.

I say narrowly selfish here rather than just selfish because, as noted in Ch. 2, one might get great personal satisfaction out of others' happiness; in that case it might be argued that acting for others' benefit is a less narrow kind of selfishness. So is acting on others' goals because they are interdependent with one's own.

4. For a skeptical view of the justification of actual and hypothetical social contracts see Schmidtz (1991), especially Ch. 1. Schmidtz argues that there is an "emergent" justification for a social contract only if there is reason to believe that reasonable parties would have bought into it. In the absence of that, a "teleological" justification is required: that is, the contract must serve some good purpose. But if it does, then a story about a hypothetical original agreement adds nothing to the justification of the state or institution in question; if it does not, then what difference does it make that somebody might have had reason at some time to make this deal? To ask ourselves whether it would have been reasonable for some hypothetical forebears to buy into an institutional contract seems an unnecessary step. Let's just ask ourselves whether we have anything to gain from buying in. I do not think these criticisms apply to Rawls's view, which does not really amount to a contract theory. Those who believe organizations are complexes of real contracts seem prepared to consider teleological justifications for them.

5. Solomon (1992) takes a dim view of the contract as metaphor for organizational obligation. I shall discuss, and to a considerable degree accept, his views in Ch. 4. I think contract theory makes more sense as a view about employment in organizations than as a view about citizenship in communities, since employees often sign actual employment contracts and citizens do not sign citizenship contracts.

6. Donaldson and Dunfee envisage hypothetical propounders of second-order "macrosocial contracts" that set certain conditions for local contracts and govern situations in which communities with different extant local contracts deal with each other. The macrosocial contracts must comply with the hypernorms, about which I shall raise doubts in Ch. 4.

7. In Chs. 4 and 7 I shall introduce some modifications. The focus on local social contracts turns out to be different, but not radically, from Rawls's focus on what he calls the basic structure.

To anticipate Ch. 6: one of the functions of corporate culture is to get people to want to meet their local obligations; another is to assure each participant that all or most other participants are doing their fair share.

8. Waters (1989) discusses how structural characteristics of an organization can have bad consequences from a moral point of view. The structure and the systems are of course the result of people's intentions, and somebody is responsible for them even if not all their results are what anybody intended. On people's willingness to avoid responsibility by blaming the structure and other impersonal items, see Klein (1989). I am morally responsible if I yield to temptation, but the competent manager of morality will reduce temptations insofar as possible.

9. For an argument to the contrary, see Wolff (1970), who defends anarchism by arguing that citizens have not signed any contract and that, if they did, they would be consigning themselves to "voluntary slavery." The latter point seems unduly hard on self-binding, but the former may encourage a healthy skepticism about the natural rights of governments.

10. And certainly not Werhane (1993).

11. Many of the most interesting issues in business ethics arise where the assumptions of perfect competition do not hold, as they normally do not. Business ethics has at least that much in common with business strategy.

12. It may turn out that what appears to be moral behavior is not, precisely because of its environment. We shall discuss that sort of situation further in Ch. 4.

13. One thing it does not show, so far as I can see, is that rational and self-interested people will ipso facto behave morally. But it does play a crucial role in the arguments of Gauthier and others to that effect.

14. For the account on which this one is largely based, see Hardin (1968, 1977).

15. Cox (1985) shows that Hardin's account does not describe what actually happened to common grazing land in medieval England. She says nothing damaging to my view of the commons problem.

16. Sen (1987, pp. 79ff.; see Ch. 1, n. 26) holds that the frequently denied assumption that makes best sense of people's commons-preserving behavior is that one may act on others' goals as well as one's own if (but not only if) they are interdependent. That people do follow cooperative strategies because we are better off even when it is not the case that I am better off for it is supported by

experimental evidence, although in some cases there is room for differing interpretations.

17. One can hold that this aggregate is not strictly speaking a public good, yet still agree that the organization is analogously a commons. The collective action problems are no different, and my proffered solutions no less applicable. The metaphorical use of the model is no less appropriate than the use of the Prisoner's Dilemma to explain the behavior of people who are not strictly maximizers, or not really in prison.

Pastin (1986) shows the usefulness of thinking of the organization as a commons. One might read Gauthier (1986) as arguing that all of life is a commons and that the truly rational person is also moral—that is, contributes rather than take a free ride.

18. Rapoport and Chammah (1965) give evidence that the best strategy in a prisoner's dilemma game is tit-for-tat. Dixit and Nalebuff (1991, pp. 106–115) argue that where there is a possibility of misperception—or, they might have added, disagreement about what is an appropriate response—tit-for-tat is too unforgiving a strategy.

19. Friedman does not much discuss the Prisoner's Dilemma and the commons. He alludes to them (1982, pp. 30ff., for example), but his primary concern is to limit the application of the lesson they teach.

20. Buchanan (1994) sees these devices as ways of perfecting so-called imperfect duties. In discussing the assurance problem he records his debt to Schmidtz (1991), as I have done. In Chs. 4 and 6 I shall suggest that corporate culture helps create adequate assurance.

21. There are some cases in which the best outcome is the result of some people's—not all and not none—doing something. With South Africa, for example, it was probably a good thing for some companies to cease to do business, so as to teach the racist government a punitive lesson, while other companies continued to do business, so as to keep alive the possibility of further punishment if things did not improve, as well as deliverance from it if things did. For that matter, we may not want everyone to stay to work on the aforementioned proposal: if too many people get involved, some of them will just get in the way. I do not know how to make clear rules that solve all these collective action problems.

22. Gauthier's book, which addresses this question in some detail, generated a useful symposium in the July 1987 issue of *Ethics*. I am indebted to the critical work of the symposiasts: Kraus, Coleman, Braybrooke, and Mendola.

23. On the point I raise here, the criticisms of Dixit and Nalebuff are not damaging. Frank's observations, discussed in Ch. 2, support the point I am making.

24. Schmidtz makes much of this. One of the interesting features of the argument for reciprocity as a cardinal form of justice is the extent to which it rests on practical and utilitarian grounds. I suggested in Ch. 2 that that must be true to some degree of any defensible account of justice.

25. Which, a true Kantian would probably respond, is a good example of what is wrong with being practical. It is just this Kantian attitude that tempts some people to say that ethics not only does not but should not have much to do with business. We shall discuss this and related issues in Ch. 4.

26. No community should demand that everyone adhere to a certain narrowly defined conception of the good life; Rawls (1993) is surely right about that. Promoting certain broad kinds of conception and their associated virtues, however, is appropriate.

27. Of course they will not behave the same always and everywhere. Where people's motivation differs, the appropriateness of some familiar ethical concepts, such as reciprocity, will differ as well.

28. The Rawlsian view barely qualifies as a social contract theory. Early contract theories offered to provide some basis for morality, but Rawls's does not. He differs from Hobbes, for example, in not using his device to argue that morality can be derived from self-interest. Rather than try to find a basis of any kind for morality, Rawls makes significant assumptions about morality and about what a moral government would be like; if one thinks, as he does not, that it is really important to get everyone to agree to a certain conception of the good, Rawls does not undertake to change one's mind. He does offer a striking way of modeling the kind of impartiality that he thinks is essential to justice.

29. In the next section and elsewhere we shall discuss the reasons Rawls offers for not trying to extend his device to cover organizations.

30. Certain religious communities fit the criteria better than some nation states. It may be more difficult to leave a religion than a country, and it may be nearly impossible to imagine what one would be like without one's religious beliefs.

4

Business, Ethics, and Business Ethics

What are a businessperson's moral obligations? One might argue that being in business does not excuse immoral behavior and that therefore a businessperson's moral obligations are essentially the same as those of anyone else; one might then infer that there are no interesting moral issues that relate just to business. Alternatively, one might argue that a businessperson acting in a business capacity does not have an obligation to be moral in an ordinary sense: in the long run, in fact, the important stakeholders in the business system are best off if its individual participants faithfully and even ruthlessly serve their managers and stockholders.

If either claim is true, the study of business ethics loses much of its point. If a businessperson's moral obligations all derive just from being a person, then business ethics is nothing more than ethics, essentially the same whether applied to businesspeople or others. If, on the other hand, a businessperson had better not be moral, then business ethics is truly an oxymoron. To defeat these claims requires that we address an issue we have already discussed in a slightly different guise: what is the relationship between the moral obligations that come with one's role in the business system and the moral obligations that one normally has anyway?

The usual practice is to think of business ethics as a branch of applied ethics, which shows how certain institutions and practices in business do or do not conform to the standards set by theoretical ethics. If that is right, then applied ethics shows how and to what extent the great principles apply in business situations. A businessperson should therefore be moral for the same reason anyone should, but what is the moral thing to do is a function of contractual obligations and other states characteristic of business. I do not accept this view of business ethics or, for that matter, of theoretical ethics.

We know that a course in business ethics does not usually make bad people good. If John Shad gave millions to the Harvard Business School in hopes of improving the moral tone of its MBAs, he will probably be disappointed. But surely it is no small accomplishment for a course in business ethics to make well-meaning people better and more reliable at doing what is right, particularly as morality is not simply a matter of being well-meaning. After all, a finance course does not usually make people greedy.[1] One of the arguments made in this chapter is that the study and the practice of business do involve certain presuppositions that are not ethically neutral. Among them is the standard economist's view that people are already greedy.

The very question whether business ethics is a field separate from business and ethics suggests what is not true: that knowledge arranges itself into subjects and fields for our convenience. On that view science is, in Plato's words, a matter of carving the world at its joints; universities and professional societies are organized along the lines dictated by nature as it has been revealed to us so far. In fact, fields are just human taxonomic devices, areas in which theoreticians and practitioners can communicate about a cluster of problems or practices because they share certain methods and assumptions and beliefs and definitions, hence criteria for what is properly empirical as opposed to necessary or normative.[2] As assumptions, practices, and problems change, disciplinary lines shift, too. Inevitably, our views of whether there should be any shifting will be influenced by considerations of available funding and student enrollment.[3]

AGAINST BUSINESS ETHICS

A famous objection to businesspeople's behaving ethically is put forward by Albert Z. Carr in a pair of articles that appeared in the *Harvard Business Review* in 1968 and 1970 but that represent a viewpoint still much in vogue.[4] Carr's point is that it is not a good idea to be ethical—by the usual standards, he apparently means—in business, except insofar as doing so makes one's organization competitive. He suggests that, where there is a choice between being ethical and being competitive, it is reasonable to choose the latter; otherwise, there is no point in being in business, and in any case one won't be there for long. Carr more than suggests that successful competitors are unethical.

Carr might have told the story of Judge Emil Fuchs, for many years the owner of the Boston Braves, who tried managing his team in 1929 despite his unfamiliarity with the subtleties of baseball. One day when the Braves had the tying run on third base with two out in a late inning and a weak hitter at bat, Fuchs wondered aloud what to do. One of his coaches suggested the stratagem, then standard for that situation, of attempting to steal home. "Never!" cried the judge. "We shall score our runs in an honorable way!"[5]

An economic system may indeed produce a morally praiseworthy situation because individuals do things that, considered in themselves and without reference to context, are not morally praiseworthy. This is a corollary of a familiar point I argued in Chapter 2: that individual actions taken on a utilitarian basis may not create a utilitarian result and are therefore not necessarily correct from a moral point of view. It is at least possible that establishing or maintaining a morally praiseworthy community requires the contribution of some people who are ruthless, driven, even unscrupulous, even as maintaining the domestic tranquility of a democracy may require an authoritarian military force.

The crucial flaw in Carr's Machiavellian view that an organization requires cunning and ruthless leadership is that it presupposes that the manager who is truly a morally good person cannot set priorities when principles appear to conflict in application or weigh the consequences of any contemplated actions as part of moral deliberation. On the contrary, we have noted that not only one's position in business but also one's status as a citizen or a parent or a friend creates obligations. We have noted too that it may sometimes be wrong to do what would be right in a world in which there are no irrational people and no free riders, or in an uncompetitive situation. It makes a difference that that is not always the way things are; it is a mistake to suppose that ethics is essentially about the few situations in which the world is that way. Setting priorities and weighing in the more common kinds of situation are not always easy.

From the point of view of the social contract theory we have been discussing, Carr is judging the behavior of businesspeople by standards appropriate elsewhere or by second-order standards that should be applied not directly to behavior but to local standards. To say that that is inappropriate is not to say that one may simply abandon one's own moral standards because business is business. The moral businessperson must be aware of the tacit agreements that constitute the rules of the game and has a *prima facie* obligation to play accordingly; at the same time, he or she must be prepared to criticize the rules and even abandon the game if its standards and practices clearly fall short of the applicable ethical principles so that some other moral consideration overrides the obligation that the rules entail.

Carr assumes that the system of which the contract is a part is a productive and roughly fair economic system; that is a justification of the usual ruthless rules. It does not occur to him that business ethics might involve anything like investigating and interpreting the terms of the social contract on which business operates or that moral philosophy as a whole critically investigates the terms of broader social agreements and practices and their relationship to our view of the self and the good life.

If a productive business system requires people of bad character doing bad deeds, we must at the very least try to determine the benefits of that productivity and its costs to the moral fabric of society. At the very least; it is not at all obvious that a business system is morally justifiable if it is optimally productive from some economic point of view; a system involving slavery, for example, might be very efficient. Nor is it obvious in any case that bad behavior in business is really essential to the success of the system. Carr's view does seem to apply to some organizations, in which ruthlessness is a requirement for success and decent people are eaten alive. In most such organizations, however, if my argument to this point has been correct, cooperative behavior of the kind that preserves the commons is impossible, with bad results for the organization's effectiveness. Carr's position as applied to the village commons would be that a rational sheep owner must put as many sheep as possible on the commons or face being cheated by the other villagers. The wholly opposite position would be that the individual should never overgraze the commons, no matter what anyone else is doing. Carr opposes that, rightly. What is wrong is that, seeing no option other than these two, he chooses the first.

It is the manager's accountability to create an organization that is not ruthless, but some organizations are nonetheless. People in such organizations are not morally obligated to cut their own throats, for example by refusing to reciprocate when others are ruthless to them. On the contrary: we have found reason for saying that cooperative behavior is morally required if and only if there is some chance it will be reciprocated. If there is not, charitable behavior—nonstrategic altruism, as Schmidtz calls it—often makes things worse by encouraging others to take further advantage. To that extent, too, Carr is right.

Similar to Carr's position is Friedman's (1984) famous dictum that the only moral responsibility of a manager is to increase the stockholders' profits legally, so some ethical obligations are overridden by the profit imperative. Ownership confers prior rights, and the employee has obligations accordingly under the employment contract. Friedman holds that the free market has fair and utilitarian consequences.[6] Even more important to Friedman, the free market respects the participants' right to autonomy: it rests on contracts made by willing parties, and it enshrines property rights. The employee's obligation flows from the contract. If the contract is unfavorable, one need not sign it; if one's job becomes untenable, one can quit. Friedman considers freedom a good thing in itself, foundational to morality, and its utilitarian and just consequences a side benefit.

According to Friedman, behavior we normally consider ethical often turns out to be justified in part by its contribution to profit, as the market punishes bad behavior. For example, if a company manufactures a defective product, would-be buyers will buy elsewhere; if it discriminates against candidates for employment or promotion or equal pay because they are female or members of ethnic minorities, its work force will be inferior or overpaid; if it treats employees shabbily, it will pay a premium for the services of those who are willing to put up with the poor treatment for a price.[7]

Friedman's view appears to be that giving people appropriate opportunities and rewarding them in proportion to their contribution to the profitability of the enterprise is moral because it contributes to the bottom line. For Friedman, then, business ethics is nothing more than legal and effective business practice, for according to him it produces utility, is just, and—most important—respects all applicable rights, most of which he apparently thinks flow from the uncoerced employment contract.

Why then should a businessperson be moral, according to Friedman? Because it is by definition an effective business practice, hence a contribution to the productivity of capitalism. In this Friedman might seem to agree with James Burke (1985), mentioned in Chapter 1, who also identifies ethics with good business. In fact, the positions of Friedman and Burke are really quite different. Burke's view is that ethical behavior, identifiable independent of its business results, has generally good results in business. Friedman's view is that ethical behavior is not identifiable independent of its business results but instead is to be identified with whatever has good (i.e., profitable) results in business. In answer to the question, Why should I as a businessperson do what standard morality requires when standard morality diverges from effective business practice? Friedman would reply, You shouldn't; Burke would reply, It doesn't.

One important point central to Friedman's analysis is surely right: the contractual relationships that play a large part in markets and organizations entail moral obligations. Less sound is his claim that, because the parties enter into the contracts voluntarily, meeting the terms of one's contract fulfills the moral obligations of any party in business unless public officials and managers interfere with the workings of free markets. If Friedman were right, there would be little philosophical or practical need of business ethics.

Peter Drucker (1981) takes a view roughly opposite to that of Friedman but compatible with Burke's: that one has essentially the same moral responsibilities in business as elsewhere. Hence he wonders why all the fuss about business ethics. There would be no point to business ethics if one's employment in an organization either settled all moral issues and left one with the choice of obeying (e.g., an instruction to lie) or resigning or left all moral obligations, including those having to do with lying and charity and the Golden Rule and so on, unaffected by any rights or obligations attaching to one's employment in the organization. The former position follows from Carr's; the latter Drucker takes in effect, apparently along with the assumption that an act can be evaluated morally apart from its context.

Drucker's argument suggests that one does not have any moral obligations in virtue of being in some position in business, since morality is a matter of adherence to univeral moral principles: no exceptions are made for business necessity. Presumably he would say the same about professional ethics. Drucker sees no problem about balancing the obligations that come with one's role in the organization against the moral obligations that one normally has; apparently the latter always override. This means that employment contracts, for example, create no moral obligations. Drucker also quite clearly assumes that genuine moral principles take no account of special circumstances or utilitarian considerations.

The ethical employee would seem to be in roughly the same position as the ethical citizen, who has moral problems insofar as public duties conflict with the dictates of conscience. If that is right, business ethics has a status as respectable as that of political theory. Here Friedman must demur, for he needs to maintain a clear distinction between employment and citizenship; that much follows from his view that a firm has a single clear purpose—the enrichment of the owners[8]—whereas a political entity does not. Hence he denies business ethics the respectable status of political theory. Devices like the Rawlsian myth of the impartial but not disinterested lawgivers working behind a veil of ignorance do not work for organizations, if Friedman is right. If political theory is about the just consent of the governed, then business ethics is not about anything interesting, since one gives one's just consent by signing the contract. So Friedman can argue, I think not successfully.

If Friedman were right in believing the clear purpose of a firm to be to make a profit for the stockholders, his minimalist view of business ethics would be vastly more plausible. In the next section I shall argue that he is wrong. The argument is important in our consideration of Rawls as well, since Rawls (1993) declines to apply his method to firms in part because they have a clear purpose. If they do not, then we are the more justified in applying the Rawlsian device in business.

THE PURPOSE OF THE ORGANIZATION

Friedman in effect invites us to think of an organization as a purposive system and of its end as profit,[9] but need we? Smith manufactures something and sells it for profit. To increase her profit she hires Jones to work for her in exchange for pay. The purpose of the organization, one is inclined to say, is Smith's profit; Jones's compensation is a side benefit that keeps him a party to the employment contract. Now suppose Jones is an inventor who offers Smith, a venture capitalist, a majority of the stock in his company in exchange for her financial support. In this case what is the purpose of the enterprise, and what is relegated to the status of side benefit? Where there are agreements that spell out the rights and obligations of all the parties, talk about ownership and the purpose of the enterprise adds nothing.[10]

It is not the owners' benefit that justifies inducing people to cooperate when they otherwise would not (e.g., by paying them), but the benefit to the cooperators and others—possibly different benefits to different stakeholders—that derive from so cooperating.[11] The organization is, among other things, a network of implicit and explicit arrangements and agreements among the participants, who have their separate reasons for signing on. For many employees the purpose of work is compensation or personal fulfillment; these may, in turn, be related to the achievement of some corporate goals. The organization exists, and management has a job, because people must cooperate to achieve the goals that benefit them all or are means to achieving goals that do.[12] But the reasons for the organization's creation are not the only basis of its obligations, which extend to a range of stakeholders.[13]

An organization differs from a civil polity in its degree of focus on shared goals whose benefits, along with the individual's freedom to seek an employment contract elsewhere, justify a measure of management authority that exceeds what a good civil polity would grant its office-holders. The difference is not a radical one however: as no possible benefits can justify tyranny, it is far from clear that the benefits that the organization creates can justify coercion. Enforced agreements that preserve the commons and thereby the ends that people have chosen for themselves and have entered the commons in order to enjoy are not necessarily coercive. On the contrary, they may make it possible for people to have what they want.[14]

One would expect Friedman, of all people, to advocate limited management in the name of freedom, but his view that democracy does not normally trump property rights requires a clear distinction between citizenship and employment. He claims (1982, p. 3) that one justification for granting more authority to local than to national government is that it is easier to leave town than to leave the country. Here, as also in his opinion that the appropriate recourse for the unsatisfied employee is to leave the company and get another job elsewhere, he implies that ease of exit justifies greater managerial control and less democracy. On the whole, Rawls (1993; see, for example, pp. 40–42 and 276) agrees. But we are dealing with matters of degree: today it is sometimes easier to change one's citizenship than to detach oneself from one's employer. (Chapter 7 will deal further with this issue, which is the subject of Hirschman [1970].) If so, then Friedman's view of the employment contract is greatly oversimplified, and Rawls need not be so reluctant to apply his device to organizations.

Organizations that are productive from the point of view of all or most participants do require relationships of subordination, which they induce people to accept by offering them a share of what is produced. Whether that is a fair bargain we cannot determine just by reference to how productive the organization is or whether people stay on their jobs. Organizational goals and means as well are legitimized by their value as means to all the stakeholders' ends. The organization preserves the rights of the participants only where every contract in an organization is a fair one at least in that it provides for the fair distribution of the goods that are the fruit of cooperative work.[15]

CONTRACTARIAN VIEWS AND APPLIED ETHICS

Keeley (1988), Dunfee (1991), and Donaldson and Dunfee (1994, 1995) agree that contractual relationships are essential to organizations and entail special moral obligations (contrary to Drucker), but not the obligation to be ruthless (contrary to Carr), and not just any obligation stipulated in the employment contract (contrary to Friedman).[16] They do not agree that the employment contract is the only one in play or that just any contract between uncoerced parties guarantees fairness and rights. Dunfee recommends applying the standard ethical principles to these contracts, not directly to the behavior that complies with them. As I noted in Chapter 3, Donaldson and Dunfee argue that the legitimacy of local contracts is ultimately a matter of whether they are consistent with "hypernorms" that apply to all possible contracts. Moral behavior is then behavior consistent with legitimate contracts. So there is business ethics.

Contract theorists will grant Carr that competitiveness may require behavior that under some circumstances would be bad but that is necessary for the individual's survival and the organization's fulfillment of its noble purposes, but they do not assume that all contracts are morally legitimate. Their theory leaves one with the problem of balancing the obligations entailed by one's role in the organization against the moral obligations one otherwise has. In this respect the ethical employee is in roughly the same position as the ethical citizen, who has some public duties that may seem to conflict with the dictates of conscience. In this way, too, business ethics seems to have a status as respectable as that of political theory.

Subtler contract theories do see business ethics as being about something interesting. On their view it is a form of applied, as opposed to theoretical, philosophy: the former is about what happens under certain assumptions, the latter about what holds whatever the world is like.[17] The distinction implies that ethical principles—for example, the hypernorms of Donaldson and Dunfee—do not change with circumstances but that different judgments become appropriate as the facts change. Theoretical ethics is about universal principles that have to do with well-being, fairness, and rights: for example, one should treat other people as ends, and not as means only. We might then infer that it is wrong to mislead, since in doing so one is treating others merely as means. But discharging one's obligation to stockholders may require deceiving competitors. The contractual account applies universal principles to tacit agreements, such as an understanding that competitors may mislead each other in certain ways, and presumably deems it acceptable. Thus, members of organizations and communities have moral obligations that do not apply elsewhere. A good organization, or any good community, is one whose contracts pass muster with respect to the time-honored principles of morality: it preserves its citizens' rights and maintains appropriate standards of utility and justice. Different communities may have (somewhat) different local standards, since moral principles allow significant leeway in reaching agreements.[18]

Yet there are problems with the analogy of the contract.[19] One of them is the assumption, found in some versions of contract theory, that participants bargain to get the outcome that best serves their interests, which are set before they enter into an organization or any community.[20] In fact, the culture in a community helps determine how we conceive of the good life.[21] One possible result is that one's interests encompass the well-being of others.[22] So one may be loyal to a community not just because one has made a deal and will suffer if one does not continue to comply, but because one comes to care about the community and its members and trust them. In other ways, too, one's community may alter one's interests.

It is in any case not so easy to evaluate the contracts in force in an organization from the point of view of the time-honored moral principles that transcend all possible communities. There is no good reason to assume that these principles, or the Donaldson-Dunfee hypernorms for that matter, will generate compatible results in practice.[23] To deal with this problem we might propound a metatheory that justifies giving utilitarianism priority over (say) Kantianism under certain conditions. If someone else then were to propound an incompatible metatheory showing the contrary, there would have to be a metametatheory—and so on ad infinitum. And there are questions about the truth of these theories as well.[24] Nor can we even readily identify the contracts, or the concepts for that matter, in force. That is the task of the corporate anthropologist.[25]

CONTEXTS AND CONSEQUENCES

Understanding an action requires understanding its context. In particular, making judgments on the actions, institutions, rules, and language of a culture alien to ours requires understanding the local thick concepts (Geertz [1983 and elsewhere])—including virtues, which in my view are thick moral concepts—that one can understand only by seeing how they are embedded in a culture's complex practices, which may incorporate moral and factual presuppositions.

We may come to understand the aliens' actions and thick concepts by investigating this network of connections and by identifying certain assumptions and values that seem not wholly unreasonable, even if not acceptable to us. We may, for example, understand the point of saying that it would have been dishonorable for Hamilton to refuse Burr's challenge to a duel but reject that concept of honor, as we would the concept embodied in the claim that the mobster Joseph Valachi acted dishonorably in discussing his business activities with federal authorities. If we cannot construe an action or an institution in a way that makes any sense whatever to us—understanding, for example, that it is supposed to ward off evil spirits—we cannot interpret it.[26]

By what he calls symbolic analysis, Geertz seeks to "establish the layered multiple networks of meaning carried by words, acts, conceptions, and other symbolic forms" (Marcus and Fischer [1986, pp. 27–29]). Geertz does this for Bali and other exotic communities but then suggests we can do the same for our own community and for organizations. This is one of the functions of the analysis of corporate culture, and practitioners of business ethics ought to attend to it. One looks at the *meaning* of an act or practice, hence of any thick concept that may apply to it: the way other people react to it and interpret it; how it fits with people's tacit agreements and relationships; the rules that govern it; the roles it plays; its consequences; its history; the intention with which it is done. If people in a community share certain objectives or are agreed on a certain conception of the good life, then part of the meaning of the act will be the way in which it contributes, or is intended or believed to contribute, to those objectives or that life.

Consider a promise: what makes it the act it is is that it has a role in a language and in a morally significant agreement people have bought into. We do not judge promise keeping or promise breaking only by the actual consequences in a particular case; we do not look only to utility to decide whether to break a certain promise. Consequences are not irrelevant, however, for we cannot make responsible moral judgments about promises without thoroughly understanding the institution of promising, and that surely includes knowing something of its usual consequences as well as much else, particularly the expectations people have for it and the demands these expectations make on it in a community.[27]

The same is true of acts and institutions and offices that get some of their meaning from the role they play in business. Many acts performed by managers and employees of organizations are the acts that they are by virtue of the agents' roles in the organization. If a pitcher throws a ball under certain circumstances, his act is not only a throw but a pitch, and an inning-ending third strike as well. A treasurer moves her hands in a certain way and thereby a company makes a payment and discharges a debt.[28] In making some sounds a manager humiliates and demotes a subordinate and provokes a wave of dissent. The context, including but not limited to roles, rules (of language, for example), intentions, and consequences, makes a physical movement an action of a certain sort and may give it some moral properties as well. The context also makes a person a treasurer or a pitcher or honorable. The assessment—prudential, moral, or any other kind—of a complex act requires an understanding of that context. At a minimum, we must be able to answer the now-familiar question, What is the point of doing that? The question may include but go beyond the individual actor's intention on that occasion. Clearly it follows that business ethics requires an understanding of business, as one cannot make ethical judgments about an act without this sort of understanding of its context, and in particular its purpose.[29] But while understanding the context that makes movements actions of certain kinds is not a sufficient condition of criticizing the community's associated moral views, it is a necessary one.

This is not to say that there is one context per act. Within an organization a certain remark may constitute sexual harassment when made to certain people, but the speaker may think of the remark as an expression of the kind of free speech permitted by our national culture or as a move in a very ancient two-person game. It is appropriate to call it harassment when it is unwelcome and not to permit it. But a manager who wants to discourage harassment effectively must also understand the various ways in which the speaker might understand the remark and help him (or her) see why in this context one description of the speech act must be dominant.

CRITICIZING COMMUNITIES: RELATIVISM AGAIN

A certain kind of relativist will claim that this sort of understanding is indeed sufficient for moral criticism, that there is nothing more to moral philosophy than interpreting the thick moral concepts of a culture and seeing what purposes its institutions and its complex tacit social contracts are supposed to serve. Williams (1985), who gives signs of being this sort of relativist, argues that morality should be studied from the ground up, much as anthropology is, and for some of the same reasons: practices, rules, institutions, and intuitions differ from one community to another. If all ethics is local, if different communities have their own views of the good life and the good person, then we may wonder why one would postulate cross-culturally applicable moral principles of the sort that contractarians and others have traditionally sought. In the absence of such principles, there is such a thing as business ethics—or, on a radical account, there are various versions of business ethics for various organizations—and there are other ethical systems for other communities, but mere ethics is an oxymoron.

Yet, as I argued in Chapter 1, there are limitations on relativism; any ethical system, however alien to ours, must have something to do with what we can recognize as a candidate for the good life, justice, and arguably rights as well; otherwise, we have no basis for calling it an ethical system, as opposed to just a way of organizing a community.[30] I suggested earlier that the very idea of interpretation presupposes that the aliens' institutions and beliefs must make some kind of sense to us, that we can discover some purpose for the former and some reason for the latter. It does not follow that the purposes are good on the whole, or the beliefs true. To understand a concept like corporate loyalty or even a questionable one such as manliness or phlogiston is to see that it has not been wholly pointless. Our ability to see how the notion connects to the local notion of the good life does not imply that it is acceptable under current circumstances, or any for that matter. We can see why people postulated phlogiston; we can see why in some societies people have a sense of self in which clitoridectomy or making $200 million a year plays a role. But we need not think them right.

Let us not assume, however, that an argument about morality with an alien would necessarily be a waste of time. An outsider's interpretation of a certain practice or personal quality might show that it has broken free of its original justification and has a kind of functional autonomy. Even where physical courage has ceased to be very useful, for example, it may still be an honored virtue. Similarly, young men might be proud of their tribal markings or expensive suits long after their purpose had faded. Some ancient sense of professional responsibility may now cause more trouble than it is worth. Certain sexual mores may be outdated and dysfunctional, hence objectionable on broadly moral grounds.

I do not claim that the disappearance of immediate reasons justifies the elimination of the practice. People may still expect adherence and feel betrayed when there is a lapse. In considering practices that smack of clannishness or undue filial piety, we may fail to note that for many people families have a profound moral status, and family life is simply more important than any other aspect of life: it is the sort of thing that, far from being subject to utilitarian evaluation, is the basis of it. So it is, as I argued in Chapter 2, with other principles that govern intimate matters: abiding by them makes some people happy because it is right, and not the other way around.[31] Even from a utilitarian point of view, the criticism may fail. To violate even apparently outmoded feelings of familial or corporate loyalty is to risk undermining the bonds of trust and respect that bind communities; since it takes considerable interpretive skill to see all the ramifications of a practice, it is not to be assumed that one can readily evaluate its consequences—not that the consequences alone count.[32] But surely with some care it can be done? Can we not evaluate local principles and practices according to the higher-order principles of morality?

THE PRINCIPLES OF MORALITY

There is a problem with such evaluations. Morality's time-honored principles of utility, justice, and rights cannot be neutral arbiters among communities. More broadly, utility cannot always support us in comparing communities from a moral point of view because using a utilitarian standard presupposes some conception of the good life, and conceptions of the good life vary from one community to another, and even from one person to another: think of extended family relations, a life of ease, personal power. Consider esteem: insofar as the esteem of others is of value, as it is to most people,[33] and insofar as the sort of life that earns esteem differs from one community to another, so does the nature of the good life. Utilitarian considerations are thus not always of much help where there is an argument between two sets of community standards.[34]

The time-honored principles of justice and rights have some of the same crippling shortcomings as utility. They are incapable of being neutral arbiters among communities for at least two reasons: they conflict in practice, and different communities may have different conceptions of what these principles imply.[35] So it is extraordinarily difficult to find a basis for cross-cultural criticism.

Consider rights. Morality demands respect for them, hence for autonomy, but how do we identify autonomy? It is hard to see how one could hold that a certain action is autonomous, even intentional, without having some basis for saying that it is somehow reasonable.[36] Hence we are likely to agree on what is autonomous if and only if we agree on what is reasonable motivation, and so to a significant degree about the nature of the good life as well.[37] It is a further problem that opposing ideologies may have different views of freedom and coercion. Note how differently a socialist and a libertarian will view coercion: the former, not the latter, will claim to find it in a competitive market.

Consider justice. It fails as a basis for comparison insofar as it is possible for different communities to have different criteria for deserving. Socialists and capitalists, for example, differ over whether it is just that people with greater native talent are paid more. From one organization to another there will be still further differences over what justifies discrimination.

The difficulty of using the standard moral principles for moral evaluation of different communities' views on morality is not a merely theoretical one; our actual moral arguments illustrate the problems. There are champions of fairness on both sides of the issue of affirmative action. There are advocates of freedom on all sides of the issue of employee rights. The emerging consensus about the equality of women is not a result of a great many people's suddenly noticing that the basic principle of fairness has for some reason or other not been applied. Instead, among other things, over time many women adopted a different notion of the good life for themselves and therefore espoused a different set of fairly specific principles governing the basis on which discrimination is allowable.[38]

As in science, we adopt a new theory if new questions or new data create sufficient dissatisfaction with the old one and if the new theory answers the old questions equally well and the new ones better. Change in our moral rules—for example, the adoption of rules like "no one should be denied a job on account of gender," rather than any supposed first principles of morality—comes about, perhaps suddenly, for similar reasons, with two differences at least. First, in science we can more readily agree not only about what the data are but also about what works better, since we have a clearer view of what we want from science than of what ethics should do for us. Second, as I argued earlier, our moral rules may go on creating expectations and even utility after their original point is lost. For these reasons, in the case of morality the dissatisfaction associated with the old theory must be great enough to make it worthwhile to undertake significant reorganization of one's values, a difficult process, as all reorganization is. In prospect its results are unclear, and the case for theoretical satisficing may be strong; in retrospect one may wonder, as many feminists have, why it took one so long to see the light.

But don't we still have the great principles of ethics to guide us, even though interpreting and applying them is difficult? I want to cast still further doubt on them.

AGAINST THEORETICAL ETHICS

Consider the principles that are supposed to govern scientific theorizing. According to the likes of Quine, Kuhn, and Rorty, we know of no self-evidently correct universal principles, substantive or methodological, that will always enable us to distinguish readily between good scientific theories and bad ones.[39] Yes, a good theory is coherent, simple, general, conservative, modest, and falsifiable without having been falsified, but these criteria may conflict or raise controversy in application, particularly over time. (On the criteria themselves and the difficulties I discuss here see Quine and Ullian [1978, esp. pp. 64–82].) For example, we favor certain theories on the grounds of conservatism relative to other theories we believe, generality, and simplicity, among other features. But it is characteristic of scientific revolutions that they pit modesty and conservatism against generality and simplicity and favor the latter pair (Quine and Ullian, pp. 74f.). And simplicity itself is a hard criterion to apply with confidence (pp. 71f.). What counts as a single, unified story? What is the principle of individuation of stories?

Most important, the criteria will sometimes yield when we find good science that does not fit them. For example, some theories are not at all simple; some cannot be definitively falsified. (Think of natural selection.) The criteria are not after all guaranteed a priori: we derive them from what we know about successful scientific theories, not the other way around. Yet these criteria are neither arbitrary nor useless. There is a difference between good science and bad science, and there is such a thing as scientific progress. By the same token, there is a difference between good and bad moral philosophy, and moral progress is possible.[40] And it is possible to criticize a culture's thick concepts and characteristic practices.

A traditional Cartesian philosopher would deny that we arrive at principles of knowledge—that is, the fundamentals of epistemology—by looking at the criteria implicit in what scientists do but would in effect argue that philosophy of science is just applied epistemology. An antifoundationalist would argue that that is backwards: philosophy of science is what epistemology purports to be.[41] We arrive at principles of knowledge—that is, the fundamentals of epistemology—by first looking at the criteria implicit in what successful scientists do. These criteria can then be used to criticize particular theories. Neither the criteria nor the theories are clearly prior in all respects.

I claim that business ethics is in much the same state: it is not applied ethics in just the way the philosophy of science is not applied epistemology. We[42] do not make moral progress by getting ever clearer on the details of the foundational principles of ethics. We do it by testing principles and intuitions against each other on two assumptions: that we cannot be altogether wrong about what is and is not moral and that none of us is altogether right.[43] Neither our principles nor our intuitions are prior; nor are they permanent.

It is impossible to predict which principles may be revised. The only ones we cannot imagine undergoing revision are the ones so broad that they are more useful for indicating what morality is about than for guiding action. The principle that we should treat people equally unless there is good reason not to seems unlikely to be revised, or ever to be of much help; what is eligible for revision is the list of good reasons.

As a practical matter, managers can promote morality more effectively in most organizations by finding processes of adjudication and dispute resolution that command widespread respect among those who want to be good citizens in the organization than by trying to police people according to the time-honored moral principles.[44] That would be true, however, even if business ethics were a search for the perfect application of ethical principles to business, and that is not what business ethics is. For *nothing would count* as the perfect application of ethical principles to business. What would it mean to say that the socialist's or the capitalist's or anyone else's notion of justice is the perfect application of the principle, or not?[45] We cannot answer questions like that in business ethics courses, or in any ethics courses.

It is no doubt possible to propound a moral theory that gives determinate results so that no question of application or of conflict of principles arises; some form of utilitarianism might be that way. But all such attempts of which I am aware have counterintuitive consequences that raise serious questions about why anyone should accept the theory. Yes, our intuitions may be wrong, but on what basis do we abandon many of them to embrace a theory? (Shall we propound a metatheory to deal with this question?)

As we seek principles and virtues that work more satisfactorily within our community, we sometimes reconsider our notion of what is satisfactory. We do not work from the top down: we find evidence for these principles and virtues in new intuitions and insights given by experience, literature, and case studies. Over time people in a community develop agreements on dealing with moral problems. The process never ends: there will always be good reasons to reflect on our principles and intuitions.

Whether we side with moral realism or with Bernard Williams, our moral assessment of any culture, in business or elsewhere, should rest on a thorough familiarity with that culture's thick concepts and characteristic practices. This may involve focusing on what the language of a culture presupposes without argument.

TACIT IDEOLOGY

Interpretation does not permit us to evaluate others' principles and vocabularies, or our own, against the time-honored moral principles. Yet we can note what others' vocabulary assumes about ethical matters and with some difficulty do the same for our own. There is no reason to hope that we shall ever speak in a vocabulary that provides a morally neutral perspective on other vocabularies we find lacking, but we can consider reasons for and against accepting implications of the language heard in organizations.

In claiming that the discourse of business, with its characteristic thick concepts, presupposes some ethical views, I am aware of the current tendency to make ideological points cheaply by pointing out that even those who try modestly to stick to evident facts are themselves prisoners of some unexamined ideology that privileges questionable views and empowers the wrong people and that therefore one should be equally heavy-handed in some different cause. Bad arguments aside, it is true that there is no theory about organizations or anything else that is a compilation of observed facts and that in the absence of at least rudimentary theorizing there can be no observed facts worthy of the name. (I elaborate in Hartman [1988].) One of the uses of philosophical analysis is to identify philosophical positions that hide in apparently empirical statements and theories, in part because these inevitably oversimplify the world. They assume, for example, that things move frictionlessly, or that Euclidean geometry is true, or that the money supply alone drives inflation. These falsehoods are often not only harmless but useful or even necessary for predicting some state or event or otherwise understanding it. But the use of standard economic assumptions in discussing ethics shows that a false assumption that is useful for one purpose may be a disaster for another.

The assumption, for example, that individuals are rational maximizers of their own selfish interests enables economists to make some useful, although inexact, predictions about large groups of people. To base a moral judgment on the assumption that some individual will necessarily act in his or her own narrowly selfish interests, however, would be most reckless. Not much better is the assumption—in criticizing the notion of comparable worth, for example—that managers normally try to maximize profits as faithful agents of stockholders. One (e.g., Friedman) might then believe, without further evidence, that companies foolish enough to discriminate on the basis of race or sex or to permit

sexual harassment would pay a stiff price in the labor market and ultimately become uncompetitive and that consequently we need not worry
about that happening. One might hold that a commons, being a cartel,
could not be preserved or that regulation aimed at preserving a
commons would infringe intolerably on its participants' freedom. One
might deny that brainwashing was logically possible or consider it
morally permissible. One might believe that everybody has perfect information. One might consider economics and ethics identical, as some
old utilitarians did.

The morally freighted assumptions of economics do not normally
appear in such egregious form. Traditional utilitarianism does not usually state outright the psychological theory that is essential to it and
whose evident absurdity would raise doubts about utilitarianism. It is typically, although not exclusively, a philosophical task to explicate the
assumptions that animate a theory, particularly if they are assumptions
about what is moral or immoral. Hence, if a libertarian argues that freedom is the preeminent human right, it is appropriate and most
important for a philosopher to see what the libertarian counts as freedom and to judge whether freedom in that sense is such a good thing as
its honored name implies. And so we shall, in Chapter 5.

Who, after all, could argue with the notion that a legitimate contract
involves a willing buyer and a willing seller? But a great deal depends on
the basis on which one attributes willingness to a party. What conditions
would create doubts about whether a party is willing in a sense that can
legitimize a contract? An answer to that question is presupposed by a
statement that a party to a contract is willing. The problem is not that the
standard libertarian gives a strange answer to the characteristically philosophical question but that the standard libertarian does not address the
question squarely.[46]

The language of the human resources profession hardly respects the
distinction between giving people good reason for a belief or desire and
manipulating them.[47] To identify this feature and show how it relates to
the presuppositions of standard libertarianism does not by itself prove
much. There remains the task of showing why the distinction is important, and that in turn requires giving an account of good reasons for
belief and action—the essence, I have suggested and shall argue in Chapter 5, of a definition of autonomy. It is also part of an explication of the
Kantian distinction, central to morality, between treating someone as an
end and treating someone as merely a means; that distinction is a crucial
one in business, where people do treat one another as means.[48] Identifying presuppositions is thus only the first step in a long process of
argumentation.

As economists generate useful theories on the assumption that the individual is selfish and rational, organization theorists usefully assume
roughly the opposite: that individual states of perception, thought,
belief, and desire can be cancelled out. (See Pfeffer [1982] and, for an

opposing point of view, Hartman [1988].) For similar reasons a traffic engineer might propound a theory about traffic flow that bypasses the individual perceptual state that a psychologist postulates to explain what happens when someone with normal vision looks at a stoplight. But traffic engineers do not normally claim to have shown that individual states of perception are eliminable postulates. From the point of view of ethics, the problem is that the individual conceived by certain organization theorists is one about whom questions of autonomy and rights can barely arise.

PRINCIPLES FOR GOOD ORGANIZATIONS: A RAWLSIAN PROPOSAL

If the arguments in the previous section are sound, we cannot address the great ethical issues of business by applying foundational moral principles to individual behavior or to local rules and practices. How then do we determine what is morally good? I have suggested that the practice of successful scientists should guide us in propounding principles of sound scientific methodology. If the topic is business ethics, we might consider moral managers.[49] The best of them, with no very specific a priori principles to guide them, create communities that generate opportunities for people to make moral progress and enjoy some version of the good life. But then how do we know in advance who the best ones are?

Contract theory is supposed to help here. We might say that the indeterminacy of application of the time-honored moral principles makes it possible for different local institutions and rules to fare equally well from the point of view of utility, justice, and rights. It is not a relativist view that different communities may have different rules based on different agreements—recall that Donaldson and Dunfee speak of moral free space—so long as we do not go on to say that any old agreement is all right. So what makes an agreement good from a moral point of view?

I argued first, against Friedman, that absence of coercion does not suffice: an agreement can be made among free parties and still be unfair. The right to exit does not entail fairness. Then I argued, against Donaldson and Dunfee, that we cannot readily distinguish good agreements from bad ones by applying the time-honored principles of morality, or hypernorms. If we cannot know exactly what a morally good agreement looks like, then perhaps the best we can do is to try to describe a good procedure for reaching agreement. We might say, for example, that a morally legitimate agreement is one that would be made by rationally self-interested people, each of whom is prevented by the rules of negotiation from getting an unfair advantage. The problem with this move is that it is not clear that people have set and permanent interests in advance of their living together in a community. What features, then, would legitimize a procedure for developing agreements on how a community is to be governed?

I think the later Rawls (1993) has a useful approach. He does not assume that people's values predate their living in communities, nor does he claim that the procedure he offers is certified by the time-honored principles of morality. On the contrary, he argues that we inevitably face a plurality of reasonable[50] "comprehensive moral theories," which may be utilitarian or religious or something else, and that a state has no justification for demanding that citizens accept any comprehensive view of what utility or justice requires. The best that politicians can do is to design political institutions that embody an "overlapping consensus" that accommodates the plurality of reasonable comprehensive theories likely to be found in a modern state. Rawls's use of the famous "original position" bears little resemblance to traditional contract theory. It does not, for example, promise to conjure a just state from ignorant self-interest in a moral vacuum. Modestly, it models the procedure by which reasonable people who value freedom and equality (without initially being able to say exactly what these entail) arrive at principles and institutions acceptable to them—that is, compatible with their various comprehensive doctrines. The principles and institutions thus acceptable are the best we can get from a moral point of view. This approach does not make political theory a form of applied ethics; Rawls is rejecting the possibility of judging a state morally good or bad according to whether its laws and institutions meet the standards of utilitarianism or any other comprehensive doctrine, which is just what applied ethics is supposed to do.

At this point one might object that Rawls is defining freedom and equality arbitrarily and making them foundational. I think this objection fails. The original position models equality as discrimination on bases that an impartial and reasonable person puts forward. There is no guarantee that the result of the procedure will be self-evidently just—Rawls does not claim it will be—but it is a good basis for further negotiation, and it is the best we can do. As for freedom: Rawls in effect defines a free person as one who can decide what his or her own best interests are; that, as I shall argue in Chapter 5, is not a bad definition. In any case, freedom and equality are not foundational, since Rawls does not claim to have an answer to (or any interest in) anyone who does not care about them or who thinks they have nothing to do with morality.

There is a further sense in which justice is not foundational. Rawls does not believe that justice can be defined the same way in a family as in a community, or in a community as in an organization, since these different entities impose different requirements for justice.[51]

Despite the difficulties Rawls mentions, the main ones of which we addressed at the end of Chapter 3, a broadly Rawlsian approach is not out of place for business ethics. Knowing what the right moral principles are for a community, an organization for example, is a matter of knowing how one would design a community that does effectively what it has to do—not the same thing in every community—but also protects justice and freedom, even though the founders of an organization may not embrace the so-called difference principle that would appeal to impartial founders of a state and may see basic rights differently.[52] Insofar as business ethics describes the features of the good organization, it is not an application of "real" ethical principles.

According to the Rawlsian approach, then, a morally sound organization is one that would be designed by a group of people who value being free and politically equal and desire to be responsible citizens, who know they are going to represent stakeholders of the organization but do not know which kind. They are a kind of ideal board of directors. We can assume that those in the original position would try to design an organization that would not be brutally hard on any stakeholder and that would produce an overlapping consensus on certain matters but leave room for differences on others.[53]

One of the complications of transplanting this machinery to organizations is that we must develop an account of political equality that would be appropriate for organizations. Whether an organization should be more or less tolerant than a state of a range of views on nonpublic moral issues is not an obvious call. We might argue that these are none of the organization's business, or on the other hand that the relative ease of entering and leaving organizations permits less tolerance of diversity, while the greater need to focus on certain goals requires it.[54]

We cannot assume that the Rawlsian method would create an organization that would be considered good in all times and places—Rawls himself is not so bold[55]—or even put to rest once and for all this issue of tolerance, but it shows how people like us might go about constructing the morally best organization we can imagine. That would surely be an organization that would be hospitable to a variety of rational views on moral issues. Over time, Rawls suggests (especially in 1993, Lecture VII), the participants might criticize and revise their behavior and renegotiate the agreements that bind them. Rawls would not object to differing agreements in different organizations, or in the same one at different times.[56]

We associate with Aristotle the views that morality should be generally consistent with commonsense intuitions[57] and that moral principles arise out of the experience of people of practical wisdom, which encompasses at least two virtues: ethical sensibility, the ability to see the ethical aspects of a situation, and moral imagination, the ability to identify ways to deal with conflicting moral obligations.[58] The case study method is one way of honing these faculties, as well as the overlapping faculties of the effective manager. After all, people are not good managers primarily because they know and can apply general principles about how to manage.[59]

What can we say from this point of view about the great issues of business ethics? That is a large subject, but I offer a few brief programmatic remarks about what goes on in a just organization, with no guarantees at all that we are moving towards defining Justice.

SOME MODEST REMARKS ON JUSTICE AND RIGHTS

In considering what justice demands in an organization, we might be tempted to begin at a broad theoretical level and hold that here and everywhere justice demands that people be treated equally unless there is some special reason why they deserve something more or less than equal treatment. That is not a very useful view.

If we are doing applied ethics, we face the question of how this principle is to be applied. Capitalists typically claim to apply this principle of justice by rewarding productivity: the capitalist's intuition is that it is just that the brilliant inventor and the entrepreneur who creates the market for the invention get rich; they deserve it. Socialists consider it just to distribute wealth on the basis of need; talent is no basis of desert. Which application is the right one? My argument is that there is no way to answer this question definitively, no defensible foundational theory of justice or of human nature that one can apply confidently to decide the issue, despite the efforts of generations of Marxists and Aristotelians[60] and others.

As a modest Rawlsian alternative, we might postulate founders who define distributive justice as rewarding talent-based contribution but only insofar as doing so benefits the untalented as well.[61] The decision would be based to a great degree on knowing how most people of our acquaintance are motivated. They are sufficiently self-interested to respond to incentives that reward greater effort more greatly. They are not, however, the rational maximizers of standard economic theory. So, for example, most people will cooperate even when they could be better off if they were free riders, so long as others do not take undue advantage of them. Most people are sufficiently concerned with fairness to be indignant about (others') free riding; they will punish noncooperators and those who try to get more than their fair share, even at a significant cost to themselves.[62] Yet the founders might well become aware that there can be catastrophic results if people make a practice of punishing any failure to reciprocate cooperative behavior (Dixit and Nalebuff [1991]). For a community of people motivated as are most people we know, they would probably establish as a community principle that patient reciprocity is a virtue but being a patsy is a vice, with many victims. The community would therefore reap the benefits of a notion of justice seasoned by mercy.

To judge that people are not classical rational maximizers requires some understanding of psychology. To judge that rewarding talent would benefit the least talented in the long run requires the same, and some understanding of economics, too. Evidently, it is easier than some philosophers have believed to get an *ought* from an *is*.

It is less clear what well-informed founders would do about affirmative action, perhaps the busiest current arena for arguments about justice. Those who accept Rawls's "principle of fair and equal opportunity" for communities may differ among themselves about what people in the original position will propound for organizations. The founders will have to be sensitive to the long-term benefits of affirmative action, but to its abrasions, too; they will need a sense of what citizens can accept and still respect each other. Note, however, this important point, here and in the case of rewarding talent: beyond appeals to the initial procedural and to such factual considerations, the Rawlsian view does not entertain the further question, "Yes, but is affirmative action [or pay for talent, or whatever] *really fair?*"[63]

It is not surprising that our imagined founders design organizations that please our liberal capitalist intuitions. This is the sort of organization that is best for people like us, and it may not be in all ways appropriate for people who are motivated differently, as those accustomed to life in a different sort of community might be.[64] We may infer, too, that some of our central moral principles are more ephemeral than we might have supposed: they depend on how people are motivated and will change as people's motivation changes. Over time saints and artists and philosophers and managers too will make us rethink what our interests are. Over time some people (some women, for example) may well come to believe that the old understandings of what is fair and appropriate are unsatisfactory. Among other things, they presuppose that people are motivated in certain ways; those presuppositions may become obsolete as social conditions change or as we scrutinize our intuitions, our principles, and our vocabulary and see that there are different ways of looking at the world. It is conceivable, for example, that there might be communities in which peer pressure against letting one's friends down is a stronger motivator than individual pay and in which it might therefore be appropriate to have a different conception of justice, as well as of the demands of loyalty.[65]

Which of these conceptions is really the best possible one? On that issue, standard theoretical ethics has nothing useful to say.

PROSPECTS

Chapter 7 addresses some of the problems that social contract theory is supposed to solve, and some that it raises. I hold to the view that the Rawlsian approach is a promising one.

The next chapters focus on motivation, a topic on which ideology runs free. Do not expect to find there (or anywhere) a view of motivation that stands austerely outside all parochial points of view. The best we can hope is that we shall notice some of the presuppositions of our own talk about the world and about the person, that rational and political animal.

The shortcomings of the economist's notion of rationality will become more evident.

On that notion, the standard solution to the problem of the commons is this: in order to serve everyone's interests, the participants make a contract and then enforce compliance. It will turn out that a contract is not by itself the best way to preserve the commons in a complex organization. This commons requires that participants in the organization have an interest in one another's well-being.

NOTES

1. There are some—mostly people unacquainted with ethical theory—who argue that business ethics should be taught in every course, since to have separate courses in business ethics is to suggest the absurdity that ethics is something separate from the rest of business. They do not make the parallel argument that one should teach finance in every course rather than in separate courses so as not to suggest that finance is something separate. This is probably because they think teaching finance requires some knowledge of theory.

2. In saying this I do indeed mean to imply that different fields have their different and characteristic ways of dividing the necessary from the contingent and *is* from *ought*. They do after all have different definitions, hence different views of what is true by definition.

3. Is management a discipline separate from sociology? That is a question not about knowledge but about academic politics.

4. The articles have been reprinted and appear in the bibliography under the dates 1984 and 1989. Carr's argument is not particularly subtle, but it is a clear, forceful, well-known exposition of a point with which many businesspeople with whom I have worked heartily agree, and they are not shy about saying so.

5. During World War II the hidden ball trick was illegal in Japanese baseball because it was regarded as dishonorable—just the sort of thing you would expect of Americans (Whiting [1989], p. 46). One thinks of the famous remark attributed to Leo Durocher: "Nice guys finish last."

6. Recall from Ch. 2 that Friedman does not have much to say about the Prisoner's Dilemma and the commons.

7. In this argument Friedman appears to be a kind of hard-nosed rule utilitarian, for it is not clear that he regards fairness in itself as able to justify or condemn business practices. Perhaps fairness smacks too much of the kind of equality libertarians do not advocate. Insofar as Friedman countenances any sort of fairness, it is the sort we would expect a capitalist to accept: to each according to his contribution.

8. Note the title of Friedman (1984): "The Social Responsibility of Business is to Increase its Profits."

9. One thinks of such famous names as Simon and Mintzberg. There is a vast literature on the cybernetic approach to organizations and other systems, but there are many other ways to think of organizations. Morgan (1986) discusses several organizational "paradigms" and emphasizes their incommensurability. Hartman (1988) argues that different organizational theories and analogies may be answers to different questions or tools for different tasks. Keeley (1988) takes a position on that issue that is closer to mine, but he criticizes the view of the organization as a purposive system because it encourages a morally inadequate

treatment of rights, and he supports the view of the organization as a nexus of contracts. Keeley's influence on this section is extensive and valuable, even though I disagree with him on a number of issues. For a similar and equally respectful dissent, see Herman (1991), to whom my debt will be evident.

10. From Hegelians like John R. Commons to neoconservatives like Richard Epstein, there is agreement that ownership is a bundle of rights, not a simple two-term relationship. A contract rearranges those rights and spells them out in greater detail. Edel et al. (1994, pp. 198ff.) show how over time our views about private property must be elaborated to keep up with new developments, for example in technology. They suggest that merely appealing to property rights is a move of limited and diminishing value.

11. Here I believe I have the support of Freeman and Gilbert (1988, p. 18), who argue that "purpose emerges as a web of semiautonomous bargains, among individuals." To claim that profit is the overriding purpose is like saying that the overriding purpose of one's life is to breathe.

12. As I have already argued and shall argue further in Chs. 6 and 7, however, an organization will be the more effective insofar as its participants are disposed to cooperate beyond the requirements of narrow self-interest.

13. There is a vast literature on stakeholders as well, and on what they are morally owed. The issue became truly hot with the publication of Freeman (1984).

14. For a similar but finally not identical view see Herman (1991). The moral problem for management is to get people with differing interests to cooperate; the only real solution is to get them to do so voluntarily. That management characteristically orchestrates common tasks requiring cooperation does not necessarily undermine rights. I shall have more to say in Ch. 5 about having what one wants.

15. It might appear that a rational person would accept an unfair distribution of the products of labor in preference to getting nothing as a result of not entering into any contract. Recall that people sometimes choose the latter, as Frank (1988) and his sources give reason to believe: people regard unfairness itself as undesirable.

16. Donaldson and Dunfee take the idea of the contract far beyond the boundaries of the individual organization: their primary interest is ethical dealings among organizations in different national cultures.

17. Much of analytical philosophy and its successor movements in the last thirty years has been predicated upon the denial of the clear distinction, implicit here, between necessary and contingent truth.

18. Donaldson and Dunfee argue, surely correctly, that macrosocial contracts must grant what they call "moral free space." See esp. pp. 260–262.

19. Solomon (1992; see esp. pp. 50ff.) makes much of these problems. Donaldson and Dunfee do not discuss them but seem to avoid falling victim to all or most of them.

20. This criticism has more force against theories that claim that some people once actually formed a political entity by entering into a real contract than against theories about either hypothetical contracts or real contracts of a normal sort. A related criticism attacks the notion of a state of nature.

21. Rawls argues (1993, p. 276, for example) that one cannot know what one would have been like apart from one's community. I argue in Ch. 6 that there may be equal difficulty in seeing oneself apart from a strong corporate culture. Rawls's theory does not assume that interests are fixed or identifiable separately

from one's life as a citizen. Donaldson and Dunfee (1995) do not claim that any contract will be appropriate forever

22. Sen (1987, Ch. 2, esp. pp. 46ff.), Bowie (1991), Derry (1991), and others attack the standard economist's egoist assumptions to the contrary.

23. Derry and Green (1989) point out that business ethicists just don't seem to know what to say when, for example, utilitarian and Kantian theories generate different ethical imperatives in practice. Donaldson and Dunfee do not apply hypernorms directly to business practice, and in general their contractarian view shows how people can agree about ethical obligations. I do not think they need hypernorms at any level to make their most important points.

24. Williams (1985) repeatedly claims that the standard moral principles can be neither made consistent nor ordered rationally. Nussbaum (1990, pp. 55–66) notes the similarity between Williams and Aristotle on this point. She accepts the Aristotelian view that rationality does not require—nor does there exist—either a single metric by which we can make and assess every decision or a set of principles that covers all morally significant acts. This pretty well eliminates utilitarianism.

Why, in any case, do Donaldson and Dunfee (p. 266) put forward "precedence of duty over personal rights" as an attractive example of a hypernorm?

Donaldson and Dunfee give some reasons to believe (esp. at pp. 268–271) that the way to characterize the best possible local agreements is to focus on the process by which they are negotiated. As I shall hereafter argue, that idea has merit.

25. In what follows I am indebted to Phillips (1992). The point is important for those, like Donaldson and Dunfee, who hold that there are real contracts that need to be evaluated ultimately from the point of view of hypernorms.

26. Recall Ch. 2. The parallel for statements of fact, familiar since Quine (1960), is that a translation of an alien language according to which everything the aliens say is false cannot be regarded as an accurate translation.

27. The difficulty with the deontological view of ethics, which advertises itself as opposing the consequentialist view, is not so much that it requires the notion of a mere action's being moral or not as that it requires the notion of a mere action, identifiable apart from its consequences, or even its intended consequences (e.g., "He shot at the fleeing burglar."). See if you can say where act ends and consequence begins in this sequence: Prinzip's nerves twitch; his muscles twitch; his finger crooks; the trigger moves; a man is shot; a man is killed; the Archduke is assassinated; the Austro-Hungarian Empire is deprived of a great figure; the Great War is started. One could go on, beginning earlier or ending later. Kant seems confident about our being able to identify the maxim of an act, but it is not clear that there is only one. One of the conditions of solving a problem is that we be aware of the possibility of alternative accurate descriptions of the situation. (See further Edel et al. [1994], pp. 112ff.)

28. Here is a crux in the argument over whether an organization can literally act. The notion of corporate intention is problematical, certainly; the extreme nominalist claim that the only actions are those of certain individuals suggests that it is literally true that Alexandra Harkness moves her hands but not literally true that a payment gets made. Then, somewhat as in the case of Prinzip's act at Sarajevo, one must wonder how we decide which level of description is the real or natural one. It may be true that a corporation cannot act immorally, but it seems undebatable that individuals can undertake moral or immoral acts that

cannot be described, much less morally assessed, without essential reference to some corporation.

29. The claim that one can make such ethical judgments without knowledge of the context makes sense if and only if one accepts the implausible nominalism that countenances only physical movements and not such events as payments and promotions.

30. My argument here would probably be congenial not only to Arrington (1989, pp. 241f.) but to Rorty (1991) as well. See especially vol. I, pp. 27–30, where he defends what he calls his ethnocentrism with characteristic ironic modesty. The chapter titled "The Priority of Democracy to Philosophy" (pp. 175–196 in the same volume) has influenced this whole essay. In the end I do not believe we can establish ultimate principles that are more action-guiding than are the broad principles that define morality, which are hardly action-guiding at all.

31. Williams (1981, 1985, and elsewhere) argues that utilitarianism cannot account for personal attachments of great moral importance. Nussbaum (1993) notes that Aristotle regards these experiences as paradigmatic. Donaldson and Dunfee (1994a, p. 6, n. 9) note Parfit's example of the woman who cultivates dispositions that will have good consequences. These include a strong maternal instinct, which however then leads her to favor her children's interest over others'. In that sense utilitarianism is self-defeating. Here, as in Ch. 2, the utilitarian can invoke Scanlon's (1982) distinction between normative and philosophical utilitarianism and embrace the latter.

32. American baseball players who move to Japan to play find incredible the Japanese insistence on working a pitcher's arm to exhaustion even as treatment for soreness, since in many cases it aggravates the problem. But the practice also helps support the prevailing and in many respects valuable attitude of selfless determination that characterizes Japanese players. (See Whiting [1989, pp. 65f.].)

33. Maslow (1970) makes a great deal of this point. One wonders what he would say about Mersault, the existential protagonist in Sartre's *L'Etranger:* esteem is the last thing he wants.

34. Recall Rawls's (1993) view that rational conceptions of the good vary from one person to another and that each individual is entitled to his or her own conception, subject to others having the same right.

35. For more on this point, see Hartman (1994). Lippke (1991) criticizes the use business ethicists make of standard principles. Lacking any theory of justice, they have no way to deal with cases in which, for example, utility and justice appear to compete, no way to justify a proposed distribution scheme, in general no way to settle arguments. I would add that if they did have one, questions would arise about whether it was any good. Similar observations appear throughout Williams (1985).

36. Here too the famous Quine (1960) argument applies.

37. Reasonableness is not only about the relationship between ends and means, *pace* Hume and his many successors.

The question of the nature of autonomy, and in particular what if anything it has to do with rationality, has been controversial for a long time. It is hard to see how an act could be autonomous if not somehow rational, and it is hard to see how one could take an act to be somehow rational if there were no evidence that it aimed at anything one could conceivably find desirable. It appears, then, that some of the difficulties in utilitarianism having to do with the nature of the good life affect issues of rights as well. Ch. 5 pursues this and related issues.

38. What is desirable is a function of what is available. In matters relating to gender, as elsewhere, technological progress encourages moral progress. It seems to have mattered that cooking and ironing need not take hours daily and that it is not necessary to hunt dangerous animals for food each day or fight wars by hand. Consider, too, how reproductive technology has changed sexual practices and therefore some people's values as well. Yet, as with all intimate matters, expectations and values remain long after the consequences of our actions and institutions have changed.

39. These would be analogous to the principles that Donaldson and Dunfee want to apply to contracts in organizations. The tempting but wrong analogy here is between actual scientific laws (rather than these broad criteria for good science) that apply imperfectly to the world and moral principles that allegedly do the same.

40. Contemporary moral realists claim that there are moral statements that have as much right to be called true as do the statements of science—however much right that is. The realists are mostly not foundationalists, however. See, for example, Sturgeon (1988), who believes that scientific reasoning is dialectical as moral reasoning is. Williams, an opponent of the realists, resists the assimilation of scientific to moral reasoning (1985, Ch. 8).

Kuhn argues, in effect, that good science is not science that mirrors the world but instead science that is done under conditions that encourage useful results and make room for further progress. To understand what makes science good, start by considering those conditions. Aristotle argues not very differently about good action: it is not action that obeys some general principle but rather action that a certain sort of person—a person with a certain kind of experience, character, education, and temperament—would take. To understand morality, start by considering virtue. Contract theorists argue that we should start by considering the procedures for arriving at moral judgments, but they had better understand, as Kuhn does in the analogous case, that it is appropriate for the procedures to change as time goes by.

41. Consider this similarity of philosophy of science to business ethics. There is such a thing as epistemology, and most theorists of knowledge will say that the field is distinct from science and the philosophy of science. But Quine has famously raised the question whether epistemology is anything other than philosophy of science. I am not prepared to argue that ethics culminates in politics, as Aristotle claims, or that ethics overlaps with sociology, as MacIntyre (1981) claims; that requires the kind of skepticism about the is-ought distinction that Quine has sponsored about the analytic-synthetic distinction. For my purposes it is enough to point out that it is as absurd to say that there is no such thing as philosophy of science, that there is just philosophy (including epistemology) and then there is science, as it is to say that there is no such thing as business ethics. As to the question whether competent work in business ethics requires a knowledge of business: would anyone doubt that one needs to know something about science to be a good philosopher of science?

42. That is, you and I and those who can generally understand us when we adduce moral considerations.

43. Rawls's reflective equilibrium is a sophisticated way of doing this. Derry and Green (1989) single out this device as holding some promise for business ethics. The crucial point is that neither our principles nor our intuitions can be altogether prior to the other. I do not think we can say in advance how broad will be the principles that we can agree on and actually use.

44. Insofar as morality is a matter of acting virtuously and not merely according to right principles, managers can promote morality by attending to corporate culture, which affects people's motivations. Management by culture, hence by propagating certain virtues, is particularly effective in large, complex organizations, where individuals' behavior cannot be closely monitored.

45. We cannot easily settle arguments about how to apply a rule. We might try to find a metarule governing its application, but then if we could not agree about the application of that metarule, we would have to find a metametarule—and so on *ad infinitum*. This Wittgensteinian argument suggests that, as there is no such thing as *the* application of a rule, the best we can do is try to reach a (perhaps temporary) procedure for adjudicating questions that arise. Procedures themselves may raise metaquestions, for example about whether a situation is one in which a certain procedure ought to be invoked, but they raise fewer of them. We can agree to a moral duty to abide by all decisions of the U.S. Supreme Court without agreeing that whatever the Court decides is right.

46. Some libertarians do go remarkably far in the direction of explicating their less plausible positions. Posner (1983), for example, states that the notion of fairness is contentless because there is no evidence that considerations of fairness motivate people, but we have noted just such evidence in Ch. 2 (see Frank [1988, pp. 167f.], who targets Posner specifically). He also faults fairness on the grounds of disagreement about its application. Since that kind of disagreement is one of the engines of scientific as well as moral progress, Posner's unreflective empiricism has little to recommend it.

47. MacIntyre (1981) makes much of this, but since he wrote his book the notion of empowerment has entered the language of human resources scholarship and surely brings with it a suggestion of autonomy.

48. There is nothing wrong with treating someone as a means; if there were, commerce itself would be immoral. Kant's stricture is aimed at treating people as though they were only means, nothing else, with no ends of their own.

49. It is characteristic of Aristotle to define ethics by reference to the excellent man. To many critics this is exasperating question begging, never mind sexism, but in the current context it may seem less so. For our purposes the important point is not to claim that our knowledge concerning the excellent man has some sort of priority but to avoid claiming that any level of moral knowledge is prior to any other. Aristotle himself often makes the point that we can start a philosophical exploration by considering something without implying that that something is truly prior.

50. In Lecture II, sec. 2, pp. 54ff., of *Political Liberalism*, Rawls explains and defends his view that I may have good reason to consider your moral view reasonable even if I do not accept it.

51. Rawls discusses this point mainly in Lecture VII. In this respect justice differs from utility, which is the basis of the best-known family of comprehensive doctrines. A utilitarian believes that a morally superior family, state, and organization all do have in common that they characteristically generate happiness. The idea of justice *tout court* makes no more sense than the notion of a hypothetical agreement made for an organization by founders who have no information at all about history, psychology, sociology, the organization, or their clients' actual or possible preferences, or their own.

52. Rawls gives the good nation-state responsibility for protecting the basic goods that any rational and reasonable person would want despite their differences concerning what is good. It is far from clear that all organizations have the

same affirmative responsibility, but they surely ought not to reduce people's basic goods.

53. The people in the original position must design not only an organization but a significant part of its environment, since the design of an organization is far more dependent upon its environment than is that of the average nation state. For his purposes Rawls can regard the latter as sealed off from the rest of the world. We cannot similarly ignore external stakeholders, even when in the first instance we are discussing internal matters. We cannot say what a just organization is like without saying a great deal about what a just economic system is like.

54. MacIntyre (1981, for example) and others, finding liberalism to be thin moral gruel, seem to prefer communities in which people are agreed about what is most important. Even one who shares MacIntyre's nostalgia, however, as I do not, can question whether organizations should demand consensus on nonpublic matters.

One of the advantages of the Rawlsian approach is that we can think of each of the many organizations there are as a kind of experiment in morality. If one works in an organization whose founders make rules one considers oppressive, one can usually look elsewhere. This is a point to Friedman (1982), who however is wrong in suggesting that the possibility of exit is a sufficient condition of a morally responsible organization. (Hirschman [1970] has a subtler view, which we shall consider in Ch. 7.) A problem about relying on exit as sufficient is that there may be only a few organizations that grant due process or respect loyalty, and they may get chased out of the market in the short run. (Here I agree with the criticisms of employment at will in Werhane [1994].)

55. He is consistent in this respect throughout the 1985 article, whose title is "Justice as Fairness: Political not Metaphysical." In 1993, especially in Lecture VII, he argues that his system is superior to any alternative in adjusting to changing circumstances.

56. Donaldson and Dunfee seem to agree. They sound Rawlsian when (at p. 260) they ask this hypothetical question: "What general principles, if any, would contractors who are aware of the strongly bounded nature of moral rationality in economic affairs choose to govern economic morality?" Rawls goes into some detail about the conditions and procedures under which his founders (we need not call them contractors) operate and emphatically does not advocate evaluating the results of their work by reference to any independent norms of utility, justice, or rights. Donaldson and Dunfee bring in hypernorms at this point, in my view not very helpfully. We should see hypernorms as emerging from our negotiations rather than standing in independent judgment of them, as I gather Donaldson and Dunfee would agree; hence, hypernorms are subject to change, but not rapid change.

57. Solomon (1992) and Duska (1991, 1993) have noted this with approval. A pragmatist way of making the corresponding point is this: in social policy, what is right just *is* whatever consensus permits accommodation. Rorty (1991, p. 184) claims support from Rawls in neither embracing nor rejecting pragmatist minimalism on this point. Rawls (esp. 1985, 1993) simply wants to present a feasible consensus that permits accommodation among rational and reasonable people; whether it is truly just beyond that is not a question that concerns him. In a Rawlsian Utopia, people's views of what is moral change as they go along; I believe he means to say that the moral views of such a community at any given time are as

close as people can get to morality at that time. For those who want to be moral while the search for moral truth goes on, that will just have to do.

58. For an account of the former, see Paine (1990, pp. 77–80), who notes that the ability to recognize a situation as morally problematical often needs to be supplemented by the ability—unfortunately, none too common—to bring the appropriate moral principles to bear in deciding what to do and in justifying one's decision to others who may criticize it or take it as a guide to action. (Of course there is no reason to believe there will always be a single moral principle that should be brought to bear.) The latter is the subject of Ciulla (1990) and strongly resembles the practical wisdom that characterizes successful managers. To the extent that one considers these (or any) virtues significant, one is not likely to think it possible for someone ignorant of business to have anything helpful to say about business ethics.

On Nussbaum's (1990, esp. Ch. 2) interpretation, Aristotle would largely agree with both Paine and Ciulla. Nussbaum points out (pp. 66–72) that Aristotle holds that apprehension of the particular case is prior to that of the general and that one's belief about the particular can be accurate in a way no general belief can be. Aristotle's theory of knowledge has notorious difficulties, and in discussing ethics we are probably better off adopting something like reflective equilibrium, which gives clear priority to neither principles nor particular intuitions. But there is much to be said for the view that general principles are a deficient guide to action when not accompanied by the practical wisdom that comes of experience.

59. Even if we did educate managers by teaching them principles, it would do no good to teach them principles like "See to it that your organization always maximizes the present value of its future cash flow."

60. Aristotle bases his moral views on a conception of human nature that he does not consider ephemeral, and to that extent he is a foundationalist. But as Nussbaum (1990, esp. pp. 56–66) notes, he differs from certain foundationalists —utilitarians, for example—in his denial that there must be some single metric of moral goodness, even within a particular choice situation.

61. Rawls (1993; for example, pp. 279f.) permits differential rights based on differential contributions to associations but emphatically does not do the same for rights based on differential contributions to society as a whole, since it violates the notion of the equal worth of all citizens.

62. Frank (1988) notes the evidence to this effect and argues that there is something to be said from the point of view of self-interest for what looks like vindictiveness: if your determination to punish that sort of behavior is known, people are less likely to mess with you. Schmidtz (1991) goes so far as to argue that reciprocity is and for pragmatic reasons ought to be central to our notion of justice. This would not appeal to Kant, whose very term *Categorical Imperative* seems designed to rule out such practical considerations. If all ethics were Kantian, Carr would be closer to the truth than he is.

63. In both 1971, p. 88, and 1993, p. 282, Rawls argues that in a social structure arranged according to his rules there is no question about whether a particular distribution of goods is fair after it has been determined that it has been done according to the rules.

I do not wish to suggest that there is no point in arguing about affirmative action. A defender of it might be able to get an opponent to agree that we ought to discriminate on the basis of personal qualities in ways that make an organization more effective, then demand to know why we ought not to discriminate on the basis of personal qualities in ways that make a society more effective in the long run. The opponent might reply that in a good society we encourage organizations to aim at what makes them more effective rather than at what makes society more effective.

64. For reasons by now familiar, there are limits to what we can imagine might motivate people, and these limits imply limits on what we can imagine might be reasonably considered moral.

65. Nothing I have said implies that any kind of motivation is as good from a moral point of view as any other. Extreme individualism, for example, will probably destroy trust and loyalty, hence any possibility of cooperation, in any community.

McCloskey (1994) argues for bourgeois virtue, which he claims is appropriate to an era and an area in which we bourgeois greatly outnumber both aristocrats and peasants and commerce is here to stay.

5

Morality and Autonomy

It is possible for morality to be in the moral person's best interests, not because all rational people must be moral, but because there is a certain kind of good life in which rationality and morality are compatible. It is characteristic of the good community that in several ways it makes this compatibility possible for those who live there. So does the good organization for those who work there. It is therefore the moral task of the manager to create a productive organization in which, on the whole, it is rational to be moral.

Morality is in the first instance about acting in others' interests rather than just in one's own, but, as I argued in Chapter 2, the notion of interests is subtler than the one implied by the utilitarianism that goes with standard economic theory. In particular, neither one's values nor one's interests need be narrowly selfish or otherwise inimical to others' interests. That the moral life is a matter of acting in others' interests is therefore compatible with the moral life's being a happy life, a life lived for the most part to good advantage.

It is a good life—not necessarily the only possible good life—to live morally in a community that propagates the good life for all. There is a problem here, however: in addition to being hospitable to morality or not, a community may greatly influence what people want. If a community gives people what they want, however, and what they want is itself a result of the effect of the community on them, how can the community then be acting in the people's best interests? This is a particularly difficult problem when the community in question is an organization.

It seems reasonable to say that a good community provides not simply what people want but what is genuinely desirable and will give them true happiness. Standard utilitarianism has little to say about genuine desirability and true happiness, as opposed to what one wants. Are there some things that humans ought by nature to desire, things truly desirable whether everyone knows it or not? Is there such a thing as *the* good life?[1] This essay defends a theory of human nature that takes people to be rational and reflective, to have fairly but not entirely stable preferences of which some are preferable to others, to be social animals, and to be capable of emotion. On this theory, free will, a characteristic but not universal human trait, is a significant part of the good life.

The ways in which one's community influences one's nature and motivation may destroy one's autonomy, especially where the community is an organization. That is the subject of Chapter 6, which is about corporate culture. Chapter 7 considers how the community may help create one's autonomy. That is not an entirely new thought; Aristotle claims, pertinently, that a person is a rational animal but also a civilized animal.[2] I think Aristotle is essentially right, but his view requires elaboration and defense. If autonomy and rationality imply doing what one wants, free of social constraint, there is a problem about how community influence could either support or destroy one's autonomy. And how much of what we believe about the good life can be independent of whatever an organization or some other community has caused us to believe?

A necessary condition of addressing those issues is an account of the autonomous person.

PERSONS

Any moral system of which we can make sense assumes the importance of individual persons.[3] So do the notions of responsibility, the good life, punishment, education, intention, autonomy, even community. This is true in spite of the imperfection in every person's unity, the occasional uncertainty over whether some purported individual meets the criteria for personhood, the importance of one's community to one's identity and one's well-being. For certain purposes, including some related to management, it may make sense not to think of persons as unitary entities, but morality is not among those purposes.

Views about personal identity—about what makes the person unitary—have moral content, and social implications as well. Should someone who committed a crime but then developed amnesia and underwent a radical personality change be punished? In a well-ordered society, what sort of change would justify the judgment that Smith does not deserve punishment for what she did before undergoing the personality alteration? Is she still Smith? The answer requires considering the social consequences of various possible legal arrangements, hence the proper functioning of a well-ordered society. We may try to distinguish the philosophical issue of personal identity from practical and even moral issues, but it is not clear how cleanly that distinction can be made.

When we say a thing has changed, we are presupposing that in some essential ways it remains the same throughout the changes. So with persons, who change with respect not only to their physical properties but also to their emotions, attitudes, and memories and sometimes to their values and personalities. Death, on the other hand, is an essential change. Recent philosophical writing on the problem of personal identity (starting with Nagel [1971] and Parfit [1971]) has made psychological connectedness the favored criterion of personal identity, or rather of what is important about personal identity. If person A at time t_1 forms an intention that is carried out by person B at t_2, person B credibly claims to remember what person A experienced, and person B is indistinguishable in personality and emotion and character from person A, then practically and morally A and B are the same person.[4] It follows that it is continuity of intention, memory, and emotion that justifies attributions of personal survival through time.[5] It follows too that the self is not something separate from one's abiding desires and beliefs and other states that constitute one's character. On the other hand, most people do not have entirely coherent preferences at a time or stable preferences through time, contrary to what economists normally assume. We identify with certain important, long-term, general desires and principles, to the extent in some cases that we would have difficulty saying why we have them. Some acts, as we have noted, we consider beneath us; some slights are so intolerable that we need not and cannot say why we do not like them. But our views about even these may also change over time. In that sense, what is most important about personal identity is a matter of degree of coherence and continuity.

People do have histories. Jones is a unitary person because he can remember some of his past and maintain fairly consistent desires, values, principles, and traits at a time and over a period of time; his identity over time involves fairly consistent emotional predispositions, with no sudden radical changes. Jones deliberates and makes decisions that will serve what he takes to be his abiding interests. It follows that, since he does not know exactly what his future preferences will be, his rational course in some cases will be to work for an arrangement that does not necessarily give first priority to all of his current preferences. (See Gauthier [1986, p. 343] for a version of this view of self-management.) He resents wrongs done to him in the past and acts accordingly; in that way he identifies his current self and interests with his past self. His continuity consists in part in the execution of intentions, which entails orderly change against a background of fairly consistent values, emotions, and beliefs.

If he is particularly reflective, Jones can also consider what kind of person he wants to be and try to make a future for himself accordingly: he can project himself intentionally into the future and weave together intentions to make long-term projects and a good life. He may then develop his character accordingly and seek ways to bind his conduct to the standards he sets for himself, for example by making public wagers or promises or taking steps to avoid temptation.[6] Yet since at time t_1 he may not know exactly what he will desire at time t_2, he does not necessarily act on a consistent set of values throughout his life, for learning through experience may—no doubt should—lead him to alter some of his views about what is most important. He creates his own history, of which an unfolding narrative is a better description than is a snapshot taken at any particular time.

There are rational connections, although not necessarily very tight ones, among Jones's reasons, between his reasons and his intentions, and between his intentions and his actions. His reasoning may not be perfectly consistent, he may act intentionally against what he knows to be good reasons, and he may form an intention and then not act on it, but if he is a being to which intending can be attributed, he will act on reasons at least much of the time. If Jones is particularly rational, he critically reviews his preferences among possible as well as actual courses of action with a view to determining not only which action is best but also which preference is most reasonable, and pursues ends preemptively and indirectly through complex and nonobvious intermediate steps.[7] Very rational people bind themselves to certain values and principles and forswear opportunities for certain short-term gains that impose long-term losses. They may even leave open the possibility of changing certain of their values after having contemplated the various forms the good life might take, particularly if they agree with Rawls and me that a good community does not insist on any one particular form for all its participants.

Because some people are capable of this sort of self-management, and because what makes people happy is in part a matter of what they learn to be happy with and what dispositions they cultivate, we can say that the best self-managers are capable of determining, within limits, what will make them happy. Jones might decide that he should cultivate a greater concern for his family at the expense of worrying constantly about his job; that may happen over time, although not everyone can do it, for people are characteristically but not always rational. If they are rational only to a very small degree, questions arise about whether they can act intentionally.

People have a presumptive right to manage themselves this way; for a community to interfere with their doing so requires some overriding justification. But is it in one's best interests to be a rational self-manager? One can imagine an unreflective person being happy, not minding being stupid, living from one pleasant moment to the next like the elevator operator in *Brave New World*. Such a person, having become reflective, might regret the loss of innocence. But being happy without knowing what makes one happy is a matter of luck, and that can change. The same is true of having a string of happy moments without being clever enough to plan for them. People's clarity and coherence on the subject of what will make their lives better is valuable because the ability to calculate or decide the value of things is itself valuable; if morality is about treating people as ends and not merely as means, then morality should promote people's capacity to decide what their chief ends should be, subject to others having the same right. There is in any case something counterintuitive about the notion that a person can be better off by virtue of being less of a person, in the sense of exercising human faculties to a lesser degree.

PLEASURE AND ACTION: THE UTILITARIAN SELF

My argument to this point is clearly incompatible with a view of persons familiar to economists and others who espouse a certain kind of rational individualism as a basis for method and morality. On the whole, according to this view, people know what they want; they know its nature and the costs and the consequences of getting it. They want what is best for them: that is, they are rational and their desires are selfish; nor would it make any sense to distinguish between what they value and what they want right now. Their desires are coherent: if they want something, they want to want it, in the sense that they do not have desires they would prefer not to have, and their desires do not otherwise contradict. They are also constant: their preferences change little, their most important preferences not at all. The notion of management of one's desires can therefore get no purchase. The traditional notion of rationality involves psychological egoism: one's welfare is strictly selfish and is not a function of how well off anyone else is; one is motivated only by one's own objectives; one's choices are based on one's own goals and do not take others' into account. (Recall from Chapter 1 that Sen [1987, pp. 79ff.] distinguishes here among three positions not always seen as distinct.)

The desires people have can, according to this view, be inferred from the way they act, since a desire is a disposition to act in a certain way; it follows that one necessarily acts on one's strongest desire. The view is therefore behaviorist; the objection that intention is a function of desire and belief, and so cannot be reduced to either, is answered by the assumption that agents have perfect information. On the whole, then, one acts so as to achieve one's own happiness; self-interest is thus the motivator of intentional action. What people want makes them happy or is an efficient means to ends that do. There is no problem about knowing what will make one happy, no problem about believing one is happy when one is not, no problem about embracing some inferior grade of happiness. Freedom is accordingly good because it is a matter of being able to do and to have what one wants and what will make one happy. People ought to be allowed to exercise their free will because the purpose of morality is to provide individuals with good lives within constraints of equity. Equity, in turn, is primarily a matter of getting what one deserves on the basis of the value of one's contribution to productivity, with the welcome result that equity has the utilitarian advantage of giving people an incentive to contribute.

On these assumptions, some combination of utilitarianism and libertarianism seems attractive, even inevitable. The best institutions will be those that generate the most happiness; they will be the ones in which people are allowed to do as they wish so long as they do not interfere with others doing the same. That arrangement will lead to the best outcome for them, since what they want to do and what is best for them as individuals will coincide. People will not create chaos by acting this way, since a market provides for everyone's freedom, as Adam Smith (allegedly) argued. To regulate people's behavior in their best interests is futile, since individuals know best what is in their best interests; those who claim otherwise turn out to have some selfish agenda.

These assumptions are, as is utilitarianism itself, problematical in part because freedom and happiness are far more complicated matters than this common view supposes. People do not always know the nature, costs, and consequences of what they aim at. What they want is not always what is best for them; some of their desires may be unselfish and even sacrificial, and some are irrational. They may want something but wish they did not, because they know it will only make them unhappy. And there are other problems.

Freedom does not always have good consequences, but it is morally important all the same. It is hard to imagine a conception of the good life in which choice is not permitted; even for a utilitarian, it is easy to see how denying people freedom for their own good as determined by somebody else encourages paternalism and, in due course, repression. People are characteristically autonomous agents, owed respect for their autonomy and leeway for their pursuit of happiness. But autonomous action is a more complicated matter than utilitarian economists believe. In particular, it is not true that its only motivator is narrow self-interest. That is, psychological egoism is false.

Proponents of psychological egoism can argue for their view on at least two grounds: first, that certain successful economic theories assume it; second, that close inspection of examples of apparently selfless acts reveals that the agent's actual (selfish) goal is to be, say, a martyr or an admired philanthropist. Neither argument succeeds. As to the first: successful theories—and economic theories, even more obviously than most others, are successful only within certain limits and for certain ranges—often make false assumptions.[8] The assumption of rationality has approximately the same status as that of perfect information, but the absurdity of the latter assumption is more obvious, ignorance being easier to recognize than irrationality.

As to the selfishness allegedly hidden in apparently selfless acts: this view rests on something like a tautology, wherein what one wants to do is by stipulation identified with one's intention on the one hand and one's interests on the other. (LaFollette [1989] gives a slightly more generous reconstruction of that view.) The usual behaviorist assumptions make this identification easier still. In the end, however, the theory is impervious to any possible counterexample, and that is not a sign of a good theory.[9]

Economists normally use the obvious criteria for determining examples of one's interests and bring in trivializing desiderata like the warm glow of charity or martyrdom only when falsification threatens the theory. But the trivial argument that any act can be construed as selfish suggests a different and genuinely important point: there is a great variety of states, including for example another's well-being, that may make the appropriately disposed person happy.

Partly for that reason, even if psychological egoism were true, it would not undermine morality. A particularly subtle kind of psychological egoist can deny that self-interest necessarily leads to nasty acts and can argue that, on the contrary, the theory is compatible with the most wonderfully beneficial behavior. All that is required is that the agent's self-interest overlap sufficiently with the interests of others; that is something for a wise agent to desire whether psychological egoism is true or not. A good person might accordingly undertake to maximize the overlap by cultivating a disposition to behave morally (even though, as I argued in Chapter 3, it would probably be a good idea not always to suffer wrong without retaliating).

We come again to that great practical moral problem for managers and those who hold political office, a problem central to this essay: since morality is sometimes personally costly, how does a community encourage morality among people who are not saintly and, for that matter, not hyperrational? What can a manager do, under the constraints of morality and organizational effectiveness, to cause people in an organization to behave morally? Aside from the usual incentives, can employees or for that matter people in any community be given any other sort of reason to believe that it makes sense for them to be moral even when no one is watching? Is a closely supervised system of rewards and punishments the only possible answer? I call this a practical problem, but it is as much a philosophical one as is the corresponding problem about rational maximizers.

The solution to this problem lies in seeing the role that morality may play in the good life of the moral person. In Chapter 3 I lent some support to the notion of morality as involving self-interest when I argued that unbridled selfish action harms everyone by ruining the commons. There, and in this chapter as well, I have suggested that one might accommodate one's environment and one's interests at the same time by managing one's inclinations. In any case, if psychological egoism is false—even if it is mildly complicated—one can act not only to serve one's interests but also to achieve some other sort of objective or to conform to some standard; hence, one can value some state of affairs independent of whether it does one any good.[10] That happens with humans more often than with dumb animals, with grown-ups more often than with children, with reflective people more often than with impulsive or shallow ones. It happens with those who have a significant measure of autonomy and consequently do not act merely from the prospect of pleasure. And it happens with those who get pleasure from quite a variety of things. All this requires some elaboration and argument.

AUTONOMY

The concept of autonomy is sufficiently complex and controversial that one cannot begin an account of it with an adequate definition: addressing the problem of free will requires not only stating one's conception of freedom but also defending it. That is what I undertake in this section, but I begin with a preview. Autonomy, which for present purposes I do not distinguish from freedom of the will, is a property of actions first of all. An autonomous person is one who is usually capable of autonomous action, but one may be rendered incapable of autonomy merely by someone's interference. ("Sorry, I'm just not a free agent in this case.") Autonomy is a matter of degree: some acts, hence some people, are more autonomous than others. When we say that an act is autonomous, we might more strictly say that it is largely autonomous. In acting autonomously one does what one wants; in fact, an action that is not at all autonomous is not an intentional act. The desire that animates an autonomous act is one that the agent desires to have and that is ultimately based on values that are part of a coherent conception of the good life; reflection is therefore characteristically involved in an autonomous act. Planned actions, which are typically part of some personal project, are usually autonomous. We have reason to attribute autonomy to acts insofar as they are rational; in that respect, attributing autonomy is like attributing knowledge and is potentially controversial. The least degree of autonomy involves that modicum of rationality that we must attribute to another in order to understand what that other says. A highly autonomous person may be able to decide what kind of person to be. Constraints, irrationality, weakness of will, manipulation by people with their own agendas, and ignorance are among the chief barriers to autonomous action. Whether an act is causally determined is not an issue; the question is, What sort of state of the person caused it? Autonomy is prima facie good, and a person has a right to all autonomy that is compatible with a like degree for others. In some organizations this right is not honored; others enhance people's autonomy. Violations of one's rights typically entail violation of one's autonomy.

When you say that Smith does something (say, action A) intentionally, you are attributing to her the belief that there is some reason for doing A. You are also doing more than describing what Smith has done: you are implying that her action was reasonable in the sense that there was some reason (not necessarily a strong reason) for Aing, that from Smith's point of view there was something to be said for it; otherwise, you would have no basis for claiming that Smith had done it intentionally rather than accidentally.[11] (The reasoning here is similar to that produced in our discussions of interpretation. For example, see Chapter 2.) To say that an act is not autonomous at all is to say that it is not an intentional act.

Yet not all intentional actions are autonomous to any great degree. If you threaten to fire Smith unless she agrees to the allocation of some capital to a project of which she does not approve, her subsequently doing it because she prefers doing so to being fired does not make the action autonomous. If you drug Smith or tell her some credible lie with the result that she allocates the funds, she is not acting autonomously. But if you demonstrate to her that the investment will generate a rate of return far above that of Treasury bills at minimal risk, there is no reason to doubt her autonomy if what you say causes her to act accordingly.[12]

Even if she makes the investment because she believes such investments are good, if she believes this because she is drugged or deceived concerning the project's chances, then her acting on it falls short of autonomy for the same reason the operative belief falls short of being a piece of knowledge. Her action is autonomous if its cause is her understanding of the issues and her well-placed trust in your judgment. In calling her action autonomous, therefore, you are implicitly assessing it as at least minimally reasonable.

Nor is Smith free to do what is not feasible.[13] In discussing freedom of the will we tend to forget this, and to forget as well that one's autonomy may be increased by many kinds of support in achieving one's objectives. This means, among other things, that we should be reluctant to agree that regulation that preserves the commons and its benefits interferes with people's autonomy. And so with certain other political arrangements.

Libertarians, particularly those who hold the standard utilitarian economist's view discussed in the previous section, are more likely to hold that autonomy is just a matter of not being coerced; for them there is no threat to freedom where what one wants has been heavily influenced by considerations that are not rational, brought to bear by those who are not one's friends, or where one wishes one did not want what one wants, as in the case of a reflective addict. Libertarians are right to be wary of arguments—from Marxists, for example—that one is not truly free unless one's consciousness is appropriately enlightened—by Marxism, for example;[14] but they can hardly deny that brainwashing exists or that it happens in some organizations.

The key to understanding autonomy—it is sometimes proffered as an essential part of the solution to the problem of the freedom of the will[15]—is to see that an action can be both caused and intended and that there is no mystery about events that admit of more than one kind of explanation. Is the person really free or only the subject of science? One may be both, but there are moral reasons, most famously expressed by Kant, for not treating anybody as only the subject of science—particularly if the "science" in question is management.[16]

To say that caused action cannot be free is a bit like saying that caused belief cannot be knowledge. It can, of course, if it is caused by good evidence understood by an agent who can infer the true belief.[17] The attribution of knowledge to Smith is an implicit evaluation of the soundness of her reasoning; in that sense it rests on standards of acceptability of evidence that may not be universally considered self-evident or easily confirmable. These standards are beliefs about beliefs—about the kind of belief that is acceptable—and can therefore be called *second-order* beliefs. (We encountered something like these in Chapter 4 in the discussion of how the canons of scientific method come out of successful science and not only the other way around.) Contrary to empiricist epistemology, your belief that the cat is on the mat rests not merely on perception of the cat on the mat but on a network of second-order beliefs that provide satisfactory ways of deriving first-order beliefs from evidence.

The attribution of autonomy or even of intention is similar: it implies reasoning that is sound according to standards of acceptability, at least to the agent in a cool moment. "Jones argued with the police officer because he didn't want to get another ticket" attributes at least some autonomy. "Jones insulted the police officer because he didn't want to get another ticket" attributes a great deal less. As I have argued several times, we explain an action or an institution or practice only insofar as we can answer the question "What is the point?" in a way that appeals, albeit perhaps indirectly and distantly, to our own view of what is good. If our best attempt at explanation of an intentional action attributes a wholly bizarre objective to the agent, then we ought to question whether we really have an explanation that attributes intention, much less autonomy.

It is characteristic of humans that they can form not only simple intentions but fairly elaborate agendas and complex strategies. We plan our lives. If autonomy does have to do with strategically designing one's life, it must therefore have to do with recognizing constraints as well as opportunities and dealing with them effectively. Freeman's (1984) view that relationships with stakeholders are at the heart of strategy has been widely accepted. For similar reasons we should accept that personal autonomy has to do with effectively confronting one's environment. Autonomy does not imply the absence of any environmental effects on one's choice: on the contrary, for an organization or an individual, one's surroundings may contain the means to fulfill one's plans as well as some constraints to bear in mind while making them.[18] Clearly there are some environments that are more supportive of one's strategic efforts than others; one's autonomy is thus a function of certain features of one's community. For example, an organization in which one cannot survive without lying and cheating may severely curtail one's freedom to act as one wishes, and do so in a way that violates one's moral rights.[19]

Autonomy requires the ability not only to act on desires but to reflect on them.[20] I may desire to smoke but regard this sort of desire with disapproval and wish I did not have it. The desire to smoke is then a first-order desire, and the desire not to want to smoke is a desire about a desire, hence a second-order desire. If I am neurotic or just weak-willed, I may have a great many first-order desires that are inconsistent with my second-order desires but on which I act all the same. That I am autonomous means not that my first- and second-order desires are consistent but that where they are not, I normally[21] act on the second-order ones, for example by not smoking. In exercising second-order desires we exert some control over our first-order ones, for example by overriding them, or avoiding situations in which they might arise, or cultivating different first-order desires. Some of the "important, long-term, general desires" with which we identify, as I argued earlier, are second-order desires.[22]

On the assumption that one can desire to have certain second-order desires, we can speak of third-order desires.[23] To simplify, I shall sometimes speak of higher-order desires, which include desires of the second, third, and higher orders. Insofar as one has the will to fulfill one's highest-order desires, they are part of one's character.[24]

Among our very general and strong higher-order desires, values constitute an important special case. If I value something, I not only want it but consider it the sort of thing I have good reason to want; hence I want to want it. Normally I also have a first-order desire for it, but there are cases in which one values something but finds oneself desiring its contrary, probably to one's regret and embarrassment: consider the faithful spouse hankering after an affair. In that case, too, the value is a second-order desire. It is characteristic of values, as opposed to just any old desires, that they give the agent some actual reason for action, by virtue of some rational connection to a coherent conception of the good life;[25] that is not true of all second-order desires.

Just having first-order desires that are consistent with one's second-order desires is no guarantee of autonomy. One of the striking features of most of the higher-echelon characters in Brave New World is that their first-order desires fit their second-order ones very well, but we are not at all tempted to claim that they are autonomous. It is not only that all their higher-order desires are designed by the community and in its interests, although that feature does suggest that they are being treated primarily as means rather than ends. It is also that they do not arrive at their higher-order desires through reflection; they cannot reflect critically on them and by the rules of their community are not allowed—and in most cases are not able—to develop a coherent set of values. One is not permitted, for example, to consider whether a life of challenges is superior to a life of easy pleasure. They cannot therefore plan their own lives in the way autonomous people characteristically do.

That is an extreme and fictional case, to be sure, but in fact our highest-order desires are always susceptible to community pressure. Churches, schools, political entities, and not least managers try to get at what essentially motivates us, and they often succeed in affecting our desires, including our second-order ones. We are urged to love God and do as we please, or to be motivated by patriotism, or to feel loyal to the company. The shaping of our attitudes toward our desires is seldom done by appeals to our reason. Extreme cases of this kind of influence constitute brainwashing, which does not make people autonomous.[26]

Even where one is not under another's immediate influence, the nature and provenance of one's second-order desires may make them other than autonomous. Suppose I unconsciously and irrationally believe I was responsible for my mother's death. I may then exercise great self-discipline in hardening myself against desires of which I believe my mother, whom I remember as censorious and punitive, would have disapproved: sexual attraction, interest in nonclassical music, enjoyment of sports. I may even go the murderous way of Norman Bates in Hitchcock's *Psycho.* Here the operative second-order desires are likely the product of serious psychological problems, not at all the sort of desire we would consider autonomous, second-order though they be. In a case like this I am not operating on the basis of values that incorporate some essential reference to a coherent conception of the good life.

But is it not possible for me to have at least a coherent worldview that includes the proposition that the virtue of filial piety overrides all other considerations in discussions of morality and prudence, so that for example anything I suffer is preferable to my mother scratching her finger? If one takes a Humean view of reason as characterizing the relationship between means and ends and not the ends themselves (see Chapter 1), one gives an affirmative answer here. My answer should be predictable from what I have said in similar situations, beginning in Chapter 1: if we cannot see why anyone would adopt a certain conception of the good life, then we have no reason to consider it a conception of the good life, hence no reason to dignify Norman Bates's high-order impulses by calling them values, and no reason to believe that decisions he makes on the basis of them are autonomous.[27] (It does not follow, however, that such people have no rights: it is bad policy to coerce people purely because we believe they are incapable of autonomous behavior.)

It is even possible, although not highly probable, that this dutiful son has reflected on his desires and his values and is satisfied with them. As one reflects on successive orders of desire, one may or may not arrive at certain values with which one identifies so closely as to be unable to answer the question "Why is that so important to you?" There is no reason to believe these values are unaffected by one's environment, but that they are so affected does not by itself have any bearing on whether they are a basis of autonomous action. At the same time, they may be fundamental in this way and yet still not be a basis of autonomous action because they are irrational. We may be tempted to believe that if we keep asking why, and so ascend through the orders of desire, we finally come to the foundational self that has all these desires and considers them all from the point of view of no further desires. That would be a false picture of the self, and of autonomy.

It is fair to say that autonomy as I have defined it admits of degrees. Some people have value systems that are stupid or incoherent or based on wildly false beliefs. It is not clear that we should attribute autonomy to, for example, a man whose fanatical zeal in the name of masculinity leads him to commit acts of extraordinary recklessness and cruelty. Some people have insane values; some people, unable to act on their values, act on impulse, instead. In a few cases it may be impossible to say what the salient values are or to know whether it makes sense to attribute a value to someone who so often violates it. What is clear in such cases is that the agent is less than fully autonomous. But even fairly autonomous people do not always act in character, or on principle, or according to values they do hold; they may succumb to weakness of the will, one of the great enemies of autonomy.

To a behaviorist, which is what I claimed as early as Chapter 2 the proponent of the standard economic theory of behavior is, all this can make no sense. But it comes pretty close to being a plain fact of life. There is such a thing as regret, which usually follows acting according to some first-order desire that violates a second-order one. There is such a thing as admiring people who act according to a certain principle, such a thing as trying to act that way but sometimes failing, such a thing as binding oneself in a cool hour and trying to remain faithful to one's values in a warmer one.

We bind ourselves to our principles by such devices as promises and enforceable contracts; when temptation comes, we are denied the object of our first-order desire. Although that desire is frustrated, it would nonetheless be an oversimplification to say that we cannot do what we want to do and a mistake to say that in such a situation we have lost our autonomy. On the contrary, if what I have said about the nature of the person is true, we can more readily identify ourselves with those relatively permanent higher-order desires rather than with the first-order ones that are frustrated on this occasion.[28]

In general, then, we should not infer from the mere existence of restrictions on Smith that her autonomy is being abridged. To make that judgment requires some assessment of the way in which she has come to be bound. If she has done so voluntarily, and if the binding instrument (for example, a contract) does not otherwise violate her rights or exploit her, then her autonomy is not violated by her being compelled to get up early in the morning to go to work, although it may be violated by her being compelled to submit to random drug testing.[29] Smith's agreeing, even under pressure, to act in support of the commons would surely not by itself violate her autonomy; in fact, in some circumstances the absence of such an agreement would, since it would reduce the probability of her getting what she wanted.

We sometimes bind ourselves in obedience to higher-order desires, through a public contract or otherwise, and in that way we are able to act coherently and strategically and design our lives, some of us more successfully than others. Your ability to communicate and to act intentionally presupposes a degree of consistency in your desires and beliefs, but keeping your first-order desires consistent with your second-order ones requires a thorough understanding of the relations among your second-order desires and between them and your more immediate ones, and a critical attitude toward both kinds.

In obvious ways our first-order preferences are not stable. The higher-order ones are more stable, but even these change, contrary to standard economic theory; if they never did, one would be denied the possibility of moral growth. On the other hand, as I have argued in this chapter, if preferences were not stable to a significant degree through time, then there would be a problem about personal identity—in fact, in a few cases there is. We can say that one's character is essential to one's identity. It is therefore misleading to think of yourself as essentially something separate from all of your desires, as is suggested in our saying that a person *has* these desires; it is nonetheless true that there are some desires with which you do not identify, on which you may or may not normally act, that you would like to alter.[30]

CHOOSING ONE'S DESIRES

If Smith is a particularly rational and reflective and in that sense a highly autonomous person, she may be able to consider what highest-order desires, values, and principles should govern her life. (Recall our discussion of a similar point in Chapter 3.) Within limits she can cultivate certain higher-order desires, for example the desire to enjoy reading great literature or the desire to enjoy volunteering her services to those in need. She can also cultivate values and even adherence to principles by reflection and disciplined habituation.[31] In making decisions about values and principles she is deciding how to be motivated, what to want, what sort of person to be: that is, she is choosing her character and deciding what is in her best interests. This process, which takes a great deal of time and is never wholly successful or complete, is one objective of education in the liberal arts.

As I claimed in Chapter 3, Smith not only need not but cannot make decisions of this sort entirely on the basis of self-interest, for one of the objectives of the process is to decide what she wants her interests to be. It follows that there is a range of very important choices that cannot be made in a straightforwardly self-interested way; some of one's interests (or principles or values or desires) cannot be chosen on the basis of any higher interests, on pain of infinite regress. Yet whatever interests you choose, they will be served best if they are consistent, attainable, potentially long-lasting, unlikely to create subsequent problems and frustrations for yourself or anyone else, and generally compatible with the interests of those with whom you associate. (Note the implication that the nature of a reasonable person's environment will significantly affect what interests are worth cultivating.) At the same time it seems reasonable to prefer interests that do not diminish one's capacity to be reasonable or any other capacity that is necessary for characteristically human pleasure.[32]

Two caveats seem obvious but worth mentioning. First, not many people are so reflective or, therefore, so autonomous; nor are most people's desires sorted so neatly into separate orders. Second, even reflective people will be influenced by their environment, in particular their workplace; when they are, the influence will not always address their rational faculties. But, as I suggested earlier, the mere existence of that causal influence does not undermine autonomy. On the contrary, just as the right educational environment supports the acquisition of knowledge, one's environment may encourage rational reflection and reduce the incompatibility of the goals of the people in the environment and thus contribute to one's autonomy. This point is important for my forthcoming argument that autonomy is a function of being in the right kind of community. On the other hand, one's environment may affect one's values as well as one's lower-order desires by operating through emotions.

EMOTION

To this point I have sketched a largely rationalistic, hence incomplete, view of human nature. An autonomous person can resist acting on first-order desires that violate second-order ones: such a person has second-order desires and values and principles that are consistent and at least to some degree feasible under the probable circumstances. It follows that a certain emotional strength is part of autonomy, as weakness of the will is its enemy. It is characteristic of the autonomous person to be able to decide to some extent what to desire, but many people are as much influenced by appeals to emotion, such as through symbols and rituals of the kind that support a corporate culture, as by discursive argument, and only a few are capable of deciding what to want and making it stick. Even the latter requires emotional strength as well as rationality.

This is not to say that most emotions support rationality. Under the pressure of fear, for example, one may abandon a principle in obedience to a first-order desire to run. Similarly, fear may cause one to have a second-order desire to enjoy the company of only people of one's own race, hence to feel ashamed of finding oneself seeking out someone of another race. In extreme cases, fear may impair one's ability to draw an unwelcome factual conclusion. My point is just that it does not always happen this way.

The suggestion that autonomy requires emotional support recalls the Aristotelian view that habituation is a way to become virtuous. Aristotle does not put reason in opposition to emotion: on the contrary, he regards good character as a matter not of reason being strong enough to defeat emotion, but of emotion being reason's ally. Virtue is a matter of being pleased by the right things and disposed to act accordingly.

Shaping one's character therefore requires training one's desires and emotions, not just one's power of reasoning. This is a part of moral education crucial to building the similarity of intuitions required by a community in which people trust each other, as I suggested in Chapter 2.

The scope of rational reflection in dealing with other people is surely limited in any case: one can never be certain what the outcome of other people's reflection, rational or irrational, will be if one's own action will affect others' action and reflection and vice versa. There can thus never be enough evidence for a rational person to be certain of the effect of his or her actions on others or on the commons, even on the implausible assumption that all other people involved are selfishly rational.[33] From a selfishly rational point of view, therefore, there cannot be any conclusive reason for the individual to act so as to preserve the commons.[34] To make up for the inevitable shortfall in evidence, the commons needs emotional support in the form of some kind of community spirit.

Recall Frank's (1988) embrace of the argument that emotion may support behavior that is not rationally self-interested but does preserve the commons, although he and his predecessors do not put it quite that way. As in the example cited in Chapter 2, pride or indignation may lead me to refuse a deal that is in my interests but unfair; my reputation as proud or indignant may induce the other party to offer a fair deal. In a similar way, affection may lead us to trust each other when there is no evidence that that is the rational course; in the event, however, mutual trust proves useful. We may be tempted to say that it is sometimes rational not to be rational; let us say rather that apparent short-term rationality is often not the most useful course.

Affection, a human emotional state that can hardly be called unnatural and can surely be a component of the good life, differs from trust in that the latter does alter when it alteration finds and does bend with the remover to remove, whereas affection does not, as Shakespeare's Sonnet 116 rightly claims. On the contrary, to have affection is to regard the loved one's interests as a particularly good reason for action. If we as community members have affection for one another, not only will your interests affect my actions, but my affection will influence my (second-order) beliefs about how to interpret behavior so that I will consider you trustworthy even on little evidence and may disregard contrary evidence as anomalous; since you will be doing the same for me, our interpretations will both be on the mark. The radical unpredictability characteristic of human relations in game-theoretical situations is reduced or eliminated where people are not entirely self-regarding and can therefore rely on each other. Love is blind no more than a self-fulfilling statement is a lie; on the contrary, regard for one another's interests increases our knowledge about one another. And loyalty is not necessarily irrational, as standard economic theory implies it is. (In the last two chapters of this essay I shall have a great deal more to say about loyalty.)

There is nothing unnatural about all this if, as I have argued more than once, the individual's concerns and values are not by nature entirely selfish or free of emotions, as those characteristic of affection are not. Nor would moral action be helped if people were unemotional: remember, emotion is to be reason's ally. We feel an obligation to each other when we share rules, traditions, role models, and other cultural artifacts. Without the pangs of conscience, the sympathy, the need to justify our actions to each other, the emotional attachments that affect just those intimate and important areas of life in which utilitarian calculation is least appropriate, we are less likely not only to behave appropriately but to care, hence to take the trouble to work out what is appropriate.[35] And we do both: Frank (1988, especially Chapter 7) cites evidence that the most plausible explanation of certain common patterns of play in two-person games is that one wants the other to do well, presumably because of the natural sympathy cited by Adam Smith.

All this implies that one ought to cultivate that concern for others' welfare in one's own dispositions, that communities ought to cultivate it as well, and that one ought to want to live in a community of people who are thus disposed. We see in this the importance of Elster's (1985) view, which can be summarized this way: a wise person is one who exercises the rational self-mastery required to decide (second-order) to acquire and cultivate and stick with the desire (first-order) to associate harmoniously with the people in one's environment and is thus equipped to deal stoically and happily with life. One shapes one's character so as to take pleasure in what contributes to the community and generally in what is right and produces wealth.[36] One has what Scanlon (1982, p. 111) calls "the desire to find and agree on principles which no one who had this desire could reasonably reject."

This view of the good life, however, seems to lend itself to abuse: one is almost asking to be exploited if one undertakes to become the sort of person who accommodates one's community. That seems to be a way of giving up one's autonomy. So the question persists, How does one lead the good and appropriately autonomous life while coping with the demands of one's community? Can we do anything more here than mention reciprocity?

PROSPECTS

The question itself suggests, what I shall deny, that your community is necessarily some sort of external threat to your autonomy and that its effect on you is to be minimized for the sake of your freedom. It should be clear by now that that is not the case. There are reasons for saying that a person is a communal animal; in fact, I shall presently argue that that is true under some natural interpretations. Rationality is not a matter of being outside any community, as autonomy is not a matter of being exempt from all causal influence. But the question of how it is possible to be communal and at the same time rational (never mind emotional as well) is central to morality, as therefore is the investigation of the appropriate relationship between the individual and the community, as therefore is the issue of the nature of the good community, which as I have argued on several grounds is a crucial question for business ethics. For the answer to the first question, the one about being both communal and rational, is this, in its broadest terms: you are communal but also rational and autonomous if you are appropriately influenced by the right sort of community. Some communities support morality; some, including that of the Ik, are lethally inhospitable to it.

In Chapter 6 we shall discuss how corporate culture may work on people's values and undermine morality as well as autonomy. Although a strong corporate culture can have that effect, it need not. The issue is what kind of community supports the good life—including autonomy, which seems threatened by the great effect the community will have on one's desires. Since our community affects our interests, our answer to that question requires that we consider how it should affect them, hence what we should want our interests to be. That last is an odd question, difficult to answer—in fact, if standard economic theory is true, impossible to ask. But it will prove to be a crucial one as we consider the features of the good community, hence the good organization.

NOTES

1. These two questions are not identical. My view is that the answer to the first is yes. The answer to the second is that there is no sort of life describable in detail that is better than any other sort of life, but there are various sorts of life that are good and clearly better than some others.

2. I think mine is a better translation than the usual one: man is a political animal. Whether we are thinking of the Roman *civis* or the Greek *polis,* the point is that a fully developed human being is a citizen.

3. Some understanding of human nature is a necessary condition of making sense of morality. It does not follow that the study of ethics is primarily about individual virtue, or about individuals, rather than about principles.

4. The trouble with bodily identity as a criterion is this: if we were able to section Jones's brain and transplant a half each in Smith and Johnson so that both Smith and Johnson bore the relationship of psychological continuity with Jones (as they would, approximately, if the sectioning were done right), we would have every reason to call them personally continuous with Jones. But neither successor could be identical with him; if one were, both would be, and that would make them identical with each other, as they cannot be on the bodily criterion. The most influential sponsor of this argument has been Parfit (1971).

5. The situation with respect to personal identity at a time is similar. If the brain is sectioned at the corpus callosum, the brain's owner shows signs of serious dissociation in intentions, memory, and emotion; for example, a message communicated to the side of the brain that controls some emotions but not

speech may cause the brain's owner to be excited or embarrassed without being able to say why. For a discussion of such cases, see Nagel (1971), whose views continue to be influential.

6. Schelling (1984) and Elster (1984, 1985) have written extensively about the rationality of binding oneself to protect one's true interests against short-term inclination.

7. This is the way Elster (1984, 1985) likes to describe characteristically human action.

8. There is controversy about the nature and the extent of a good theory's possible embrace of what is false. In Ch. 2, fn. 30, I mentioned the view, advocated by Cartwright (1983), that most physical laws are rough approximations of the truth. Nothing I say here requires me to go quite as far as she does. See also Friedman (1953), who proposes a somewhat casual relationship between the best possible economic theory and the truth. Pragmatists characteristically see difficulties in the attempt to distinguish the notion of truth from that of theoretical adequacy.

9. Gauthier (1986, p. 23) claims that utility is a measure, not an explanation, of preference. Braybrooke (1987) argues in effect that it is neither, and he surely would have the support of Aristotle.

10. In a pinch, the defender of psychological egoism can claim that what we value does us good and in effect make that a necessary truth. What that really is is a bad description of what is involved in valuing something. What lies behind the crudest forms of psychological egoism seems to be the view that what motivates us is the jolt of pleasure we receive as a result of getting something that we value.

11. In Chapter 1 I argued that Smith could have a reason for doing something she did not want to do. What I am arguing now, quite consistently with that view, is that Smith has a reason for action if she thinks there is something to be said for it, even if she turns out to be wrong. She might think there is something to be said for a certain action even though she knows it will not be to her advantage. She might think there is on balance good reason to do something but not want to do it. (That will happen under some circumstances discussed later in this section.)

12. It is possible that some of the management theorists who deny that it makes theoretical sense to attribute rationality to individual agents (Pfeffer, 1982, for example) think there is some contradiction between the notion of a caused action and that of a rational one. That was once a popular philosophical position, but it is quite wrong.

13. G. Dworkin (1988), whose account is similar to mine, is at pains to distinguish freedom from autonomy. On his account, one loses the former but not the latter when one binds oneself to an agreement, with oneself or with someone else, since one is then not free to do certain things. I do not know that they need to be distinguished, but I agree with Dworkin in this respect: what I call autonomy is indeed compatible with binding or committing oneself.

14. For a sophisticated version of this argument see Keeley (1988), who notes the ease with which talk of false consciousness can pervert the notion of autonomy. He cashes the concept of voluntariness in terms of rights. The least we can say about that move is that it avoids the facile assumption that we can determine what rights people have by saying simply that they must be permitted to be autonomous.

15. See, for example, Dennett (1984) and, by inference, most of the articles in Watson (1982), with the conspicuous exception of van Inwagen's.

16. One of the more interesting implications of this discussion is that free will and political freedom—the kind of thing a well-run democracy provides—are more closely related than has been widely realized. You have free will to the extent that you are able to act on reasons you can call your own, and you have political freedom to the same extent. A good polity, or a good organization, protects the free will of its citizenry, up to a point.

17. There is more to the definition of knowledge than that. Gettier (1963) gained fame by pointing out that justified true belief is not knowledge if a false premise plays a role in one's reaching the true conclusion by good luck. Nor would we call an act autonomous if the agent only appeared to act on a good reason but reaped good consequences anyway.

18. One of the themes of Pfeffer (1982) is that managerial decisions have little to do with corporate success or failure—it's all in the environment. He goes on to argue that managerial decisions are in effect a nonentity.

19. Earlier I quoted Freeman and Gilbert (1988, p. 18) to the effect that "purpose emerges as a web of semiautonomous bargains" in organizations. The bargains are less than fully autonomous in the sense that one does not usually get everything one wants at no cost. Normally, however, we enter into bargains that increase our autonomy in some way: as Rawls notes, organizations can create more of what we want than can individuals separately.

20. In what follows I am in debt to Frankfurt (1981), especially for his account of first- and second-order desires, and to Elster (1985), especially for his views about rational self-management. Schopenhauer (1989; work first published in 1841) noticed second-order desires but did not think they had anything to do with freedom of the will.

21. A little spontaneity is compatible with autonomy. Anyway, as I shall argue, it is possible to have second-order desires that do not enhance one's autonomy.

22. The parallel between beliefs and desires of the second order is certainly imperfect. For example, I may have a desire and wish I did not have that particular desire. It is not so clear that I can have a belief and believe that that particular belief is false, although I can believe that I have at least one false belief. There are cases in which one believes something in disobedience to the voice of reason in the back of one's mind, but these are far less common and more puzzling than cases in which one has a desire one would rather not have. A second-order desire concerning a particular first-order desire is fairly common; a second-order belief is nearly always directed at a *kind* of first-order belief, and the kind is determined by its origin (e.g., don't believe a general proposition on the basis of a single confirming event).

23. Elster (1989, p. 37, n. 11) points out that one may have a desire to eat a piece of cake, a higher-order desire not to crave something so fattening, and a still higher-order desire not to be so concerned about one's weight. This is an elegant example, but I am inclined to concede to Solomon (1994) that our desires are not all neatly organized into orders.

24. Of course, it may be part of one's character that one often cannot act on one's second-order desires. On desires and character see Taylor (1977) and Williams (1981). This view of desires clearly differs from the one on which the utilitarianism of standard economic theory is based; the latter does not even

countenance the possibility of acting against one's best interests in doing what one wants to do.

25. In what follows I am influenced to some degree by Watson (1982). Notice that, as in Ch. 1, I am taking the position that there is a distinction between wanting something and having a reason for having it. I also distinguish between principles and values in that, unlike some values, principles entail a moral stance (even though it might be a morally deficient stance). Every principle, however, must be or entail a value, since it is hard to see how one could hold to a principle without also holding to a corresponding value, for in such a case one would have to wish one did not intend to act on the principle in question, in which case there would be no good reason for saying that one did actually hold to the principle in question. More likely, one would be responding to pressure, hence acting just prudentially rather than in a truly principled way.

26. Exactly what counts as brainwashing turns out, as we shall see, not to be a simple issue.

27. This move makes autonomy contingent on reasonableness and so raises the possible claim that anybody who does anything wrong or stupid is not acting freely and that therefore wrong-thinking people ought to be "forced to be free," in Rousseau's unpleasant words. (See n. 14 for a similar point.) This is a danger only if my position is applied in a particularly heavy-handed way. After all, one cannot be said to act even intentionally who acts in a radically irrational way. Along similar lines, I have argued that if we understand people in a linguistic community to be constantly making wildly false statements, we have no basis for claiming we understand what they say; if we have no reason for believing there is any remotely sensible goal to a person's behavior, we have no reason for calling it intentional. Neither of these considerations, however, gives us any reason to believe that false statements or unreasonable intentions are impossible.

28. On the other hand I have not implied, nor is it true, that one should always be identified with one's second-order desires. If you were raised by fanatics of some sort, you might find yourself detesting your own natural spontaneity and enjoyment of the companionship of the sort of person your parents despised. In such a case it is far from clear that this censoriousness is characteristic of the real you.

29. Particularly when we bring rights into the account, the definition of free will seems not entirely devoid of moral considerations. When we bring rationality in, the definition seems not entirely separate from epistemology.

30. I think Rawls (1993, p. 280) is right in arguing that free people are not "indissolubly tied to any particular final end, or family of such ends, but regard themselves as always capable of appraising and revising their aims in the light of reasonable considerations." A free person could not be entirely without highest-order desires, but no one (or small number) of them need be permanent. A highly autonomous person can choose among the various conceptions of the good that a moral community countenances.

31. Augustine, not yet a saint, was probably sincere in praying, "Lord, make me chaste and continent, but not yet." One can want to be but not be a charitable person; in that sense one can value charity without being motivated by charitable desires. This seems a fairly straightforward case of a desire of a very high order being inconsistent with a second-order one. If you find your generous impulses an irritation and an embarrassment but act on them anyway, you may

have first-order desires that are inconsistent with your second-order ones but consistent with your third-order ones.

32. Rawls (1993, p. 280) suggests that highly autonomous people can choose what their best interests are to be and have "a highest-order interest in regulating all their other interests, even their fundamental ones, by reason. . . . " In Hartman (1994) I raised the question whether people in the original position could know what was in their interests—or rather the interests of their constituents—before they know what values their life in the envisaged state will lead them to develop. I suggested the founders be asked this: if, not knowing the values you will develop in that state, you could choose what your best interests would be, what would you choose? In the passage just cited, Rawls seems to allow that the founders might consider that very question. See also his discussion of second-order desires in Lecture II, sec. 7, pp. 81ff.

33. One thing game theory has done, as in this case, is to provide another reason for saying that the social sciences are not sciences: in many familiar situations people's rationality will not determine an outcome. The structure of the situation is familiar from traditional discussions of free will: you and I cannot predict each other's actions if they are interdependent. I can predict what you will do only given what I will do only given what you will do, and so on. That is one reason why strategy, corporate and otherwise, is a difficult matter.

34. This is what Gauthier (1986) so ingeniously but controversially denies, in part by bringing to bear a notion of rationality so demanding that it seems to exclude all possible people. He does laudably emphasize the training of one's dispositions, for reasons similar to those I have given.

35. Recall from Chs. 2 and 3 that Scanlon takes as basic to morality that we want to justify our actions to each other. In that chapter I mention Hampshire's argument about the emotional importance of the rules that govern intimate associations in a culture.

36. Robert Frank put the point that way in correspondence.

6

Problems
of Corporate Culture

If respect for autonomy is a moral requirement, then it is good, other
things being equal, to permit people to do what they want to do. Other
things are not equal in an organization, which almost by definition creates relationships that entail obligations and other limits on autonomy,
but organizations can also increase one's autonomy, which in any case remains an important moral consideration. Autonomy is not simply a
matter of doing what one wants: if it were, then the weak-willed person,
the addict, and the victim of brainwashing would all be autonomous. The
threat to autonomy in the organization comes in part from the organization's power to compel people to do what they do not want to do and
have no legitimate obligation to do and also from people's doing exactly
what they want to do; people may act on desires they prefer not to have
or would prefer not to have if they thought about them. Chapter 5
argued that to do what one wants to do when one wants to do something
that is not the object of a rational desire is to act less than fully autonomously.

The distinction between first-order and second-order desires provides
us with an insight into human motivation but does not by itself enable us
to distinguish between autonomous desires and others, since second-
order desires too may result from addiction or brainwashing. If an
organization affects Smith's second-order desires in a way that serves the
interests of the stockholders or managers but not of Smith, then we
surely have some reason to say that her autonomy has been violated.
Defining autonomy, Chapter 5 showed, is a difficult philosophical problem; there is a practical difficulty, too, for the manager who wants to do
what every manager has a moral obligation to do, which is to manage an
organization that respects autonomy in a way that is consistent with effectively achieving legitimate corporate objectives.

THE RATIONAL AS SOCIAL

In trying to identify the kind of desire a free person acts on, we have had reason to say that the autonomous person is characteristically rational— in fact, that we can scarcely regard another being as an intender who does not act on what we can recognize as reasons. This does not mean, nor is it true, that autonomy is a matter of remaining protected in reason's cool armor from the effects of one's environment. No such protection is possible, nor is it appropriate if one's environment and its effects are of the right kind. In arguing that we can attribute intention, hence a measure of rationality, only to those we recognize as acting on reasons that make sense to us, we are making rationality a social matter, in at least this sense, which should remind you of something I have said before: if people in an alien community draw inferences in a way we cannot interpret as being rational, then we shall likely take them to be not only irrational but incomprehensible unless and until we understand the rules of the game they are playing and can therefore interpret their behavior as somehow rational.

I interpret a noise as speech only if I assume that the creature making the noise is sufficiently rational to be able to master the complexities of meaningful language and to be able at least most of the time to make appropriate commentary on his or her surroundings. If on my interpretation what is said in a particular culture is regularly false or senseless, then there is good reason to believe that my interpretation is incorrect. Before you and I can have a conversation, we have to assume a certain amount of rationality on each other's part, and a background of shared definition and belief; I recognize you as a user of language, and rational in that sense, only if you and I agree about a wide range of facts. If I cannot find anything believable in what you say, then I have no basis for claiming that I understand what you say. Of course, all this is compatible with the lamentably widespread incidence of irrationality and false belief, far beyond what standard economic theory contemplates.

Within scientific communities a degree of consensus about facts and methods—we might speak of the sharing of second-order beliefs—is required for communication, even for meaningful dissent. Every discipline has its own vocabulary; to a lesser degree of strictness, so does every community. Implicit in the vocabulary, particularly in the words for thick concepts, are guidelines on what counts as a rational inference and what does not.[1]

We have discussed a further sort of rationality I must attribute to you to understand you. I recognize you as an intending being, and at least minimally rational in that sense, only if you and I are in some significant agreement about what is desirable. If I cannot see anything desirable about what you desire, then I have no basis for claiming that you are performing a certain act intentionally, never mind rationally.[2] To call another living being rational or even human is to make an assessment that has moral weight: it says in effect that that creature is like me, has objectives I can find comprehensible (that is, I can see the point of what he or she does), and should be considered human for moral purposes.[3]

Since we attribute autonomy in part on the basis of rationality and rationality in part on the basis of our own views of what is desirable, we need to take care to avoid the tempting assumption that those who do not desire quite what we would desire must be irrational. Hence, we must be aware of the variety of ways in which one could conceive of the good life, hence of the range of things one might reasonably desire. It is important to avoid letting management, or for that matter anyone within the organization, decide what one can reasonably conceive to be good and so reserve the right to force one to be free. Maintaining the requisite detachment from local views about life in that case is by no means impossible, for it is much easier to imagine a kind of good life alien to your organization than one alien to your family and friends. Yet social pressure within an organization is strong, and it can indeed close one's mind to alternatives and open it to brainwashing.

It is a mistake in any case to suppose that one's identity is ever separable from one's past and present surroundings. To remove all the influences of the community is to remove much of one's values, one's language, one's ability to reflect, to reason, and to choose. These things are central, not peripheral, to one's personal identity, as I argued in Chapter 5. That is one reason why it is a mistake to believe that freedom is the absence of the community's influence on the agent or that the self is what would be left if all accrued influences could be removed.

Human happiness is characteristically social in this way. It is hard to imagine being without the ability to feel anything like the satisfaction at a job well done or the pride earned by a famous victory. These states are based on developed tastes and values involving social standards and the attitudes of others, like the states Maslow (1970) places highest in his needs hierarchy,[4] surely the ones with which those who have them identify most firmly. There is nothing wrong with that—there is no reason, that is, to regard the desire for food and shelter as natural and good and the desire for the esteem of others and of oneself as artificial and bad. Some things that are artificial are not bad; social desires are not wholly artificial if humans are naturally social animals.

Rather than divide a person's desires and values and principles into the natural and the social, we can think of them as being both if we believe that the human lot is life in a community, as on Aristotle's account it is. We have found reasons to claim that one lives well in a community by cultivating desires for what the community has to offer and respect for certain rules and repugnance toward breaking them even on utilitarian grounds. Yet the problem remains that shaping one's character and training one's desires and emotions to fit the environment looks like turning oneself over to whatever the community wants. Surely the power of the community to mold those roles creates the potential for manipulation of higher-order desires and beliefs through social pressure, so that in the end Winston Smith loves Big Brother. The good of the community may be invoked as a justification for this, but in an organizational context "the good of the community" may turn out to mean the financial benefit of certain senior managers or, occasionally, the stockholders.[5]

This is no mere theoretical problem; the socializing power of communities has led to moral catastrophe. One thinks of the speed and thoroughness with which the Nazis were able to induce mass moral pathology in what was in some ways a highly civilized society. Much the same can happen, even more easily, in an organization. Think of the investment banking houses in which people who had shown no inclination to criminal behavior became involved in what they knew to be wrong and illegal. In some cases, they later came to view their illegal activity with astonishment, as though someone else had done it all.[6]

One of the primary means of inducing any sort of behavior in an organization—hence, one of the dangers for morality there—is corporate culture, which is the body of shared beliefs, values, expectations, and norms of behavior characteristic of an organization. A sufficiently effective corporate culture can create support for immoral principles and practices in a way that is hard for even a moral person to discern. It may do so in two ways: by inducing straightforwardly immoral behavior and by inducing some behavior or other in a way that is immoral because it violates the employee's autonomy. If, as I have argued, it is the primary function of the moral manager to create an organization that respects the individual's autonomy and encourages moral behavior, then creating a moral culture by moral means is a large part of the moral manager's function. A moral organization in which the commons is preserved can support individual morality through the socializing influence of corporate culture.

The problem about socialization I have already introduced: our deepest values, however much and however well we reflect on them, are profoundly influenced by our community and, in that sense, apparently out of our control. The question then arises, What is the difference between a genuinely good community and one in which people are thoroughly brainwashed to be dutiful and thus preserve the commons? We want people to do the right thing, and we want them to do it freely. Under what conditions, then, can we say that the culture of an organization or any community promotes appropriate values in a way that respects autonomy?

TWO EXPERIMENTS

We can all too easily think of cases in which autonomy has been violated by brainwashing. Often it does not take long, and does not require any elaborate organizational apparatus. Two famous experiments show how it can work.

The better known of the two, in fact one of the most celebrated of experiments offering a dark view of human nature, is that of Milgram (1974). Subjects were told that they were assisting in an experiment testing the effect of negative reinforcement on memory. They were then instructed to administer shocks, as they thought, to people who failed to respond with correctly remembered nonsense syllables. The supposed victims were themselves actors, who deliberately gave wrong answers and then pretended to be in increasing and eventually terrible pain as the subjects gave them what seemed to be shocks of increasing severity. Many subjects, even though they believed they were administering shocks not only excruciating but dangerous to the apparent victims, persisted in obedience to their instructions and the urging of the experimenter.

Some of the subjects of this manipulation seem to have had conflicting second-order desires. Most of them shocked their subjects reluctantly; some were in tears as they did so. It appears that they were not disposed to shock and did not want to be disposed to shock but did believe they had some kind of duty to meet the terms of their agreement to participate in the experiment in spite of their disinclination. Had they reflectively and carefully weighed the competing principles of humaneness and obedience to the experimenter, they would likely have acted differently; this we can infer from the regret they expressed afterward with evident sincerity. We might say they had, but ignored, third-order desires about how to prioritize their second-order desires.[7]

The so-called Zimbardo experiment tells a different but no more reassuring story. Seventy-five men—no women—between the ages of seventeen and thirty volunteered for a psychological experiment conducted in 1971 at Stanford University by Haney, Zimbardo, and Banks (1973). They were tested for psychological stability, and twenty-four who tested high were chosen as subjects and offered a small stipend. On the first day of the experiment the participants were "arrested" and taken to a "prison" in the basement of a building on the Stanford campus. There half of them were named prisoners and dressed in gowns and nylon caps and made to live in cells; the other half were named guards and were given khaki uniforms and police-style mirror sunglasses to wear. The prisoners soon became passive, depressed; the guards behaved abusively towards them and seemed to relish doing so. In short, most members of both groups acted in stereotypical fashion and seemed to feel that that was appropriate, as though guards were supposed to act that way and the contemptible prisoners deserved what they got. Within thirty-six hours, serious psychological problems began to develop among the prisoners. Planned to last for two weeks, the experiment was halted after six days because most of the participants had in effect become prisoners or guards, wholly captured by their roles. The prisoners were relieved when it ended; the guards were disappointed, because they were doing their work with great enthusiasm and wanted to continue. Afterward both classes of participants expressed surprise and embarrassment over what they had done and how they had felt.

The Zimbardo experiment tells us something about corporate culture, and in particular something about ethical behavior within a strong corporate culture.[8] To begin with, the guards clearly behaved immorally. No system that countenances that sort of behavior in those circumstances has any warrant to be called a form of morality. If the guards had simply gone through the motions so convincingly that the convicts felt oppressed, they could have been justly criticized for that alone. Beyond the way they acted, however, they developed a contemptuous attitude towards the pseudoconvicts, who were not in fact criminals, as the guards knew. That attitude itself was morally inappropriate—questionable even in the case of real prisoners.

The guards' behavior was voluntary in the superficial sense that they acted on their first-order desires. One thing that makes us reluctant to call their acts autonomous is that they did not reflect before acting; if they had done so, they probably would have acted otherwise. Afterward they could not rationalize their behavior and, in some cases, found it surprising and embarrassing. We may be inclined to infer that their first-order desires did not conform to their second-order ones, because they did not want to be motivated by desires to punish and humiliate people who did not deserve it.

That is a facile explanation. The guards' immediate inclination to abuse the prisoners was based in large part on the role they assumed. As guards they accepted a duty to act in a certain way and even, as they apparently thought, to adopt a certain attitude. They wanted to be abusive; that seems clear. No one forced them to act that way, and acting that way did not seem to bother them at the time. Their inclination to act contemptuously may therefore not have been inconsistent with any second-order desire: they did not show any desire not to be motivated that way. Yet it is at least possible that on reflection they would have agreed that participation in an experiment of this sort would not justify being contemptuous and that for that reason, come to think of it, they should not have been so eager to abuse the prisoners.[9] The best explanation, I think, is that the experimenters manipulated the guards' second-order desires, which as a result were inconsistent with some of their other, still higher-order desires and with their values.

The guards seem to have been irrational as well, in the sense that they apparently acted on wholly unjustifiable and implausible beliefs about the prisoners' character. In that sense they betrayed certain of their higher-order beliefs, which would never countenance such a ludicrous inference.[10]

There are some significant differences between the experiments. The Zimbardo participants acted according to their inclinations: the guards went about their work with gusto, and the prisoners acted on their impulse to cower. The Milgram subjects overcame their inclinations, as their tears showed, and acted on higher-order desires under pressure. On the other hand, the experiments teach some common lessons. Taken together, they suggest that one's desires, whether they are of higher or lower order, are vulnerable to pressure. They suggest that lower-order beliefs can be affected, but they do not tell any very clear story about higher-order beliefs. The guards believed the prisoners were scum, probably in spite of their beliefs about what would count as evidence that someone was scum rather than because of them.[11] Social pressure affects second-order beliefs; if they were not susceptible at all to social pressure, we would have a great deal of difficulty communicating. It does not much affect them in the short run; even in the short run, first-order beliefs are less open than first-order desires to social pressure.[12]

Communities exert pressure on one's desires and beliefs at several levels. They do it by exerting authority, even when the authority cannot compel obedience by reward and punishment. More interesting to those who study organizations, they do it by assigning people positions that have accountabilities and expectations associated with them; we hardly need the Zimbardo experiment to show us that. One might take the view that one's moral duty is not to act to fulfill a role (that is, one should not aim at any sort of virtue) but instead to do what is right. That does not seem very helpful advice to someone who works for an organization: from Chapter 4 we see how one can buy into a legitimate agreement that assigns one a role. The point is not confined to organizations. Aristotle gave good reasons for saying that one ought always to fulfill the terms of the role of citizen, that the central virtue is civic virtue.[13]

Explicitly assigning roles and signing contracts, however, is not the manager's only, or always the most effective, way of affecting behavior and desires. It is sometimes more effective to create a strong corporate culture.

THE NATURE OF CULTURE

Corporate culture is the body of shared beliefs, values, expectations, and norms of behavior that shape life in the organization and account for certain observable artifacts. One postulates a culture to account for local behavior and the arrangements that anthropologists call social structure. (See for example Allaire and Firsirotu [1984]; Sathe [1985]; Schein [1985]; and Martin [1992]; the literature is vast.) Culture is communicated through socialization that proceeds by example, peer pressure, rituals, symbols, and didactic stories, true or apocryphal. The important messages are often not stated explicitly: even people most influential in keeping the cultural flame may be unable to state the rules, for the same reason fish do not feel wet. When that is the case, one cannot easily reflect on the rules. As I claimed in Chapter 4, an anthropologist will do better than an attorney in explaining an organization's rules and practices, in part by postulating certain cultural facts.

Cultural norms are not usually the result of conscious legislation, even when the community in question is an organization; once they have arisen, however, people in authority may begin to enforce them. Over time there may develop within an organization, as part of the local corporate culture, certain implicit understandings about how things are done; even if no one has consciously designed these understandings, even if they are not rationally defensible against alternatives, they may be taken very seriously and ignored at one's peril and that of others. (Think of our moral views on intimate matters, discussed in Chapter 2.) As I noted in Chapter 2, people who move from one organization to another may find that what was wit in the old organization is impudence in the new one, what was fawning is respect, what was honest confrontation is mutiny.

Corporate culture is important to business ethics because it is a vehicle for imparting and maintaining the moral principles and the values, good and bad, that animate life in the organization. Precisely for that reason, it may be difficult to detach oneself from one's corporate culture and assess it morally. Nor is it always clear what these values are. In some organizations values get taught openly and straightforwardly: Johnson and Johnson lists its most important moral principles, compels people to discuss them, and supports them with incentives as well as examples. More frequently, particularly in smaller organizations, the principles are conveyed only by examples, from which in due course one learns the kind of thing that is permitted and even successful. The principles that are actually in force may be elaborations on the espoused rules or inconsistent with them. In the latter case, there may or may not be strong sentiment in favor of the stated rules and sanctions against those who violate them. The task of the corporate anthropologist parallels that of the psychologist: to notice, or if necessary postulate, the entities and events that account for what we observe in the behavior of people in the organization.

Culture affects language and in some cases makes language its vehicle.[14] I have argued that we understand each other only if we hold a range of beliefs, including second-order beliefs, in common; in the extreme case, we cannot tell whether some alien speaker is saying something crazy or being translated wrong. I have extended the point to the moral realm: we can understand each other only if we share some views about the nature of the good life and about what counts as an appropriate answer to a question of the form, What is the point of that? If Jxnzs, an alien, says that in his culture causing pain is in itself a moral act, we may find it impossible to know whether we have translated his words correctly or whether, if he is speaking English, he has command of the language. The differences among actual cultures are less dramatic, but we can easily think of cases in which an imputation of virtue in a culture distant from ours puzzles us greatly, and may even offend us. It takes some subtle anthropology to give an account of a concept like taboo or to explain (which is, as I argued earlier, not to justify) a practice like clitoridectomy.

The differences among corporate cultures are usually more pedestrian. But it is easy to infer the assumptions in a culture in which people often use words like *strong, wimp,* and *girl,* as opposed to terms like *caring, personal space,* and *karma.* Consider what must be assumed if the word *elitist* is in play, or the word *scab,* or *blasphemy.* Or, for that matter, a term like *organizational effectiveness,* or any term that presupposes, as do names of jobs and verbs signifying actions in the name of the organization, a whole network of relationships of rights and obligations.

Suppose managers in a certain organization are quick to revile subordinates. An outsider, hearing a vice president loudly and publicly call a manager an idiot, might try to interpret the statement. To do so correctly would require that the outsider understand that the vice president does not really think the manager is an idiot but is only participating in a kind of initiation ritual, understood by both parties to the conversation, designed to foster stoicism and a sense of solidarity among managers as well as a high level of performance in the organization. Anyone familiar with military culture will recognize the pattern. It is appropriate to try to find out whether the organization's objectives require such a culture, as the military arguably does, and the answer is not always affirmative. In any case, this sort of interpretation does not imply moral justification.

If the claims I have made about language are true, it will be difficult to free oneself of the presuppositions that one's language carries with it. I argued in Chapter 4 that we cannot find some fact-neutral or value-neutral language from whose vantage point we can criticize our own language. It follows that it is difficult to criticize a culture from within, since as natives we shall have difficulty formulating alternative principles and beliefs and understanding them when they have been formulated. Seeing why the alternatives ought to be accepted will be more difficult still. It also follows that making moral progress is not easy, since it requires getting free of the limits imposed by the local language. A pedestrian but significant example: in a corporate culture that values decisiveness and calls it strength, the statement that it takes a strong man to change his mind on the basis of a sound argument would be hard to comprehend—rather like saying that a real man enjoys wearing a dress. Looking at a culture significantly (but not radically) different from one's own may contribute to just the kind of reflection that moral progress requires and so better equip one to criticize one's own culture. But although it is usually easier to interpret the words and action in another corporate culture than in a remote society, what I have just claimed about language and culture implies that the former is not always a trivial undertaking, especially if there are widespread superficial similarities.[15]

CULTURE AS A WAY OF MANAGING

Organizations have always had cultures, but attention to corporate culture is a fairly recent phenomenon. One reason for its current prominence is that the alternatives to managing by way of culture have become less viable. In a turbulent environment in which change has accelerated and competition comes from new and unexpected quarters, the organization that imposes stable and specific job descriptions with little room for discretion will have difficulty adapting. Particularly in large and diversified organizations, corporate management will not be able to supervise closely, nor will it be competent to set narrow limits within which people in the divisions must make decisions; sometimes managers will have no good grounds for reviewing the decisions made in the divisions or for fairly and effectively compensating the decision makers. Where opportunities come unexpectedly and demand skills that exceed those of the accountable position—for how can we know, when we are designing the job, exactly what will be needed to solve the unforeseeable problems of an increasingly unpredictable future?—the best response will often be to assemble a task force of people with the needed skills, whatever their official job descriptions are.[16] To manage an organization in which teamwork is a preferred means of management requires a shared sense of larger corporate objectives and of How We Do Things Around Here. Johnson and Johnson corporate cannot micromanage its foreign subsidiaries; it can, and does, address the difficult task of nurturing carefully designed values in them.[17]

To show how a strong culture can be deployed as a management instrument requires reference back to the theory about desires and beliefs argued in Chapter 5. A strong culture can affect one's values and moral sensibilities in a number of ways. It can operate straightforwardly through rewards and punishments—that is, by motivating managers to provide what people want and administer what they do not want or withhold what they do. Over time certain kinds of behavior get reinforced or extinguished, not only through pay and promotion but through the less visible devices of socialization: myths, rituals, special terms, and so on.

Culture may also significantly determine one's wants and then satisfy them. Like culture in the broadest sense, corporate culture has a significant role in determining what sort of thing makes one happy, even what sort of person one wants to be, in part by determining what counts as success. Management can sometimes manage effectively by creating a social context that determines what people need, or at any rate what they greatly desire.

Culture at its most powerful works on one's second-order as well as first-order desires: it causes one to want, consciously or not, to be a certain sort of person with desires, tastes, and projects of a certain kind. One may even make a planned and concerted effort, through self-binding for example, to become the sort of person that the right people in the organization respect. To the extent that the workplace has replaced other community institutions, organizations accumulate greater power to socialize. We think of religion as teaching people to strive to be a certain sort of person, to try to have the right dispositions. Now corporate culture performs that function. It should not be surprising, therefore, that corporate cultures are supported by myths, symbols, and rituals, much as religious groups are.[18]

A standard system of rewards and punishments takes one's second-order desires as given and causes one to desire (first-order) to assist in the achievement of certain organizational goals, owing to the consequences to oneself of so doing. A direct instruction determines what one does; a compensation system determines what one wants to do, in order to get paid. A strong culture sometimes determines, or at any rate significantly affects, what one wants to want; its influence can reach to one's values. If I am a malleable personality in an organization that values toughness and aggressiveness, I shall likely want not only to act accordingly but actually to be tough—that is, to be the sort of person who is motivated by the demands of success rather than by sensitivity to the hurts and needs of others. In Joseph Heller's novel *Something Happened* (1974, p. 67), the protagonist says, "And I find that I am being groomed for a better job. And I find—God help me—that I want it." Had he been thoroughly socialized, he would not be appalled at wanting it.

A common theme in the corporate culture literature is that culture gives people's lives meaning; that is, it creates values that guide people's aspirations and, when they are being serious, their behavior. In giving an account of personal identity in Chapter 5 I emphasized the centrality of values and principles to the self and its continuity and thereby suggested that it would be a mistake to think of one's deepest preferences as accidental features of the self, although one might gain or lose one or two of them while remaining oneself. To the extent that one's principles are determined by one's corporate environment, one is a corporate creation.[19] Success and prestige are among culture's devices for affecting second-order desires—and strongly too, where people are prepared to devote their lives to these things. Where these are major rewards, there is as much leeway in what may make one happy as there is variety in the activities that may be prestigious, and management may have much to do with determining which activities those are.

Culture also affects people's beliefs, including second-order ones, the ones about what sort of thing we should believe and on the basis of which we reflect on first-order beliefs and make corrections to them. I argued earlier in this chapter that a linguistic community necessarily pressures its members towards consensus on second-order beliefs. In a similar but more pedestrian way, a strong corporate culture produces second-order beliefs in part by filtering what people see and hear and how they talk, by training their expectations, and by influencing their interpretations of others' behavior as courageous, or insubordinate, or insolent.

A culture's propagation of interpretive second-order beliefs gives people in the organization meaning, not quite in the way the propagation of second-order desires does. It not only commits them to definitions of words, particularly for thick concepts, which in turn commit them to a certain view of how things are and ought to be. An organization, like many human institutions, is a complex network not only of contracts but of shared intentions, expectations, and conventions that create thick concepts and sort people into roles that create obligations. In that sense communities and organizations create or enact reality and divide the world in certain ways rather than others.[20] But there is a further reason for saying that what is the case in an organization is a function of corporate culture: it is a function of what people believe, because what is the case is a function of what people intentionally do, and that is a function of what they believe. Beliefs also create facts by virtue of being self-fulfilling, and self-fulfilling beliefs may preserve the commons or destroy it. For example, that people in a community or on a team believe that others are free riders will affect people's decisions about whether to ride free themselves and so will affect the truth of their beliefs about one another.

CULTURE AND A THEORY OF MOTIVATION

It is important to understand what theories of corporate culture are not. Most important, for our purposes, they are not just theories about job enrichment or anything else that comes under the broad umbrella of the human relations approach to management. In particular, McGregor's (1960) distinction between Theory X and Theory Y rests on a view of motivation that I have claimed is inadequate from the point of view of both explanation and justification. McGregor claims that the capital distinction is between theories of motivation that assume that work is unnatural and unwelcome and must be elicited by the use of fear (Theory X) and theories that assume that work is or can be natural and even fulfilling (Theory Y). While it is true that a corporate culture might be more or less consistent with Theory Y management, culture does not operate on the same level as management by either theory.

Theory Y purports to be more benign as well as more realistic than Theory X because it portrays people, and in particular employees, as naturally inclined to be productive, rather than as lazy by nature and reachable only by intimidation. This does seem an improvement over crude psychological egoism, at any rate. It seems clear, however—to Hart (1988), for one, and to me—that the view of human nature that McGregor assumes without much investigation of the available options is rather narrow psychological egoism of a less crude form, according to which one wants what is best for oneself.[21] It is surely true that in the transaction between the organization and the individual, what the former gives and the latter gets is not, as in the case of Theory X, simply money; it is instead some sort of fulfillment—for example, of one's innate desire to be productive, or of one's desire for security and participation. From this point of view it makes perfect sense for Maitland (1989), for example, to argue that the satisfaction one gets directly from one's work is not one's by right but simply part of one's compensation package.

According to Theory Y, an organization may provide meaning to an employee's life; in this case, what is meant is that the organization may fulfill some desires of an important sort. Although the words sound familiar, that is not the sense—not, at any rate, the only sense—in which a strong culture provides meaning: it provides meaning not simply by fulfilling people's desires but also by significantly determining what their desires and even their values are. There is no suggestion in McGregor's work that life in the organization or elsewhere might alter what people desire, much less what they want to desire. On the contrary, McGregor wants to argue that Theory Y and its characteristic desires apply to most people as a matter of course and that the standard mistake of managers has been to suppose that Theory X is or ever was true. In that sense, McGregor appears to be operating under some of the familiar standard economist's utilitarian assumptions.

That is not the only way in which culture theory differs from the likes of Theory Y. In embracing a form of psychological egoism, as Hart points out, McGregor declines to consider that the employee might be motivated by loyalty to the organization or concern for the well-being of others in it. That is not surprising: according to the standard economist's psychological egoism, uncompensated loyalty is irrational if it is possible at all. The organization remains essentially a marketplace rather than a community. In fact, McGregor lays little emphasis on motivation based on moral considerations: the employee is obligated to provide labor—though it turns out that working isn't as unpleasant as we thought—and the manager is obligated to compensate the employee and otherwise do what most effectively achieves corporate objectives. The compensation turns out to be a matter of a certain self-realization in the employees.[22]

JAPANESE CULTURE

Theory Z management, as Ouchi (1981) famously calls it, to contrast with McGregor's theories, really does have to do with culture. Japanese management aims at creating second-order desires; the objective is that the employee will want to be a certain sort of person, will want to have such attitudes as respect and cooperativeness and be motivated by concern for the interests of the organization and the others in it. Typically American workers intuitively regard this as a greater infringement on autonomy than is simply telling them what to do. The Americans' desire not to be in that position is itself a second-order desire, and it is the kind of desire that Japanese management seeks to alter in the long run.

Fucini and Fucini (1990, p. 104) give a telling example of a characteristically Japanese attitude toward worker autonomy. Management at Mazda's new Flat Rock manufacturing facility in Michigan wanted its American employees to wear Mazda caps but made wearing the caps voluntary. The employees did not wear them, and their managers were unhappy with what they considered a sign of disrespect for the company. The employees responded by pointing out that the caps were after all voluntary, but what the managers wanted was precisely that the employees wear the caps voluntarily, and they tried to persuade the employees to do so. The employees, who would have worn the caps with minimal grumbling if so instructed, were offended at being expected to want to do it. What is characteristic of Japanese management in this incident is that it was not only actions but desires that were being managed. The employees were expected to adopt certain desires, and the Americans did not (second-order) want to have these desires. As one might expect of employees accustomed to adversarial collective bargaining, the Americans did not want their desires managed or their attitudes preempted.

The other thing one might expect of veterans of collective bargaining is that they would not regard the good of the organization and its other stakeholders as a reason for action. To that extent the psychological egoism assumed in the McGregor theories is true in the case of the typical employee in an American auto factory. Insofar as it is true, we would not expect Americans to buy readily into a culture that preserves the commons. But the Fucinis do not portray Mazda's Americans as in all ways fanatical individualists: they indicate that most employees participated in teamwork without resorting to free riding and objected when it turned out that decisions were not jointly but centrally made, mostly by Japanese nationals. (Of course, the employees had been selected with great care.)

There is not necessarily anything wrong with taking another person's interests as a reason for action; on the contrary, that is characteristic of morality and definitive of a community. There is indeed something wrong with a corporate culture that causes people to ignore their own interests in favor of those of the organization. A corporate culture can do something else, however: it can cause people to change their views about what their own interests are and even change what their own interests actually are. Japanese workers identify their own success with that of the organization far more than do their American counterparts,[23] and they consider it appropriate for the company to take an influential interest in a far greater part of the employee's life. American workers resent this sort of paternalism; apparently, it bothers Japanese workers less. So the question is, At what point does a powerful culture go beyond what morality permits? The answer cannot be found in whether the workers like it or not; for the really powerful cultures determine what they like and even what they want to like. There can be no standard utilitarian answer to this question, which is part of the subject of Chapter 7.

A culture may be functional, hence worth some favorable comment from a utilitarian point of view, in some circumstances but not others. Gordon (1991) has shown how different industries call forth different sorts of culture from successful competitors; the same is true of principles of other kinds. Surely some of the differences between Japanese and American culture reflect the differing needs of a crowded, homogeneous island nation as opposed to those of a spacious land of immigrant opportunists. [24] And surely, as Hardin (1968) himself points out, we would have far less reason to worry about commons considerations if America were still a land of wide-open spaces. But that there is something to be said for a culture, corporate or otherwise, from the point of view of the survival of the institution is no guarantee of its moral adequacy.

THE PERILS OF CULTURE

MacIntyre (1981) suggests that organization theory does not distinguish persuasion by reference to principles from manipulation and can therefore have no concept of treating people as rational beings. The Zimbardo and the Milgram experiments imply that organizations themselves can manipulate people contrary to their higher-order desires by applying some pressure that distorts or obscures the considered priority among those desires. We describe such cases by saying that emotion— say, fear—overwhelms reason. Typically one experiences surprise and regret afterward, if one is aware of what has happened. If one habitually is not aware, then over a period of time one's higher-order desires may change to fit the way one acts; that is bad, because in a rational person second-order desires normally drive first-order ones, not the other way around. (The latter situation is often a form of rationalization.)

A strong culture permits managerial manipulation of higher-order desires and beliefs by influencing not only what people do but what they are. The greatest evil of *1984* is not that the government spies on people, lies to them, and persecutes them; it is that in the end Winston Smith loves Big Brother. Japanese managers experience anxiety and burnout, but the limited extent to which many of them complain about their lot is more worrisome than the lot itself. The kamikaze pilots were all volunteers, after all.[25] And if the Japanese worker loves Mazda, is it because Mazda has affected the worker's second-order desires? And if so, do we not have reason to believe that his autonomy has been violated? The answer depends in part on how lovable Mazda really is.

Rawls is a pluralist concerning conceptions of the good: the good state, he claims, respects the citizens' rights to their various conceptions. A strong culture may give citizens or employees virtually no choice on the question of what is of greatest value in their lives. There is no reason to grant management the right to determine this issue for employees or even to narrow down their options. Of course, they must share certain objectives, but it is not appropriate to cause them all to have the same higher-order desires. If my organization causes me to believe unreflectively that professional success counts and family life does not, something has gone wrong.

CULTURE AND THE COMMONS

The good news is that management of culture can create economic and moral value by solving the assurance problem (see Chapter 3), specifically by helping preserve the commons. I argued in Chapter 3 that the logic of the commons works within an organization when employees and management, whatever distinct interests they may have, share an interest in the organization's prosperity, with the result that organizational effectiveness serves both managers' and employees' interests; that organizational effectiveness is a function of employees' and managers' cooperative effort; and that it is possible to get a free ride by contributing less than one's share of work and reaping a full share of the fruits of others' cooperative toil. In a situation with the structure of a commons, individuals acting as maximizers will in the aggregate frustrate themselves.

I also argued in Chapter 3 that a compensation system supports the commons only insofar as it can measure individual contributions to corporate performance. That, I went on to argue, is difficult in organizations that are responsive to changes in the environment—that is, organizations in which job descriptions change as conditions do and in which some complex tasks must be done by teamwork, hence without close attention to separate accountability. As I argued in this chapter, those are the very organizations most amenable to management by culture rather than by traditional means. It is through social pressure in working groups and in the organization as a whole that a strong culture can preserve the commons by encouraging employees to contribute to the organization and eventually to themselves, rather than take the rationally maximizing free (or at any rate cheap) ride.

The belief that one's commons-supporting behavior will be supported by like behavior on the part of other employees and managers is self-fulfilling, I claimed earlier; the organization's culture affects the interpretations of behavior that lead to that belief. This situation by itself does not necessarily constitute an interesting form of brainwashing, for it is what any culture, any linguistic community does: contrary to empiricist myth, we never develop second-order beliefs just by repeatedly looking at what is there. Where the second-order beliefs are false, there is a problem. Where they are true, it is not a problem that they are to some degree self-fulfilling, for so are many widely held beliefs that form the fabric of any cooperative unit.

I claimed earlier that a situation in which what people believe affects what is the case is characteristic of the social sciences, which are unscientific in part because beliefs about what is the case, including beliefs about what others may do or intend, affect what is the case. If it is true that the organization is a network of shared intentions, expectations, and conventions—although not necessarily anybody's fiction—then much of what is true of it is so because its enactors and its stakeholders expect and intend it to be true. There is nothing necessarily manipulative about that.

In any case, culture is never wholly within management's control. Cultural myths and symbols generate the appropriate emotion and belief only if they have some history on their side; so a culture does not usually develop purely as a conscious invention of management alone. The appropriate analogy for talking about corporate culture is not a two-person zero-sum game between management and employees: like a commons, a culture has many participants and is for that reason (among others) difficult to change quickly.

It is a damaging simplification to claim that corporate culture is a vehicle of managerial ideology constructed in the interests of the managers. Even if the culture does serve the interests of that group, it does not follow that that is its purpose, since that conclusion requires managers to have had the purpose in advance and to have designed the culture accordingly. That is not so easily done, although some highly effective managers do it; in any case, it suggests that it makes sense to talk about those interests in advance of their (partly social) development, in which corporate culture plays a significant role. We can as well claim that the culture determines the interests of the managers (and of others too) as that it serves them.

Whatever else may be true of a culture that respects autonomy, it must surely make room for the individual to reflect. I argued in Chapter 5 that only the most reflective individuals can keep their first-order desires and beliefs consistent with their second-order ones, in part because only those few are conscious of the relations between their second-order beliefs or desires and their more immediate ones and can take a critical attitude towards either kind. Most people are as much influenced by appeals to emotion, such as symbols and rituals of the kind that support a corporate culture, as by discursive argument in the formation of even higher-order beliefs. One is therefore tempted to call for more reflection and less giving in to emotion.

But it is not as simple as that. I argued in Chapter 5 and earlier, following Aristotle, that certain emotions are functional: for example, indignation may impress those who might otherwise take advantage of one, and a feeling of shame can lead one to do the right thing. I argued too that skepticism can loosen the bonds of loyalty that make the commons possible.[26] At the very least, we have reason to cultivate our emotions and the second-order desires they support so that we respond favorably to what promotes the community's solidarity and is not otherwise bad. Remember that, on the Aristotelian account, emotion is supposed to be reason's ally. In any case, on what better basis can we choose our fundamental values, even assuming that it makes sense to talk of choosing them? But then how can we reasonably reject the values that social influence presses upon us? I have suggested that it is extraordinarily difficult to take a detached and critical attitude toward those values and that it would not necessarily be a good thing in all respects for the community if its members were capable of doing so. It is difficult to say in the abstract what the appropriate balance is between detachment and loyalty, although I shall venture some thoughts in Chapter 7.

CULTURE, ROLES, SELF

In Chapter 4 I argued that circumstances can not only affect an action but also make an action the kind of action it is: a third strike, a payment, a hiring. In a similar way, circumstances can not only affect a person (make you stingy, gregarious, large-hearted) but also make you a losing pitcher, a creditor, an employee. Many roles come equipped with moral responsibilities: if you are an employee, you must do some things to earn your pay and some of the things you do are the acts they are because of the same context that makes you an employee (for example, your signature becomes an approval or a payment or an actionable offense). The roles you play are not confined to business: you are a friend, a citizen, an accountant, a sibling, a parent, a taxpayer, an Anglophone, and many other things, some of which carry *prima facie* responsibilities, or at the very least create reasonable expectations.

I have argued that the agent performs no such thing as *the act* itself, apart from its context and its consequences. Is there any such thing as *the person* apart from these roles? The quick answer is that, yes, the person may remain the same person while changing friends, moving to a new country, disowning relatives, stopping paying taxes, and acquiring an accent: these are incidental to personal identity. But that answer is too quick. Personal identity over time is, I have argued, a matter of the persistence of memories, preferences, values, and traits of intellect, personality, and character; personal identity at a time is a matter of their coherence. Many of these items essentially involve past roles, the loss of which would create serious discontinuity.

What am I apart from those properties that might have been otherwise? A human being, Aristotle says. But it is an essential characteristic of a human being to acquire and maintain but also sometimes change properties. And, as Aristotle notes, the human being is a civilized animal, hence one naturally disposed to acquire these properties from living in the community. There is nothing natural or good about having no such properties and playing no such roles. Whether it is good to play a role is, as Aristotle suggests, a function of the goodness of the institution of which the role is a part.

That is looking at things philosophically. To look at them practically, consider the Zimbardo experiment. The participants identified themselves with their role as prisoner or guard. They did not think of themselves as persons who for the moment happened to be subjects in an experiment that required them to be temporarily imprisoned or to act as guards. If the sort of identification they exhibited can happen in a short time under highly artificial conditions, one can easily see how a long tenure in an organization could have an even more radical effect.

Virtue in its traditional sense is a matter of playing a certain role well: that of a soldier or a mother, for example. Every role has its characteristic virtue, which is a matter of attitude and even emotion as well as behavior;

what role, if any, then, corresponds to just plain virtue? According to Aristotle, the answer is civic virtue—the role of citizen in a great community—and one's primary duty is to play that role well. It is not possible to distinguish what you are from all the roles you play, but some roles are more important than others, and Aristotle suggests that the role of citizen is the essential one. Nowadays, for reasons I have given in the two previous chapters, some of us think of our professional or other occupational roles as essential to us. At the least, they are very important.

Corporate culture works in part by creating or supporting a community structure that implies roles for people. Culture creates meaning for people's lives by giving them roles to play; the roles, hence the lives, are meaningful insofar as they are part of some institution. If the institution is an important one, then one can derive some self-respect from its importance, as when people cry, We're number one! If not, its role players may still regard it as important just because it is the source of their importance. To say that you are what is left when all your roles are stripped off is no more justifiable than saying that your true and free thoughts and intentions are what remains when the (artificial and socially determined) language that regiments them is stripped away. (In fact the two mistakes are quite similar, given the relationship between culture and roles—the former helping create the latter.)

We can still examine one or more of our roles and decide that it is a bad one and the virtue associated with it unvirtuous, just as we can discover upon analysis that some of the language we use is incoherent or impoverished or crude or dependent upon a bad theory. What we cannot do is find a point of view from which to assess all possible languages and find them wanting, or not; assessing the whole of our own language is extraordinarily difficult if it is possible at all. Nor can one achieve the corresponding detachment in order to evaluate one's roles, particularly not all at once.

Our salvation is not that we can get away from all roles and play none but that from time to time we can play many and diverse roles. This suggests another problem with the view that employment or even citizenship is essentially a contractual relationship. The metaphor of the contract understates the extent to which the relationship encompasses the self. [27] It therefore overstates the extent to which one is free to leave one role or contract and enter into another, and it understates the importance of one's emotional attachment to one's institution. The emphasis on roles corrects that and suggests a further reason for taking loyalty seriously: our attachments to an organization may be of this particularly deep sort, and their rupture no casual matter.

PROSPECTS

This chapter has raised the question, What is the significance of the possibility that the organization will in effect decide what constitutes happiness? Culture does preserve the commons, in part through creating emotions, in part through creating self-fulfilling beliefs, in part through creating second-order desires. But this smacks of brainwashing, and we want to say that there is something wrong with the society of *Brave New World*, something wrong with the view that good management characteristically makes one happy, for it could do that by assigning one a role in a smooth-running operation and socializing one to want to play that role. There are indeed voices in the management literature that can be interpreted this way. On MacIntyre's (1981, pp. 25f.) harsh reading, Weber holds that it is the task of management to generate behavior in the interests of the organization and that rationality is a property of means to the organization's ends, whatever they are, and not a property of those ends. MacIntyre attributes a similar view to Likert: that it is management's job to influence rather than frustrate the motives of the subordinates, presumably in the direction of corporate objectives. He reads March and Simon as claiming that for subordinates rationality is a matter of arguing from premises that will produce conclusions ordained by management. In each case the view is that the ends belong to the organization and the means to its employees; in the background lies the Humean notion that reason is about means, rather than ends. In its details the interpretation is not entirely fair, but it does suggest the difficulty of determining what constitutes autonomy for a social animal and what distinguishes manipulation from rational persuasion.

A significant part of the solution to the problem of distinguishing corporate cultural brainwashing from a benign development of shared values lies not in describing true happiness or invoking foundational moral principles but in stating what must be true of a community in which moral progress is possible and autonomy can flourish. I argued in Chapter 4 that even if moral realism is true it might still turn out that the closest we can get to stating true moral principles is to describe the environment in which people can move towards them, as we might describe scientific truth as what people can agree to under certain favorable circumstances. In Chapter 7 we shall consider some of the characteristics of what Aristotle would call the great *polis:* the community in which morality is possible. Such a community can have a strong culture even if it does not homogenize people's conception of the good life in a way that Rawls finds impermissible.

NOTES

1. My account implies that language is essential to rationality; indeed, it is language that enables me to represent my states of mind to others and theirs to myself and to exercise sophisticated capacities in reflection and other second-order activities that are directed at thoughts, possible states of affairs, desires, and principles and therefore require that I be able to identify them as such.

2. On a particular occasion I may not see anything attractive about some objective of yours, but I may judge that you are acting intentionally and even

rationally because I have evidence that you do normally desire what I can imagine myself desiring; in that case, I assume further investigation of your behavior on this occasion would answer the question, Why did Jones put lighter fluid instead of vermouth into the martini? Of course it might turn out that Jones intentionally poured *something* into the martini but only inadvertently poured lighter fluid in.

3. If we are pragmatists, we will judge others' rationality largely by the success of their undertakings. If they and we have wholly different views of the good life, however, we shall have different standards of success, hence no shared basis for attributing success or therefore rationality. So communities by their nature share a notion of the good life to a significant extent, and that they do contributes to their sharing a notion of rationality.

4. In speaking of tastes I do not mean to suggest any arbitrariness. The nature and objectives of a community may make it very important to develop certain tastes, if the arguments in Chapter 5 are correct.

5. For more along these lines see Gilbert (1991, 1992): he argues that standard theories of strategy fail to consider most people in organizations autonomous beings with values of their own.

6. Stewart (1991) is a rich source on Milken, Boesky, Levine, and others. In some ways Lewis (1989) is more revealing. Michael Lewis worked for Salomon Brothers for some years without entirely losing his grip on his own values, although he suggests that he was seldom motivated by ethical considerations. He vividly describes a corporate culture that was not lawless but in which morality played almost no part, although certain martial virtues were honored. What is perhaps most interesting is the extent to which Lewis himself, for all his detachment, bought into the culture that taught him about "trading, selling, and life" (p. 158).

7. This case too suggests that one's desires are not neatly organized into distinct orders. In any case, conflicting desires may be of the same order.

8. One standardly speaks of a corporate culture as being strong if it has a deep and pervasive uniform influence on employees' behavior. There is reason to believe that the corporate culture is strong when employees behave very differently from the way they do outside the organization—as, for example, when behavior condemned elsewhere in our society is tolerated in a particular organization. Anthropologists do not normally speak of influential or strong cultures, because the notion of a social norm from which a certain culture deviates much or little makes no sense; hence, there are no obvious criteria for how strong that sort of culture is. Yet there are large communities other than organizations that have an especially strong influence on their participants; some professions, for example. A typical Japanese company has a stronger culture than a typical American one, and the Amish have a stronger culture than the Presbyterians.

9. My analysis does not presuppose, what I have no reason to believe, that most people enjoy abusing others and are glad of the excuse to do so. Even if it were true, it would not explain the prisoners' behavior.

10. Presumably it is easier to maintain first-order beliefs (and desires) that are inconsistent with second-order ones if you are not fully conscious of the beliefs on which you are acting, as in this case the guards are not. In analyzing the case of a person doing something he or she can say is wrong, Aristotle likens this weak-willed person to a drunk reciting poetry without understanding its meaning. What he seems to think is lacking in this case is the sort of perception of the situation in all its relevant aspects that is characteristic of the person of

practical wisdom, which is not a purely cognitive faculty. (This is the same faculty that helps one choose wisely when principles conflict. See Ch. 4, n. 58.)

11. Desires are more commonly changed under pressure than are beliefs, but this seems a clear case of people having a first-order belief because of social pressure. See Ch. 5, n. 22.

12. The sociology of knowledge deals primarily with agreements on what to believe that necessarily develop over time, sometimes without much attention to possible alternatives. How susceptible first-order beliefs are to social pressure is bound to be a matter of controversy, in part because it is difficult to be sure of the sincerity with which they are reported. The Asch (1955) experiment famously showed that social pressure can cause people to report observations that are clearly false, but whether his subjects believed their own reports is uncertain. They might have been mischaracterizing their beliefs to avoid embarrassment.

13. A role may enrich one's life or impoverish it; in part for this reason, we identify with certain roles and not with others. To call oneself a janitor is to name one's occupation; to call oneself a neurosurgeon is to state something essential about oneself. (See Edel et al. [1994], pp. 176ff.)

14. Sathe (1985) holds that language is a level of culture, between behavior and other observables on one side and values on the other.

15. In analyzing culture we frame hypotheses that link the underlying beliefs and values with what is observable, but that link is not a straightforwardly causal one, for some of the artifacts *express* the culture somewhat as words express thoughts. In that sense one *interprets* observable entities in understanding the culture. It follows, given claims I have made at various points about interpretation, that one cannot understand a culture radically different from one's own. Normally, however, the differences permit interpretation, as it is possible to explain to a novice that a certain act constitutes a balk, or the payment of a bill, or insolence.

16. Even where the environment does not force organizational change, sharing and swapping tasks and blurring lines of accountability may be an effective way of getting work done. In a classic article, Trist and Bamforth (1951) describe the extraordinarily productive effects of job sharing in a coal mine. Their work led directly or indirectly to several important bodies of literature, no doubt including McGregor's Theories X and Y.

17. Insofar as moral management addresses culture rather than rules and systems, it shows us how morality has to do with virtue as well as with principles. In organizations that are necessarily adaptive to rapid change, in which therefore management by culture is more likely appropriate, a virtue-based approach to encouraging morality may be more effective than a principle-based approach. This seems an instance of the rule of thumb proposed by Edel et al. (1994, p. 165): for different kinds of community, different sorts of ethics are applicable.

18. Those who attend sales meetings of companies like Amway and Mary Kay Cosmetics often notice their revivalist flavor, which includes songs that sound as though they might have been written by Fanny J. Crosby. Such a culture may be especially important when employees cannot be closely supervised, as the ones in those companies cannot be. Many Japanese companies have songs, too.

19. Not casually does Saint Paul urge his followers to become "new beings in Christ." As the previous footnote suggests, the power of corporate culture to create people may be related to the decline of religion as a creating force in people's lives.

20. The extent to which we impose our categories on reality is a subject that seems to encourage overstatement and vagueness, to which I trust I have not con-

tributed unduly. In the organizational literature Weick (1979 and elsewhere) has some interesting observations about what he calls enactment.

21. Recall that Sen distinguishes the view that one's self-interest is always narrow from the view that nothing but self-interest motivates people. Theory Y denies the former but not the latter.

22. The two ways in which Theory Y, which is about how to motivate people, differs from a theory of culture are related. Neglect of second-order desires and of the possibility that one might manage one's own desires or not identify with them or that one's environment might affect one's desires for better or for worse is consistent with psychological egoism, because the typical psychological egoist is likely to think people straightforwardly want what makes them happy and is consequently unlikely to consider that people could be uncertain about what it is that they want to make them happy.

23. Yankelovich and Immerwahr (1983, p. 27) report that only 9 percent of American workers thought they would be the primary beneficiaries of increased corporate productivity, whereas ninety-three percent of Japanese workers thought they would benefit if their company's profits increased.

24. This is not to say, what is probably not true, that the characteristics of cultures are always or even usually functional, although, like the virtues they create, they often make or used to make some contribution to the community. In Japanese cultural traditions that go beyond baseball we can find explanations for the practice of making pitchers throw so much in practice that their arms usually wear out when they are still young (see Chapter 4, n. 32), but it would be a different and far more difficult matter to find a justification for it. To do so or to show that it is unjustified would at the very least require a great deal of interpretation of the kind anthropologists do. This particular practice makes sense against the background of the institution of *bushido,* the lifestyle of the Samurai, from which derive concepts like *yamato damashi* (fighting spirit) and *doryoku* (effort). (See Whiting, 1989, esp. Chs. 2 and 3.) To assess it just from the point of view of its effect on the typical pitcher's career would be like assessing some society's notion of honor by making superficial utilitarian objections to it, as though we would countenance as an objection the charge that people in our society foolishly regard lying as wrong even when it does no actual harm.

25. From a utilitarian point of view one could argue that the suicide missions were morally praiseworthy because they were cost-effective: the planes, loaded with far more ordnance than would have been possible if fuel had been required for the return to home base, probably did more damage per life lost than did ordinary bombing attacks. It takes some careful argument to defend the view that knowing one is about to die is such a great disadvantage from a moral point of view that one should prefer that more people die who do not expect to and who have not volunteered. The notion of respect for life does not seem to suffice for this argument, although a close analysis of Japanese wartime practices might uncover some views we would have reason to call repugnant. And not only those of the Japanese.

26. In American business individuality is a principle much espoused, but corporate cultures often suppress individuality. We seem to permit just enough individuality to endanger the commons, but not enough to encourage reflection.

27. Rawls (1993, esp. Lecture VII) emphasizes this point, but he uses it to distinguish between political entities and associations. I have argued that it applies to organizations better than he seems to believe.

7

The Good Community
and the Good Organization

I have suggested that, instead of trying to determine what the foundational principles of morality are and what communal or organizational
arrangements best encourage people to act according to them, we try to
say something about what a good community looks like and what it requires of those who live there. This chapter is about some of the
characteristics of a good community and, in particular, a good organization. Intended to be compatible with a Rawlsian approach, it focuses
largely on structures and procedures. It is in part a review of major points
I have made.[1]

Life in a community develops one's sense of what is desirable and valuable and of what constitutes a good life. Hence, standard moral theories
do not readily provide a neutral or very useful means of adjudication
among different communities. The question therefore arises, On what
basis can one evaluate a community's standards? For surely a community
or an organization may itself be morally good or bad.

The claim that each community has its own moral principles, or at
least its own versions of them, applies in a less radical way to organizations as well. I argued in Chapter 6 that corporate culture may impose a
certain conception of the good life and may pressure employees to have
desires that fit with the local definition of success, which may view, for example, the pleasure of normal family life as a consolation prize for wimps
and losers. There is also usually a shared view of fairness and of legitimate reasons for discrimination based on the purposes of the
organization and a local understanding about rights.[2] But that a community shapes people's higher-order desires and even their conception
of the good life does not imply that it warps or damages them. The difficult thing is to decide what counts as an unwarped value, what is true as
opposed to false happiness, which desires are good and which not. That,
in turn, requires making some sense of the notion of the kind of well-
being that is appropriate to an autonomous person.

166

I have argued that autonomy is not a matter of the absence of causal influence; there is the right kind of causal influence on one's desires and the right kind of support from the institutions of society, and there is the wrong kind. Gauthier (1986, pp. 339, 351) identifies at least a necessary condition of the right kind in claiming that what is desirable is socialization that encourages people to cooperate in situations of mutual advantage, presumably including commons situations. The absence of all socialization, if it were possible, would not contribute to one's autonomy, as a wholly isolated life would not. The solution to the problem of autonomy is good government, or good management. This is part of what Aristotle means by his claim that a person of virtue must live in a great *polis.*

What then counts as morally good management? Chapters 4 and 6 argue that it won't do to say that good management characteristically makes one happy or meets one's personal objectives. This is more than a philosophical point: an organization can have a profound and not necessarily good effect on what one takes to be one's ends. How then do we distinguish treating people as means from treating them as company-made ends?[3] Are there ends that are just naturally good?

The story of the elevator operator in *Brave New World* suggests that there are indeed some things that are intrinsically desirable, apart from whether one desires them, hence that there are some things one has a reason to do whether or not one wants to do them. One is inclined to infer that the attainment of such things is a component of true happiness and that therefore it is good that one freely choose them. But the notion of real or natural happiness is hardly more plausible than that of a natural language that we do not speak only because we were taught some other, artificial language as children. The Aristotelian tradition takes the view that there are properties of any possible state of happiness, just as there are properties of any possible language. Although it understates the variety of ways in which people may live a good life, the tradition makes two claims that I think are not wrong: first, that the state of happiness characteristic of human beings has something to do with rationality, and second, that human beings characteristically live in communities and that the good life is a life in a good community. Particularly in the statement that politics is the culmination of ethics, Aristotle suggests that we can understand true happiness in large part by asking ourselves what characterizes a good community—that is, one that creates the conditions for a life that is appropriate to human nature.

The Aristotelian tradition is compatible with moral realism. In the discussion of the latter in Chapter 4, I acknowledged the possibility that there are true moral propositions but argued for skepticism about foundational moral principles and about the notion that making moral progress is a matter of learning how to apply such broad principles as theoretical ethics can discover. I claimed that it is essential from a moral point of view that conditions in the community be right for people to be moral. A crucial point of this chapter is that one of the most important things we can say about morality is what kind of community permits it to flourish.

But here our account appears to be nearly circular. We note that one's community greatly determines one's values, and we ask how to distinguish appropriate from inappropriate determination of values. The answer turns out to be that the community and its influence have to be of the right sort and that rationality and autonomy are somehow factors, and related ones. I have already claimed that by preserving the commons the good community makes it possible for people to be moral without being punished for it, but I need to be able to say more about morality and hence about the good community than just this.

What more I have said about happiness, justice, and rights is that the best account of them would be given in a Rawlsian community. Here I want to discuss three characteristics that are compatible with Rawls's view, although not part of Rawls's account, and that I believe would be attractive to the Rawlsian founders of an organization.

The first is freedom to opt in or out—precisely what Rawls stipulates citizens cannot be presumed to have and what therefore distinguishes citizens from employees. Friedman and other libertarians have argued that that freedom, created by a free labor market and the ability of willing parties to make contracts, guarantees all appropriate rights and justice as well. I have argued that it is usually a necessary condition of them, but not sufficient; in any case, exit is seldom as easy as it appears to be. The second is loyalty, a sense of community that causes people not to act as narrowly selfish rational maximizers. The lesson of the commons and similar games, taught by the likes of Schmidtz, Frank, and Hardin, is that in this territory Adam Smith and his libertarian successors are wrong: even if you are a rational maximizer at heart, your best long-term bet is to be cooperative, whether or not it is required by the best deal you can make for yourself; in any case, not everyone is a rational maximizer at heart.[4] The third is a particularly broad form of freedom of speech. It should be understood not only as freedom to speak and have some voice in deciding what happens but also as the freedom to participate in discussion of the values that unite the community as well as those that do not and the freedom to have a heterodox conception of the good. The second characteristic goes beyond the rational maximizing enshrined in the first; the third characteristic goes beyond the second in doing away with the notion that we must agree on and stick with a conception of the good life—that is, a conception of what counts as maximizing.

These minimal conditions of an ethical community, including an ethical organization, are what Hirschman (1970) calls exit, loyalty, and voice.[5]

EXIT, LOYALTY, AND VOICE

While membership in a community is a significant determinant of one's sense of oneself and of one's higher-order desires, a certain detachment is usually possible, and necessary for a critical consideration of one's principles, as befits a rational deliberator. Most American employees are at least sojourners in more than one community: unlike their Japanese counterparts, they rarely spend all their working lives in a single company, nor are so many aspects of their lives bound up with work. It is therefore easier for them to maintain the appropriate detachment, which, however, may take the form of an attachment to the principles and attitudes of a broader community.[6]

From this vantage point we can see new moral significance in the claim that one has a right to leave an organization. That is the crucial right that libertarians recognize; they claim that organizations that make life needlessly unpleasant or unfair for their employees will be punished in the marketplace as good people leave and must be replaced either inadequately or at a premium. The libertarian infers that it pays to be nice, that niceness prevails in the end unless a well-meaning but heavy-handed government intervenes. Niceness aside, the employee benefits from the opportunity to look for an organization whose culture is more congenial to his or her dispositions than is the current one.

Beyond that, the theory might add, if the right of exit is granted, then one can expect that, owing to turnover, fresh breezes will blow through organizations and bring with them some views critical of the local practices. It is important that the natives be able, and permitted, to ask questions of the form "Why *do* we do it this way rather than the way they do it?" and in that way identify certain assumptions and rules they have not previously considered or possibilities that have not occurred to them. But fresh breezes are not very important unless employees have some voice in the organization's affairs—more rights, at least, than the average libertarian will demand of an organization.

A third feature of a morally adequate community seems not to fit comfortably with the other two: it is a measure of loyalty, usually based on a certain emotional attachment among the participants, usually helping to preserve the commons. Where there is loyalty, management does not fire an employee just because a better one is available; employees refrain from free riding or otherwise maximizing their narrow individual interests at the expense of those of others in the organization, and they take as reasons for action certain organizational goals that are not obviously or directly in their own narrow interests. Loyalty engenders trust and so makes people in the organization more cooperative.

Exit, voice, and loyalty are certainly not components of an algorithm for calculating how to maximize anything. They are only necessary conditions, in some combination, of building a productive and moral organization, and they admit of quite a variety of interpretations. Of particular importance is moral progress in a community: it requires sufficient agreement about morality to support essential social arrangements and attitudes, but also sufficient disagreement to stimulate criticism of what has been largely agreed to. Hence, it requires the opportunity to exit, the right to voice one's views to some effect and to participate in ongoing moral dialogue, and the appropriate amount of loyalty to preserve the commons and otherwise to create economies—and, not incidentally, to foster personal attachments that are of value in themselves.

The moral manager must also create a structure and a culture that encourages commons-preserving behavior and dispositions, rather than a snake pit where only a fool or a martyr would act otherwise than on narrow self-interest—the sort of place Carr envisages. For an individual who must live in a less benign culture or a not-so-great *polis*, or for a manager who must compete in markets where competitors are not inclined to play by the rules, the task is more complicated, and largely beyond the scope of this essay.[7]

Hirschman claims that exit is the standard remedy for a market that does not meet one's needs, whereas voice is likely more appropriate in an unsatisfactory political body. Rawls would apparently agree. If, as I have argued, an organization is more like a political entity than a market, then exit is not an adequate remedy in a morally inferior organization.

To someone who takes a standard economist's view of utility and autonomy, exit is the closest thing to a guarantor of a morally sound organization. To someone who takes the commons problem seriously, loyalty is required to prevent the kind of classically rational behavior that can make the organization ineffective, to the detriment of all. To someone who just does not accept the standard local notions of rationality and utility, the good community features a certain notion of voice. If we map the progression by the people we have discussed in these pages, it goes from Friedman to Frank to Rorty.

EXIT

Communities create moral rules that, like contracts, generate duties and obligations. We have noted contract theory's appeal for business ethics, along with its limitations as a metaphor, and Keeley's (1988) extended elaboration on the view that an organization is a network of contracts. Friedman seems to take only one contract seriously, since he considers the organization for all moral purposes a market and the relationship between employer and employee like that between shopper and merchant. The opportunity for those who do not like the organization's operations to exit or not to enter in the first place is a sufficient safeguard against improper governance and a guarantee of the morally unproblematical status of the employment contract. The stockholders' agents may be dictators if and only if that is in the long run the most efficient way to run an organization.

There is no warrant for assuming that organizations are just like markets. In fact, if they were managed as markets they would not serve well even those limited purposes for which libertarians believe they are established. To defend that view is to give reasons for saying that neither employment at will nor deliberately marginal performance on an employee's part can be morally justified, for reasons not altogether different from those we give for saying that good governments have not the moral right to expel citizens at will and good citizens have not the moral right to refuse to be concerned with government or the welfare of their fellow-citizens.

That the purpose of the organization is neither so simple nor so closely held as the likes of Friedman have claimed, as I argued in Chapter 4, lends some plausibility to the view that moral duties and obligations arise in part from the just consent of the managed, but this just consent is not necessarily given once and for all at the moment one decides to become employed. Hence, the members should have some voice in deciding what the rules should be, and members of one organization may decide differently from those of another. One characteristic of a good contract is that it is not presented on a take-it-or-leave-it basis to parties that may be at a disadvantage in securing their interests, as employees are in some respects against a company; instead, it is fair and productive for all, made on a level playing field between parties that have much information, many options, and some equality of bargaining power.

Sometimes contracts have unexpected consequences; a party to a contract may not know his or her interests at the point of deciding whether to enter into a contract or may have first-order desires that are incompatible with his or her second-order desires, possibly as a result of social pressure. There are many ways in which the playing field may not be level, or the players not ready for the game.[8]

Exit is therefore not enough, as I argued in effect in Chapter 4. Now I want to maintain that unlimited exit is sometimes too much.

LOYALTY

At several points I have argued that no community is composed of classic rational maximizers. That is true whatever the local notions of rationality and one's best interests. I have also argued that moral people have emotions that support their behavior: for example, they feel repugnance at the thought of violating some serious social norm. Here I want to argue that a good community requires sentiments of loyalty among its members, who as a result find civic virtue not only a duty but a kind of pleasure.

Loyalty would require an organization not to dispose of an employee simply because the contract permits it and there is a better employee available. On the other side, if an employee has an opportunity to leave an organization and enter another on more favorable terms, loyalty requires that in making the decision one take the current employer's interests into account beyond what the contract and self-interest dictate. This sounds like an admirable way for people to act in an extended family or even a community, but it is much less clear that an organization ought to be this way. One thinks of paternalism and worse.

Yet loyalty contributes to organizational effectiveness. It preserves the commons by forestalling at least three bad economic consequences of not taking loyalty seriously. First, increased competition among organizations for employees and among employees for employers will probably cost more than is gained from the total increment in person-job fit. Second and more important, employers and employees will be less likely to make joint or long-term investments that will be in the interests of both—for example, in employee training specific to a certain workplace. Marriage, by rough analogy, is an institution of little importance and little reliability where it is readily terminable by either party. A benefit of the marriage vow, particularly "for better, for worse," is to reduce the risk of termination and gain the fruits of mutual confidence. (Frank [1988, pp. 49f.] makes this point.) Third, one who is loyal to an organization and others in it is far less likely to be a free rider; loyalty may preserve the commons.

Organizations, like all communities, must have serious boundaries: not everyone may enter, and members do not treat other community members as they treat nonmembers in distributing obligations and resources. Otherwise, membership is of no value and there is no meaningful "we," as in "who we are" or "we are better off if we are moral." Other things being equal, loyalty varies directly with the difficulty of entry (see Wolfe [1989, pp. 247ff] and Hirschman [1970, pp. 94f. and elsewhere]). Of course, it is possible for the cost of entry to be excessive, or for the conditions of entry to be illegitimate because not appropriately related to the legitimate purposes of the community, or otherwise unfair.

Denying full rights to women or entry to racial minorities, for example, would seem to be *prima facie* wrong for any sort of association; yet it might sometimes be appropriate on balance. Might there not be an association of French war veterans or Norwegian-Americans? A rule permitting birthright entry into the community would in some cases—in a nation or a family, for example—be a good rule; in a business it would be a highly questionable one. We have traditionally considered political entities and families similarly in this respect; they have been thought to be a permanent part of the person, while places of employment have been considered voluntary and temporary. As family and habitat become less closely related in a more mobile world, this tradition will likely not maintain its force. To the extent that such a change is occurring, we can set less store by Rawls's distinction between communities and associations on the basis that the former greatly determine one's interests and other essential aspects of oneself.[9]

As the organization is neither a market nor a political entity, we cannot assume that the only or best way to distribute obligations and resources is to have an internal free market or that due process can generate a set of rules that will adequately solve all issues of allocation. If the allocation were done purely on a free market basis, Rawlsian reasonable and rational founders would be faced with the possibility of a future in which they would get no goods because they were no longer contributors; if allocation were done without regard to one's contribution, there would be a problem about sufficient incentive for effort. (See Wolfe [1989, pp. 251ff].) The ratification of the distribution rules, whatever they are, according to due process then creates new rights and obligations and, if the rules are designed well, discourages free riders. There is some reason, too, to discourage exit, lest those who have benefited from the community take all the benefits and go elsewhere and so damage the commons, but it is hard to decide on exit costs and to enforce them fairly. All of these considerations argue that loyalty and care for one another's interests are required beyond what any possible rules or contracts, however carefully designed, could specify and beyond what libertarians advocate.

Loyalty has an emotional basis that requires community support, as do all appropriate dispositions. Knowledge of moral principles does not guarantee loyalty, or morally good action in general; one needs, among other things, the right attitude.[10] Nor do work rules and evaluation systems guarantee that an organization is a good one in which the commons will be preserved against narrow self-interest; one needs a sound corporate culture.

Corporate culture performs the crucial function of feeding emotions that affect the employees' desires and beliefs. Even where affection is lacking, rituals and symbols can help generate the kind of loyalty that causes employees to act in ways that benefit the organization; this can be true even if, owing to the difficulties of distributing compensation appropriately, there is no certainty that the employees will get paid for it. The loyal employee may further the organization's interests because it feels right to do so, or out of a conviction that it is the right thing to do, or out of a combination of the two. If that happens generally, then the probability of compensation for such action is increased. (This is one of those situations, crucial to certain religions, in which one's good works are rewarded if and only if one does not perform them in order to receive the reward.) Are Japanese workers relatively loyal because they believe the company will share its profits with them, or do they just want to be loyal to the company? Either motive strengthens the other.

It is characteristic of a loyal person to have a certain kind of second-order desire, for example to want to be motivated by whatever serves the interests of the beneficiary of one's loyalty (or whatever shows respect to that person or organization; think of why the Mazda employees described in Chapter 6 were supposed to wear the caps). As neither marriage nor the employment relationship can thrive if it is understood that each party may exit the moment a better opportunity comes along, it is rational to want and to cultivate, not the ability to grit one's teeth and make the best of it, but the actual desire to be true to one's spouse or one's employer, at least until there is good reason to desire otherwise.

As to second-order beliefs: a loyal person characteristically thinks it rational to believe that the beneficiary of loyalty is loyal as well. Rituals and symbols of the kind we associate with a strong corporate culture create emotions that support the kind of loyalty that makes employees want to be good corporate citizens and also to believe others are in the same situation.[11]

This is not to deny what is utterly obvious and very important: as there can be too little loyalty to preserve the commons, so there can be too much to permit the voices of rational reflection or the appropriate readiness to exercise the exit option. Loyalty, involving as it does people's second-order desires, is particularly susceptible to influence by a strong corporate culture and to abuse. In generating loyalty and its related second-order desires and beliefs, a strong corporate culture may cause people to believe what is not true and not even self-fulfilling—to love Big Brother. Particularly if these beliefs are second-order and characteristically stable, they are not likely to be much affected in the short run if one notices instances of unexpected behavior by one's colleagues.[12]

VOICE

That an organization resembles a political entity more than it does a buyer in a labor market was noted many years before I wrote Chapter 4 of this book and will not come as news to scholars who write about consensus building and dominant coalitions or to managers who know about them firsthand. Management decisions are for practical purposes usually subject to some participation, no matter what the official reporting relationships are. Where decision making has to be dispersed in a diversified organization facing a turbulent environment, empowerment may be a cold-blooded strategy. Employees often assert political rights that have to do with protection from corporate authority as well as participation in managerial decisions. In so doing they reject the view that exit is the only legitimate means of changing one's situation and assume that an employee is not only a party to a contract but a part of a community. That the community has purposes incompatible with certain forms of democracy does not cancel its obligation to treat employees as ends in themselves. There is thus a moral presumption in favor of some process whereby members have a voice in the organization. I have noted that Rorty takes democracy to be prior to morality in a political entity; the point is that democracy comes as close as is possible to guaranteeing a moral society. The analogous claim for organizations would be that due process is the single most important factor in the moral status of an organization. Justice rests on a system of negotiation that incorporates insofar as possible the features of the original position.

As Rawls would certainly agree, it would not do for a bad government to hold that, if you don't like it in Springfield, you can always leave and go live somewhere else. A famous passage from Hume (quoted in Wills [1990, p. 264]) applies here:

> Can we seriously say that a poor peasant or artisan has a free choice to leave his country when he knows no foreign language or manners and lives from day to day, by the small wages he acquires? We may as well assert that a man, by remaining on a vessel, freely consents to the dominion of the master, though he was carried on board while asleep and must leap into the ocean and must perish the moment he leaves her.

Most employees were not carried on board while asleep, but many of them had no idea at the outset what they were getting into[13] and many have learned a language and manners as well as specific job-related skills that will not stand them in good stead elsewhere. Granted, an organization's practices and rules are supported by tacit agreements whose very existence creates obligations for those in the community, so long as it is possible to opt out of the agreements by leaving the community. But exit is a wholly adequate solution to moral problems in an organization only if the agreements are wholly adequate from a moral point of view.

What is morally adequate, like what is organizationally effective, may differ from one community to another when the communities have different histories and different networks of purpose. The New Jersey Devils, Carleton College, Youngstown, the legal department of IBM, and the Kurds should not all have the same rules, because their activities and purposes and circumstances differ. I noted in Chapter 6 that different industries require different cultures of successful competitors (see Gordon [1991]), as national differences reflect differing historical and geographical circumstances. Thurow (1994, p. 8) argues that in a dynamic environment, where moving the production-possibility curve to the right is more important than being on the curve, the Japanese strategy of reducing the individual employee's risks and putting the risks on the organization (by offering lifetime employment and seniority-based compensation) reduces individuals' otherwise rational resistance to technological change, with the result that what is good for the organization is good for the individual.[14] The prevalence of this situation may make loyalty a bourgeois virtue.

Considerations of this sort may lead us to ask whether American values might appropriately change as circumstances do. What ought to become of our concept of freedom when there is no longer so much space to spare and urban life changes our relationships much as Jefferson feared it would? The right to freedom of a certain kind and extent will depend in part on the consequences of its exercise. When cooking and ironing are no longer so time-consuming, or physical strength necessary for the family's survival, it makes sense for the relations between the genders to change over time. This is not to say, however, that survival of a moral principle or notion is a conclusive test of its legitimacy.

If it is true that American corporations are becoming uncompetitive relative to foreign counterparts against which they have not had to compete in the past, and if this is in part a result of differences in the way our companies and theirs are managed, then there is not only prudential but also moral warrant for reconsidering our ways of management. For what makes organizational effectiveness part of a moral justification is that cooperation creates a surplus that benefits all participants, particularly where the participants can withhold their cooperation if unsatisfied or influence how benefits are distributed. If the systems and structures that make the organization competitive are incompatible with the protection of certain employee rights or certain levels of fairness in distributing goods, however, then members of the community ought to have some recourse other than loyalty or departure.

Choice, before or even after the point of hiring, does not guarantee that the organization is a good community, for at least two reasons. First, there are problems about arranging things so that people's desires support one another, rather than destructively compete, as much as possible. This is much of what politics is about, and a tall order it is. Second, both freedom to choose a community and freedom to choose within a community are compatible with being acculturated to have and fulfill bad desires and so act against one's best interests. Neither problem is worrisome for libertarians, for whom there is no other sense of freedom than being permitted to indulge one's desires; hence, for libertarians communities do not in any important sense create freedom, except that they may broaden one's range of acceptable choices. Nor does another person's success at my expense bother a libertarian, unless coercion is involved.

But a good community also affects people's choices, in part by fostering and rewarding higher-order dispositions to associate with others in ways that support cooperation. This it does not just by designing and imposing principles: I have argued that we cannot find principles or codifiable practices that will grant all participants in any kind of community the sort of freedom appropriate to humans in full possession of their faculties. It is too much to expect that a good community might find stone tablets with such principles on them. On the other hand, it is not enough to expect that it will grant people some sort of vote on community decisions; democracy does not guarantee morality in the workplace any more than it does anywhere else. Least of all does it protect people from the kind of brainwashing of which a strong corporate culture is capable. A good community, whether an organization or not, encourages the kind of reflection and discussion that creates moral progress, among other ways by enhancing people's ability to contemplate the various forms the good life might take.

DEALING WITH MANY VOICES

It is characteristic of a Rawlsian community that a variety of conceptions of the good life may coexist peacefully, while at the same time the citizens are in consensus on a single set of principles that govern the laws and rules by which they govern their own public behavior. The result is supposed to be the best possible balance of freedom and civic order.[15] For reasons I have given several times, we can expect people within a community to have similar conceptions of the good life even though it is not a moral requirement. If anything, it may be an impediment to moral progress that conceptions of the good vary within a very narrow range. That people are free to discuss their moral differences and examine the public rules they share, while not guaranteeing that true morality will eventually triumph, will keep open the possibility that the community will move in the right direction.

Chapter 4 argued that a community's moral standards and practices are not simply applications of principles of utility, justice, and rights to some particular situation, as the term "applied ethics" would suggest. If that is right, then we would expect good principles and their favored applications to evolve together over time in a way that is consistent with the predominant local conception of the good life—a conception that, particularly as it is not likely unanimous, may change in part in response to changing circumstances and opportunities. Through experience over generations in dealing with one another, community members develop a shared understanding of the meanings and consequences of their actions and a sense of what they are willing to live with. Contrary to what Rawls may seem to have suggested before 1985, no set of founders, however objective, can decide in advance of their lives together what their public rules ought to be in detail, for the same reason people cannot decide in advance of anyone's having built an organization or decided on its mission what structures and processes and culture will make it most effective. The lawgivers in the original position cannot know what will succeed or even what will count as success.

Genuinely useful principles come out of our experience with each other, as scientific methodological principles come out of practicing science; they do not precede it. In the course of that experience certain values and principles may change, for the better if we make moral progress. We reach ever better principles and highest-order desires through experience and conversations and negotiations over a long time in a variety of circumstances.

For the sake of both moral progress and personal freedom, a good community will welcome differing views not only of specific rules but also of the nature of the good life and will have ways of accommodating them, particularly when they do not involve public matters, and ways of resolving disputes among them; in that sense it will be pluralistic. There will be and should always be competing honest conceptions of the good life, a plurality of views on moral issues that permits an overlapping consensus on public justice. Substantive moral disagreements will often create disagreements about how to adjudicate disputes, and no morally neutral procedure is likely to come to the fore, but we may hope that something widely acceptable does.[16]

I am not talking merely about keeping the peace, however. Conversation and interaction with one another may lead people to agree, but may also lead them to reflect on their preferences and even change their views about what is in their interests, what counts as success. (See Wolfe [1989, p. 261].) The kind of voice that is afforded by a good community not only permits expressing one's preferences but also encourages developing them. I argued in Chapter 5 that it is characteristic of humans that their second-order desires change over time in a way that violates the assumptions of standard economic theory. Our autonomy consists in part in our ability not only to get what we desire but also to decide—no doubt in part through interaction and conversation with others in the community—what is desirable.[17] We can think of a good community as one in which people negotiate and accommodate in their best interests according to rules that represent what Rawls (1993) calls an overlapping consensus and preserve the commons. We need not, however, buy all the assumptions of game theory that that conception suggests; communities, including organizations, are places in which preferences, values, and interests are not only represented but developed, even created. So I claimed in the discussion of corporate culture; so I have implied in what I have said about moral progress.[18]

I mean these claims to apply to organizations as well as political entities, but I do not minimize the differences between them. One difference is that the former will typically be closer to a consensus on nonpublic matters, in part because within the organization the line between public and nonpublic will be less clearly drawn. The libertarian view of *the* purpose of the organization is wrong, I have argued, and Rawls is therefore more reluctant than he needs to be about applying his machinery to organizations on account of relative focus on purpose. It is true that the purposes of an organization are usually fewer, more closely related, and more readily identifiable than are those of a political entity. What I have said about corporate culture implies that there may be more unanimity on moral issues, more loyalty to the community, and therefore more pressure for moral consensus in an organization than in a political entity. For that reason we may find it more rather than less wrenching to leave an organization compared to a nation-state, although it is probably true that exit from an organization is usually easier than exit from one's community, and that easier exit makes democracy less important.

I believe Hirschman would generally agree, since he thinks an organization is somewhere between a market and a political entity. Wisely,

Hirschman does not try to state the precisely appropriate balance of exit, loyalty, and voice for organizations. In Japanese organizations loyalty is more prominent; in American ones exit is more common; German organizations give voice a comparatively strong role.[19] There may be no way to state which is best or, therefore, what is the right balance among the three features. It may turn out that each is best for its national culture, as in different industries different corporate cultures work best. In any case, none is static.

How would we decide that, for example, American organizations ought to encourage more mutual loyalty? Would we apply some principles of utility or justice to this situation? The best we can do is hardly better than trial and error, since we cannot know in advance whether, for example, removing the risks associated with technological change from the individual and placing them on the organization will in fact give individuals an appropriate incentive to perform; it may be that loyalty cannot take root in soil in which it is not expected. To put the matter in terms more familiar to organizational theorists, we *satisfice* in making moral rules and developing community practices. In principle there is no way of knowing when we have the best practice we can get and no way of knowing whether further effort toward improvement will be worth what it will cost. For that matter, we have no way of knowing whether the cost of finding out whether further effort will be worth what it will cost will itself be worth what it will cost. We start from where we are and go on trying to do better, and we listen to the objections of those who believe we are not doing well enough.

One cannot distinguish a good scientific theory from a bad one by holding the theories up to the world and seeing whether they match it, and one cannot find any set of principles that permanently and definitively distinguishes good theories from bad ones. There are rules about the conduct of research, but even these, which scientists make up as they go along, will not last forever. The case of morality is much the same: the process is the key. Rorty (1991) sums up his views by claiming the priority of democracy to philosophy; Rawls (1985, 1993) calls justice political, not metaphysical.[20] The most important thing we can say about morality as a human institution is not that it follows from this or that set of principles or that it is based on this or that theory of human nature but that it is a result of a process that institutionalizes our inclination to find and agree on principles and institutions and emotions and virtues that no one who shares this inclination can reasonably reject. And what principles and so on are these? We learn only by setting the process in motion; even then, what we learn will not be true for all times and places.

The way to make moral progress, then, is to create communities in which people are able to think, speak, and act freely within broad guidelines of civility and discursiveness, in which certain moral and ideological views are not to affect policy, and in which people are loyal to the community but able to abandon ship if their loyalty is not adequately reciprocated. The results tell us something about the good life.

As I claimed in Chapter 4, "applied" ethics precedes and drives "theoretical" ethics insofar as our principles come from conventions we decide we can reasonably[21] accept, rather than the other way around. Whatever intuitions and principles we develop, new situations and new needs will affect our intuitions, and so eventually our principles. And the process does not end.

I do not mean to overstate what goes on in organizations: they are not seminars. They are, however, arenas in which preferences and values are formed. People in organizations do not propound universal moral theories as much as they simply reach agreements about how things are to be done locally. Such agreements, however, are the basis for the moral theories we do have. The process cannot happen purely rationally; it is not clear what it would mean to say that it had happened purely rationally. We do know, however, what it means for preferences and values to be formed irrationally. We know what radical authoritarianism looks like in organizations; we can recognize suppression of individuality; we can recognize certain forms of brainwashing.

We may be mistaken in believing we can describe the opposites of brainwashing and oppression. We may be inclined to believe that perfect freedom is a matter of detachment from one's organization: no identification with corporate objectives, no emotional ties to others in the organization, utter imperviousness to the influence of the local culture, self-interested rationality. And if the standard economist's assumptions were right—if, in particular, our interests were fixed and independent of our community—that view might have some merit.

In practice, the most autonomy we can have is to be members of a community in which we can vote and/or negotiate and be given maximum freedom compatible with like freedom for others to pursue our interests, while remaining free to think through with others like ourselves what we should take our interests to be. Where the community is an organization, we must take account of two additional factors: first, that there is one cluster of interests that nearly all members of the community will share and that requires members to bind themselves to cooperative effort, and second, that changing one's job is easier than changing one's citizenship. I do not believe these differences affect my claim about autonomy. In making that claim I have gone a bit beyond the letter, but not the spirit, of Aristotle: not only the good person but the autonomous one must live in the right kind of *polis*.

Moral progress cannot be rapid. If rules governing important relations could be readily changed, then the bonds of morality that make us reliable and trustworthy to each other and even to ourselves might be weakened to the detriment of our community. It follows that justifying change in the name of moral progress will be a significant task. Where the community in question is an organization, a certain useful detachment will be easier to achieve, but what we know about strong corporate cultures should not give us much confidence in people's ability to assess and criticize local norms and expectations. These are often unspoken; when they are articulated, they cannot be couched in neutral language, for there is no such thing. The good news about languages associated with particular organizational cultures, however, is that for most people in the organization there are other languages available, at least to the extent that the locals have a life outside the organization. There are, if not neutral languages, at least alternatives to any particular language, with different presuppositions. As I argued in Chapter 4, we did not experience a great change in our view of the legitimate status of women because someone noticed one day that principles of justice were not being applied properly. The change in attitude is ongoing, and it coincides with a change in language.

Moral progress requires that people look at things differently—I have argued that this is one of the functions of literature and of some case studies—and thus see them anew; to that end, the community ought to be hospitable to the voices of outsiders. In the case of companies, that would surely include women's voices, which would convey not only discursive arguments in favor of women's rights but also new perspectives historically associated with women.[22]

Even as a community permits dissent and heterodoxy, it must necessarily also rest on a degree of consensus if it is to be a community at all, as I have argued from several angles. Although disagreement within communities is a stimulus to reflection, hence an engine of moral progress, there are some necessary limits to those disagreements. Even coherent argument, as opposed to shouting, presupposes a common language and some common ground from which to argue; a moral argument presupposes that the disputants share at least some views about the nature of the good life.

The mere act of explaining your own and others' behavior presupposes the same; this too I have argued more than once. Within a community you can both explain and justify behavior (the two activities do overlap) by reference to norms of reasonableness and appropriateness that most members of the community share. It is no explanation in any community in which you and I live to say "I beat the man up because he is a heretic." Fortunately. When you deliberate you take certain considerations to be reasons for action; these reasons are normally the ones by reference to which you and your fellow-members of the community explain yourselves to one another, without the need for much interpretation.[23] As I noted in Chapter 6, communities and organizations may even be said to create or enact reality in the sense that they develop a system of definitions and beliefs as well as agreements on the moral rules. It would not be a good thing to undermine this system all at once, even if it were possible.

A good community thus encourages reflection, for example concerning the very second-order desires that the community encourages, but at the same time fosters a loyalty that reflection may in due course undermine, as well as second-order desires that let one fit into one's surroundings. What is needed is just enough reflection to keep moral progress going, hence a subtle combination of devotion to the local rules most of the time and occasional willingness to reconsider some of them. As in any community, we learn over time what balance of generosity and selfishness, of love and wariness, can support the good life in an organization. In so doing, we also balance loyalty and detachment. It is most difficult to determine the right balance in advance or in general, and it is risky to extrapolate confidently from one community to another, but the assumption loyalty makes is that we are together in the search for the appropriate rules and the appropriate attitude towards them, and not that the search has ended. As the conversation goes on, our conception of the good life may change as well; that is one way we make moral progress. If Aristotle is right, part of this process is self-discovery; it is also a lengthy and not entirely self-conscious invention of emotions and desires as well as reasons, a process of which only humans, in groups, are capable: the invention of ourselves.

THE GOOD LIFE AND THE GOOD COMMUNITY

Let us end where we began, with the question whether morality makes us better off. I believe that answering this question is primarily a matter of reviewing the ideas we have generated to this point. Since first asking that question I have argued that being better off is a state that may differ from one person to another and for one person from one time to another, depending in part on the norms of one's community, which affect what satisfies those who live there.

What makes the question pertinent to the topic of business ethics is the role of the community in the answer. I have argued against certain plausible assumptions or consequences of standard utilitarianism, individualism, and libertarianism to get to the view that a moral life is one possible form of the good life and that a good community, which can be an organization, characteristically causes the moral life and the good life to overlap. The usual way to effect the overlap is to reward moral behavior and to punish its opposite, but where the community is an organization and the issue is the individual's contribution to organizational effectiveness, that may not be possible. Because one's interests encompass others' interests, and because one's interests can be influenced by one's surroundings, however, a good community can support the overlap by helping individuals cultivate and satisfy a desire for civic virtue or its organizational equivalent. In an organization, corporate culture is an effective vehicle for doing this.

How can you tell what is in your interests? Well, suppose you could have anything you wanted, including any higher-order desires you chose to have.[24] What would you choose, and why? You might first be tempted to demand an unlimited supply of Cabernet Sauvignon, sex with certain attractive people, and an excellent sound system reproducing your favorite music. These are presumably a few of your favorite things; having them would make you happy. On sober reflection, however, you might decide that that list of gifts would not truly serve your best interests and so choose these most obviously attractive things in moderation, but also some less exciting, more lasting goods, such as health and friendship. Here, though, a difficulty might arise: assuming you could not choose away the laws of biology or those of logic, you might find yourself unable to satisfy your desire for Cabernet and at the same time maintain a healthy liver.

You could avoid this dilemma, to say nothing of improving your chances for getting what you want, if you could arrange to *desire* less extravagant prizes. In that way, by changing your desires, you would achieve the great happiness that so often comes with true autonomy—getting what you not only want but want to want. You are in effect choosing what shall be in your own best interests, and you are necessarily not doing it in a narrowly self-interested way. This is sometimes possible: one can cultivate certain desires and keep oneself away from bad influences. Might we then choose lives so circumscribed that we would be happy with little, perhaps with just a steady job running an elevator? Surely not: just being the sort of people who could deliberate about the good life would make us choose something more interesting than that.[25]

What it is rational to choose to desire depends heavily on one's circumstances, however. In a certain kind of situation, perhaps one not far removed from the state of nature and certainly familiar to people in investment banking and certain branches of the law, one might reasonably choose to want be aggressive, even brutal, in order to survive; one might take steps to keep oneself from being tempted toward mellow vulnerability. Of course, it would be preferable to be in a situation in which the commons is preserved by unselfish behavior and other-directed emotions, and it would be rational in that situation to follow suit. It is reasonable, therefore, to try to make agreements and create structures and cultures that will support that kind of situation, and that is what a moral manager does. If you are a professional, then you have reason to cultivate the appropriate professional virtues. If you have a significant chance of getting a position in a morally good organization, then it makes sense to cultivate certain bourgeois virtues, including those named by Solomon (1992) and McCloskey (1994): dependability, industry, toughness.

You may be tempted to believe instead that in a community in which every else is a contributor it would be rational for you to want to have the desires characteristic of a free rider, but there would be no advantage to you in that kind of higher-order desire. On the contrary, if you acted on that desire, you might have a subversive effect on the community and in due course on yourself. On the other hand, in a community in which some people are free riders—the usual state of affairs—it is not rational to want to want to be a contributor all the time. On the basis of what I have argued so far, following Rapoport, Dixit and Nalebuff, and Schmidtz, your wisest course would normally be to want to want to be a conditional contributor: you ought to want to be the sort of person who contributes until others clearly show they will not; then you can reciprocate by withholding your contribution. You should want your desires to combine charity and a sense of self-respect that demands fair treatment for yourself as well as for others.

We can give nearly the same answer to two apparently different questions: (1) What sort of community would be created by a self-interested but also rational individual who could choose not only the nature of the community but also his or her own nature? and (2) What sort of community would be created by a person or group of people able to be realistic but entirely objective and detached even from their own higher-order desires, as the Rawlsian founders appear to be?

Now consider the following question: (3) What would you want for yourself if you could have anything you wanted, taking desires of all orders into account? It should be answered in this way by a reasonable person: If I were in the kind of community described in response to questions (1) and (2), I would want to have higher-order desires that would lead to my being happy there and that would contribute to maintaining a good situation for everyone; thus, I would want to be a person of civic virtue rather than a free rider. In a less good community, I would still want to want to contribute to moral progress and (therefore) not be a patsy.

Does this mean that one should want to be an organization man in the sense made grimly famous by Whyte (1956)? Surely not: these desires are appropriate only in the right kind of organization; the loyalty implied in these desires is and must be given without immediate proof that it will be reciprocated, but it is not blind. There is usually some evidence available concerning the probable costs and benefits of loyalty; anyone who is unpleasantly surprised too often can change to a reciprocating strategy.

None of this argument quite shows that morality serves the moral person's interests, but it does not miss by much. It shows that what is moral is identical, or nearly so, with what a reasonable person would want to be the object of his or her highest-order desires, given the way things are. If we believe that one's community significantly determines one's interests, then the pressing question is what sort of community, if any, best determines and serves its members' interests. The moral organization does that. No less important, it leaves open for further discussion questions about what is truly desirable.

I have argued that a good organization will protect autonomy, preserve the commons, and encourage moral progress under these conditions: its employees are permitted to leave it unless it satisfies them; there is a measure of commons-preserving loyalty among the participants; and participants are encouraged to discuss and consider the principles and values that the organization presses on them. Such an organization supports its participants' search for the good life, seeks consensus among people with different values, creates significant overlaps between morality and self-interest, and reduces the probability of brainwashing, but it does not guarantee happiness for all. If Rawlsian founders knew enough about life in organizations and were able to make some choices about desires, I think they would choose this way.

The tension between individual rationality and the community's socializing power raises problems that are not new. Aristotle seems to be dealing with that same tension when he constructs a theory on which an account of the good community and an account of the good person cannot be given separately from each other. He holds that it is essential to the person to be both rational and civilized, but he places limits on the importance of rationality and emphasizes the importance of emotions and of one's surroundings in taking the view that virtue is a matter of having learned through habituation to get pleasure from the right sort of action and so, as I interpret him, to have interests of the right sort. In a good community, the interests of its participants must not be narrowly self-regarding or entirely selfless. Instead, the citizens must want what will preserve the commons; in the long run the community serves their interests well in part because it shapes their interests well, within limits.

Sam Rayburn and Lyndon Johnson were fond of saying that politics is the art of the possible. We might say the same of business ethics. It is not—in fact, ethics is not—primarily about how people ought to act in the Kingdom of Ends, where moral behavior is always reciprocated. If morality were about that, it would amount to nonstrategic altruism, and Carr would be right in saying that ethics is disastrous for businesspeople. Nor should we begin thinking about ethics by assuming that every agent is narrowly selfish. Morality is about what sort of community causes ordinary people to believe, to prefer, to feel, and to act so that they are better off on the whole.

From various sides we have heard the suggestion that both morality and autonomy have to do with what is intrinsically or even naturally desirable, apart from what people actually desire, perhaps under the questionable influence of a culture. Aristotle suggests the right approach in saying that humans are naturally political as well as rational and that politics is the culmination of ethics. What is naturally and intrinsically desirable, or as close to it as we are going to get, lies somewhere among whatever things people in the kind of community we have been discussing encourage one another to desire. That is at the core of a correct account of autonomy, of the good life, and of morality; if we believe that an organization ought to be a good community, it is important to business ethics as well.

NOTES

1. I have not tried to define the notion of community in advance of describing the good community; I think that would be doing it backwards. I did say in Ch. 1 that a number of people constitute a community if they share a language and, therefore, certain beliefs and the ability to understand each other's behavior and to communicate because they share those beliefs and certain preferences as well. Another feature of a community that is appropriately noted in this chapter is the prominence of bonds of loyalty.

2. The point is not that a community gets to decide arbitrarily what rights people have—it does not, for the local consensus may be wrong—but that even some of the important rights we have are based in part on expectations and tacit agreements that may be justified in part by their consequences. (The reasons for all these qualifications are given in Ch. 4.) More generally, what is right depends in part on expectations and feelings we develop together over a long period of time.

3. It would be hard to get Kant to take this question seriously, for his view of free will (though not of autonomy) is similar to the one I attack in Ch. 5.

4. Rawls (1993) almost never mentions loyalty, but some of his discussions of cooperation and reciprocity (for example, at 320ff.) show the importance of loyalty in a community.

5. Hirschman introduced exit, voice, and loyalty and has shown their usefulness for a variety of contexts. Wolfe (1989) has had more to say about them, and my debt to him, as well as to Hirschman, is great.

6. The ancient Cynics and Stoics, as opposed to Aristotle, celebrated the cosmopolitan, who is influenced by a variety of cultures and is consequently not the prisoner of just one. That is the modern predicament, which has its advantages. We who move among communities are more inclined than Aristotle to worry about the parochiality of community-based virtue. In part as a result, we are also more inclined to view morality as having to do with principles rather than with the more local and personal virtue of the kind Aristotle sponsors.

7. As Solomon (1992) argues, the war of all against all is not and cannot be so common in business as is often supposed; this problem is less pressing than we might think, but it is pressing enough. I suggested in Chs. 3 and 4 that a somewhat lenient version of reciprocity is called for against uncooperative stakeholders.

8. For much more along these lines, see Keeley (1988, especially Ch. 5). But Keeley worries about the notion of false consciousness, which can lead to a tendentious account of autonomy. (See Ch. 5, note 14.)

9. Even if I am overstating the extent to which organizations determine one's interests, we can still learn something about the legitimate rights of employees by imagining how stakeholders in the original position would rule.

10. This is neither obvious nor uncontroversial. Philosophers from Socrates to R. M. Hare have been remarkably faithful to the notion that knowledge of what is right is sufficient for right action.

11. Loyalty is not an emotion, but since loyalty is seldom the result of a transaction based on mutual self-interest, we have reason to believe that where there is loyalty, there are always emotions. Affection and a feeling of duty or honor, which often but not always overlap, are two of the common emotional supports of loyalty.

12. Why is one better off in the long run in a Prisoner's Dilemma game if one cuts the other player some slack rather than retaliate against each defection? The gesture is a self-fulfilling prediction that the other player is not wholly uninterested in one's welfare

13. Those who think an employment contract is typically made between a willing buyer and a willing seller would profit from reading Hamper's (1991) description of recruitment and the workplace at GM.

14. This argument helps to explain the Yankelovich-Immerwahr (1983) finding that Japanese workers are far more likely than their American counterparts to believe that they will prosper if and only if their company does. Note that Thurow shows a way of explaining their view, even though the notion of rationality he invokes is the standard economist's rather than the broader one I have supported.

15. In an organization even more than than in a political community, it is important to separate what the public (and overlapping) consensus holds and what each participant holds in private. That is because it is important for an employee to have an inviolate life apart from the organization. No less important than your right to leave your job and get another one is your right to leave your workplace every day and go home.

This private-public distinction will have only limited appeal to those who think the personal is political. In truth, the line between the public and the private is not so easy to draw, but for practical purposes we must draw it, for dictatorship and moral stagnation are the alternative.

16. Rawls does not finally claim universality for his method or its results. He acknowledges (1985) that there is something parochial about his liberal methodology, as it presupposes that the populace is made up of free and equal people, but he sees nothing preferable for people like us. Here we may recall a point from Ch. 1 and ask what we would say of aliens who claimed to come from a distant planet on which morality had nothing to do with freedom or equality.

17. The term *autonomy* is of Greek provenance; the components mean self and law. In this spirit Wolfe (esp. pp. 212, 261) claims that we are not only rule followers but rule makers and that being free is a matter not only of expressing our nature but of creating it. Wolfe has a number of criticisms of Rawls's views as of 1971 but seems to have no problems with his constructivist approach in general.

18. Socrates claimed that the unexamined life is not worth living. In contributing to our conversation, he might claim that whatever else the good life is, it has something to do with working out what the good life is.

19. The root of the term *Mitbestimmung* (codetermination) is *Stimme* (voice).

20. Rawls (1993; e.g., 338f., 357) holds that philosophical doctrines by themselves do not solve all political problems, including morally significant ones. In some cases we must simply try to find grounds for agreement among our public understandings.

21. Rawls distinguishes reasonable from rational: the former is characteristic of those who are willing to abide by appropriate principles if others are. They have the now familiar inclination to find and agree on principles that no one who has this inclination can reasonably reject.

22. One can see the significance of the title of Carol Gilligan's work on what she considers the female approach to ethics: *In a Different Voice* (1982). Gilligan's work is in part a critique of that of Kohlberg (1981), who assumes without significant argument that Kantian ethics represent an advance over Aristotelian

ethics. Evelyn Fox Keller (1983; for a shorter version, see 1985, Ch. 8) argued that it was a characteristically female faculty (something like Aristotelian practical wisdom) that made Barbara McClintock a great scientist. McClintock herself had spoken of a "feeling for the organism" but did not entirely accept Keller's analysis. Derry (1991 and elsewhere) has related her criticisms of standard rationality to feminist concerns. I do not claim that Aristotelian views come naturally to women, although I did argue earlier that practical wisdom is important, and as it happens I cited two women in so doing. In any case, a good community improves our practical wisdom.

23. The predicate " . . . is in the same community as . . ." is strictly speaking a matter of degree.

24. Rawls (1993) envisages his founders being able to do just this in the original position. See Lecture III, p. 107, and Lecture VII, p. 268, for example.

25. This does not tell us what sort of life is really good; it tells us only what sort of life people like us can find to be good. But this is the best we can do.

Bibliography

Allaire, Yvan, and Mihaela E. Firsirotu. 1984. "Theories of Organizational Culture." *Organization Studies* 5, 193–226.

Altman, Andrew. 1984. "Pragmatism and Applied Ethics." *American Philosophical Quarterly* 21, 227–235.

Aristotle. 1894. *Ethica Nicomachea.* Ed. I. Bywater. Oxford: Clarendon Press.

———. 1924. *Metaphysica.* Ed. W. D. Ross. Oxford: Clarendon Press.

———. 1957. *Politica.* Ed. W. D. Ross. Oxford: Clarendon Press.

———. 1965. *De Arte Poetica.* Ed. Rudolf Kassel. Oxford: Clarendon Press.

———. 1985. *Nicomachean Ethics.* Trans. Terence Irwin. Indianapolis: Hackett Publishing Company.

Arrington, Robert L. 1989. *Rationalism, Realism, and Relativism: Perspectives in Contemporary Moral Epistemology.* Ithaca, N.Y.: Cornell University Press.

Asch, Solomon E. 1955. "Studies of Independence and Conformity: A Minority of One Against a Unanimous Majority." *Psychological Monographs* 70. 9, Whole no. 416.

Bennett, William J. 1993. *The Book of Virtues.* New York: Simon and Schuster.

Bork, Robert H. 1971. "Neutral Principles and Some First Amendment Problems." *Indiana Law Journal* 47, 1–35.

Bowie, Norman E. 1987. "The Moral Obligations of Multinational Corporations." In *Problems of International Justice,* ed. Steven Luper-Foy, 97–113. New York: Westview Press.

———. 1991. "Challenging the Egoistic Paradigm." *Business Ethics Quarterly* 1, 1–21.

———. 1991a. "Business Ethics as a Discipline: The Search for Legitimacy." In *Business Ethics: The State of the Art,* ed. R. Edward Freeman, 17–41. New York: Oxford University Press.

Boyd, Richard N. 1988. "How to Be a Moral Realist." In *Essays on Moral Realism,* ed. Geoffrey Sayre-McCord, 181–228. Ithaca, N.Y.: Cornell University Press.

Braybrooke, David. 1987. "Social Contract Theory's Fanciest Flight." *Ethics* 97, 750–764.

Brink, David O. 1989. *Moral Realism and the Foundations of Ethics.* New York: Cambridge University Press.

Buchanan, Allen. 1985. *Ethics, Efficiency, and the Market.* Totowa, N.J.: Rowman & Allanheld.

———. 1994. "Perfecting Imperfect Duties: Collective Action to Create Moral Obligations." Unpublished.

189

Burke, James E. 1985. "Speech to the Advertising Council." In *Management of Values: The Ethical Difference in Corporate Policy and Performance*, ed. Charles S. McCoy, 325–331. Boston: Pitman.

Carr, Albert Z. 1984. "Is Business Bluffing Ethical?" In *Business Ethics: Readings and Cases in Corporate Morality*, ed. W. Michael Hoffman and Jennifer Mills Moore, 451–456. New York: McGraw-Hill Book Company.

————. 1989. "Can an Executive Afford a Conscience?" In *Contemporary Moral Controversies in Business*, ed. A. Pablo Iannone, 23–29. New York: Oxford University Press.

Cartwright, Nancy. 1983. *How the Laws of Physics Lie.* New York: Oxford University Press.

Ciulla, Joanne B. 1990. "Business Ethics as Moral Imagination." In *Business Ethics: The State of the Art*, ed. R. Edward Freeman, 212–220. New York: Oxford University Press.

Cooper, John M. 1986. *Reason and Human Good in Aristotle.* Indianapolis: Hackett Publishing Company.

Cox, Susan Jane Buck. 1985. "No Tragedy on the Commons." *Environmental Ethics* 7, 49–61.

Darwall, Stephen, Allan Gibbard, and Peter Railton. 1992. "Toward *Fin de siècle* Ethics: Some Trends." *Philosophical Review* 101, 115–189.

Davidson, Donald. 1984. "On the Very Idea of a Conceptual Scheme." In *Inquiries into Truth and Interpretation*, 183–198. Oxford: Clarendon Press.

Dennett, Daniel C. 1984. *Elbow Room: The Varieties of Free Will Worth Wanting.* Cambridge, Mass.: MIT Press.

Derry, Robbin. 1991. "Institutionalizing Ethical Motivation: Reflections on Goodpaster's Agenda." In *Business Ethics: The State of the Art*, ed. R. Edward Freeman, 121–136. New York: Oxford University Press.

Derry, Robbin, and Ronald M. Green. 1989. "Ethical Theory in Business Ethics: A Critical Assessment." *Journal of Business Ethics* 8, 521–533.

Dixit, Avinash, and Barry Nalebuff. 1991. *Thinking Strategically: The Competitive Edge in Business, Politics, and Everyday Life.* New York: W. W. Norton and Company.

Donaldson, Thomas, and Thomas W. Dunfee. 1994. "Toward a Unified Conception of Business Ethics: Integrative Social Contracts Theory." *Academy of Management Review* 19, 252–284.

————. 1995. "Integrative Social Contracts Theory: A Communitarian Conception of Economic Ethics." *Economics and Philosophy* 11, 85–112.

Drucker, Peter. 1989. "Ethical Chic." In *Contemporary Moral Controversies in Business*, ed. A. Pablo Iannone, 44–52. New York: Oxford University Press.

Dunfee, Thomas W. 1991. "Business Ethics and Extant Social Contracts." *Business Ethics Quarterly* 1, 23–51.

Duska, Ronald F. 1991. "What's the Point of a Business Ethics Course?" *Business Ethics Quarterly* 1, 335–354.

————. 1993. "Aristotle: A Pre-Modern Post-Modern? Implications for Business Ethics." *Business Ethics Quarterly* 3, 227–249.

Dworkin, Gerald. 1988. *The Theory and Practice of Autonomy.* New York: Cambridge University Press.

Dworkin, Ronald. 1985. *A Matter of Principle.* Cambridge, Mass.: Harvard University Press.

Edel, Abraham, Elizabeth Flower, and Finbarr W. O'Connor. 1994. *Critique of Applied Ethics: Reflections and Recommendations*. Philadelphia: Temple University Press.

Elster, Jon. 1984. *Ulysses and the Sirens: Studies in Rationality and Irrationality*. Rev. ed. New York: Cambridge University Press.

―――. 1985. *Sour Grapes: Studies in the Subversion of Rationality*. New York: Cambridge University Press.

―――. 1989. *The Cement of Society: A Study of Social Order*. New York: Cambridge University Press.

―――. 1989a. *Nuts and Bolts for the Social Sciences*. New York: Cambridge University Press.

Etzioni, Amitai. 1988. *The Moral Dimension: Toward a New Economics*. New York: Free Press.

Finn, Daniel Rush. 1990. "Self-Interest, Markets, and the Four Problems of Economic Life." Unpublished.

Foot, Philippa. 1979. *Virtues and Vices and Other Essays in Moral Philosophy*. Berkeley: University of California Press.

Frank, Robert H. 1988. *Passions Within Reason: The Strategic Role of the Emotions*. New York: W. W. Norton & Company.

Frankfurt, Harry G. 1981. "Freedom of the Will and the Concept of a Person." In *Free Will*, ed. Gary Watson, 81–95. New York: Oxford University Press.

Freeman, R. Edward. 1984. *Strategic Management: A Stakeholder Approach*. Boston: Pitman.

Freeman, R. Edward, and Daniel R. Gilbert Jr. 1988. *Corporate Strategy and the Search for Ethics*. Englewood Cliffs, N.J.: Prentice Hall.

French, Peter A. 1984. *Collective and Corporate Responsibility*. New York: Columbia University Press.

Friedman, Milton. 1953. "The Methodology of Positive Economics." In *Essays in Positive Economics*, part 1, 3–43. Chicago: University of Chicago Press.

―――. 1982. *Capitalism and Freedom*. 2nd ed. Chicago: University of Chicago Press.

―――. 1984. "The Social Responsibility of Business is to Increase its Profits." In *Business Ethics: Readings and Cases in Corporate Morality*, ed. W. Michael Hoffman and Jennifer Mills Moore, 126–131. New York: McGraw-Hill Book Company.

Fucini, Joseph J., and Suzy Fucini. 1990. *Working for the Japanese: Inside Mazda's American Auto Plant*. New York: Free Press.

Gauthier, David. 1986. *Morals by Agreement*. Oxford: Clarendon Press.

Geertz, Clifford. 1983. *Local Knowledge: Further Essays in Interpretive Anthropology*. New York: Basic Books.

Gettier, Edmund. 1963. "Is Justified True Belief Knowledge?" *Analysis*, 121–123.

Gewirth, Alan. 1978. *Reason and Morality*. Chicago: University of Chicago Press.

Gilbert, Daniel R. Jr.. 1991. "Respect for Persons, Management Theory, and Business Ethics." In *Business Ethics: The State of the Art*, ed. R. Edward Freeman, 111–120. New York: Oxford University Press.

―――. 1992. *The Twilight of Corporate Strategy: A Comparative Ethical Critique*. New York: Oxford University Press.

Gilligan, Carol. 1982. *In a Different Voice: Psychological Theory and Women's Development*. Cambridge, Mass.: Harvard University Press.

Gordon, George G. 1991. "Industry Determinants of Organizational Culture." *Academy of Management Review* 16, 396–415.

Griffin, James. 1991. "Modern Utilitarianism," in *Contemporary Political Theory*, ed. Philip Pettit, 73–100. New York: Macmillan Publishing Company.

Hamper, Ben. 1991. *Rivethead: Tales from the Assembly Line*. New York: Warner Books.

Hampshire, Stuart. 1982. "Morality and Convention," in *Utilitarianism and Beyond*, ed. Amartya Sen and Bernard Williams, 145–157. New York: Cambridge University Press.

Haney, Craig, Philip Zimbardo, and W. Curtis Banks. 1973. "Interpersonal Dynamics in a Simulated Prison," *International Journal of Criminology and Penology* 1, 69–97.

Hardin, Garrett. 1968. "The Tragedy of the Commons." *Science* 162, 1243–1248.

———. 1977. *Exploring New Ethics for Survival*. New York: Penguin Books.

Harman, Gilbert. 1978. "Relativistic Ethics: Morality as Politics." In *Midwest Studies*, vol. 3, 109–121.

Hart, David K. 1988. "Management and Benevolence: The Fatal Flaw in Theory Y." In *Organizations and Ethical Individualism*, ed. Konstantin Kolenda, 73–105.

Hartman, Edwin M. 1988. *Conceptual Foundations of Organization Theory*. Cambridge, Mass.: Ballinger Publishing Company.

———. 1994. "The Commons and the Moral Organization." *Business Ethics Quarterly* 4, 253–269.

———. 1994a. "The Status of Business Ethics." *Business and Professional Ethics Journal* 13, 3–30.

Heller, Joseph. 1974. *Something Happened*. New York: Alfred A. Knopf.

Herman, Stewart W. 1991. "Furthering the Coversation Between Philosophy and Organizational Theory." *Business Ethics Quarterly* 1, 121–132.

Hirschman, Albert O. 1970. *Exit, Voice, and Loyalty: Responses to Decline in Firms, Organizations, and States*. Cambridge, Mass.: Harvard University Press.

Hollis, Martin, and Edward Nell. 1975. *Rational Economic Man: A Philosophical Critique of Neo-Classical Economics*. New York: Cambridge University Press.

Huxley, Aldous. 1969. *Brave New World*. New York: Harper and Row.

Kahneman, Daniel, Jack Knetsch, and Richard Thaler. 1986. "Fairness and the Assumptions of Economics." *Journal of Business* 59, S285–S300.

Keeley, Michael. 1988. *A Social-Contract Theory of Organizations*. Notre Dame, Ind.: University of Notre Dame Press.

Keller, Evelyn Fox. 1983. *A Feeling for the Organism: The Life and Work of Barbara McClintock*. New York: Freeman.

———. 1985. *Reflections on Gender and Science*. New Haven, Conn.: Yale University Press.

Klein, Jonathan. 1989. "Science and Subterfuge." *The Academy of Management Executive* 3, 59–62.

Kohlberg, Lawrence. 1981. *The Philosophy of Moral Development*. New York: Harper and Row.

Kraus, Jody S., and Jules L. Coleman. 1987. "Morality and the Theory of Rational Choice." *Ethics* 97, 715–749.

Kuhn, Thomas H. 1971. *The Structure of Scientific Revolutions*. 2nd ed. Chicago: University of Chicago Press.

LaFollette, Hugh. 1989. "The Truth in Psychological Egoism," in *Reason and Responsibility*," 7th ed., ed. Joel Feinberg, 500–507. Belmont, Calif.: Wadsworth Publishing Company.

———. 1993. "Personal Relationships," in *A Companion to Ethics*, ed. Peter Singer, 327–332. Cambridge, Mass.: Blackwell Publishers.

Lewis, Michael. 1989. *Liar's Poker: Rising Through the Wreckage on Wall Street*. New York: W. W. Norton and Company.

Lippke, Richard L. 1991. "A Critique of Business Ethics." *Business Ethics Quarterly* 1, 367–384.

Lyons, David. 1965. *Forms and Limits of Utilitarianism*. Oxford: Oxford University Press.

MacIntyre, Alasdair. 1981. *After Virtue*. Notre Dame, Ind.: University of Notre Dame Press.

Maitland, Ian. 1989. "Rights in the Workplace: A Nozickian Argument." *Journal of Business Ethics* 8, 951–954.

Marcus, George E., and Michael M. J. Fischer. 1986. *Anthropology as Cultural Critique: An Experimental Moment in the Human Sciences*. Chicago: University of Chicago Press.

Martin, Joanne. 1992. *Cultures in Organizations: Three Perspectives*. New York: Oxford University Press.

Maslow, Abraham H. 1970. *Motivation and Personality*. 2nd ed. New York: Harper and Row.

McCloskey, Donald. 1994. "Bourgeois Virtue." *American Scholar* 63, 177–191.

McGregor, Douglas. 1960. *The Human Side of Enterprise*. New York: McGraw-Hill Book Company.

Mendola, Joseph. 1987. "Gauthier's Morals by Agreement and Two Kinds of Rationality." *Ethics* 97, 765–774.

Milgram, Stanley. 1974. *Obedience to Authority: An Experimental View*. New York: Harper and Row.

Mitnick, Barry M. 1980. *The Political Economy of Regulation: Creating, Designing, and Removing Regulatory Reforms*. New York: Columbia University Press.

Mitroff, Ian I., and Ralph H. Kilmann. 1986. "Corporate Tragedies: Teaching Companies to Cope with Evil," in *Organizational Reality: Reports from the Firing Line*, 3rd ed., ed. Peter J. Frost, Vance F. Mitchell, and Walter R. Nord, 413–420. Glenview, Ill.: Scott, Foresman and Company.

Moore, G. E. 1903. *Principia Ethica*. Cambridge: Cambridge University Press.

Morgan, Gareth. 1986. *Images of Organizations*. Beverly Hills, Calif.: Sage Publications.

Nagel, Thomas. 1970. *The Possibility of Altruism*. New York: Oxford University Press.

———. 1971. "Brain Bisection and the Unity of Consciousness." *Synthese* 22, 396–413.

Nozick, Robert. 1974. *Anarchy, State and Utopia*. New York: Basic Books.

Nussbaum, Martha C. 1990. *Love's Knowledge: Essays on Philosophy and Literature*. New York: Oxford University Press.

———. 1994. "Divided We Stand." *New Republic* 210, nos. 2 and 3 (January 10 and 17, 1994), 38–42.

Ouchi, William G. 1981. *Theory Z: How American Business Can Meet the Japanese Challenge*. Reading, Mass.: Addison-Wesley.

Paine, Lynn Sharp. 1990. "Ethics as Character Development: Reflections on the Objective of Ethics Education." In *Business Ethics: The State of the Art,* ed. R. Edward Freeman, 67–86. New York: Oxford University Press.

Parfit, Derek. 1971. "Personal Identity." *Philosophical Review* 80, 1–27.

———. 1984. *Reasons and Persons.* Oxford: Clarendon Press.

Pastin, Mark. 1986. *The Hard Problems of Management: Gaining the Ethics Edge.* San Francisco: Jossey-Bass Publishers.

Pfeffer, Jeffrey. 1982. *Organizations and Organization Theory.* Boston: Pitman.

Phillips, Nelson. 1992. "Understanding Ethics in Practice: An Ethnomethodologial Approach to the Study of Business Ethics." *Business Ethics Quarterly* 2, 225–244.

Plato. 1924. *Plato's Euthyphro, Apology of Socrates, and Crito.* Ed. John Burnet. Oxford: Clarendon Press.

———. 1958. *Res publica.* Ed. John Burnet. Oxford: Clarendon Press.

———. 1959. *Gorgias.* Ed. E. R. Dodds. Oxford: Clarendon Press.

Posner, Richard A. 1983. *The Economics of Justice.* 2nd ed. Cambridge, Mass.: Harvard University Press.

Prestowitz, Clyde V. 1988. *Trading Places: How We Allowed Japan to Take the Lead.* New York: Basic Books.

Quine, Willard Van Orman. 1960. *Word and Object.* Cambridge, Mass.: MIT Press.

———. 1961. "Two Dogmas of Empiricism." In *From a Logical Point of View,* 20–46. New York: Harper and Row.

Quine, Willard Van Orman, and Joseph S. Ullian. 1978. *The Web of Belief.* New York: Random House.

Rapoport, Anatol, and Albert M. Chammah. 1965. *Prisoner's Dilemma: A Study in Conflict and Cooperation.* Ann Arbor: University of Michigan Press.

Rawls, John. 1971. *A Theory of Justice.* Cambridge, Mass.: Harvard University Press.

———. 1985. "Justice as Fairness: Political not Metaphysical." *Philosophy and Public Affairs* 14, 223–251.

———. 1993. *Political Liberalism.* New York: Columbia University Press.

Ray, Carol Axtell. 1986. "Corporate Culture: The Last Frontier of Control?" *Journal of Management Studies* 23, 287–297.

Rorty, Richard. 1979. *Philosophy and the Mirror of Nature.* Princeton, N.J.: Princeton University Press.

———. 1989. *Contingency, Irony, and Solidarity.* New York: Cambridge University Press.

———. 1991. *Objectivity, Relativism, and Truth.* New York: Cambridge University Press.

Sathe, Vijay. 1985. *Culture and Related Corporate Realities.* Homewood, Ill.: Richard D. Irwin.

Sayre-McCord, Geoffrey ed. 1988. *Essays on Moral Realism.* Ithaca, N.Y.: Cornell University Press.

Scanlon, T. M. 1982. "Constractualism and Utilitarianism." In *Utilitarianism and Beyond,* ed. Amartya Sen and Bernard Williams, 103–128. New York: Cambridge University Press.

Schein, Edgar H. 1985. *Organizational Culture and Leadership.* San Francisco: Jossey-Bass Publishers.

Schelling, Thomas C. 1984. *Choice and Consequence: Perspectives of an Errant Economist.* Cambridge, Mass.: Harvard University Press.

Schmidtz, David. 1991. *The Limits of Government: An Essay on the Public Goods Argument*. Boulder, Colo.: Westview Press.

Schopenhauer, Arthur. 1989. "Essay on the Freedom of the Will." In *Reason and Responsibility*, 7th ed., ed. Joel Feinberg, 351–363. Belmont, Calif.: Wadsworth Publishing Co.

Schumpeter, Joseph. 1942. *Capitalism, Socialism, and Democracy*. New York: Harper and Row.

Sen, Amartya K. 1987. On *Ethics and Economics*. New York: Basil Blackwell.

———. 1989. "The Moral Standing of the Market," in *Contemporary Moral Controversies in Business*, ed. A. Pablo Iannone, 532–544. New York: Oxford University Press.

Sen, Amartya K., and Bernard Williams, eds. 1982. *Utilitarianism and Beyond*. New York: Cambridge University Press.

Smith, Adam. 1966. *The Theory of Moral Sentiments*. New York: Augustus M. Kelley Publishers.

Solomon, Richard, and John Corbit. 1974. "An Opponent-process Theory of Motivation." *Psychological Reviews* 81, 119–145.

Solomon, Robert C. 1992. *Ethics and Excellence: Cooperation and Integrity in Business*. New York: Oxford University Press.

———. 1994. "The Corporation as Community: A Reply to Ed Hartman." *Business Ethics Quarterly* 4, 271–285.

Stark, Andrew. 1993. "What's the Matter with Business Ethics?" *Harvard Business Review* 71 (May–June), 38–48.

Stewart, James. B. 1991. *Den of Thieves*. New York: Simon and Schuster.

Sturgeon, Nicholas L. 1988. "Moral Explanation." In *Essays on Moral Realism*, ed. Geoffrey Sayre-McCord, 229–255. Ithaca, N.Y.: Cornell University Press.

Taylor, Charles. 1977. "What Is Human Agency?" In *The Self: Psychological and Philosophical Issues*, ed. Theodore Mischel, 103–135. Totowa, N.J.: Rowman and Littlefield.

Thaler, Richard. 1985. "Mental Accounting and Consumer Choices." *Marketing Sciences* 4, 199–214.

Thurow, Lester. 1994. "Head to Head." In *Taking Sides*, ed. Lisa H. Newton and Maureen M. Ford, 4–14. 3rd ed. Guilford, Conn.: Dushkin Publishing Group.

Trist, E. L., and K. W. Bamforth. 1951. "Some Social and Psychological Consequences of the Longwall Method of Coal-getting." *Human Relations* 4, 3–38.

Turnbull, Colin M. 1972. *The Mountain People*. New York: Simon and Schuster.

Vogel, David. 1992. "Ethics and Profits Don't Always Go Hand in Hand." In *Business Ethics 92/93*, ed. John E. Richardson. Guilford, Conn.: Dushkin Publishing Group.

Waters, James. 1989. "Corporate Morality as an Organizational Phenomenon." In *Contemporary Moral Controversies in Business*, ed. A. Pablo Iannone, 151–163.

Watson, Gary. 1982. "Free Agency." In *Free Will*, ed. Gary Watson, 96–110. New York: Oxford University Press.

Weick, Karl E. 1979. *The Social Psychology of Organizing*. 2nd ed. New York: Random House.

Werhane, Patricia H. 1993. *The Legacy of Adam Smith*. New York: Oxford University Press.

———. 1994. "Justice, Impartiality, and Reciprocity: A Response to Edwin Hartman." *Business Ethics Quarterly* 4, 287–290.

———. 1994b. "Moral Character and Moral Reasoning: A Reply to Robert Solomon." in *Business as a Humanity*, ed. Thomas J. Donaldson and R. Edward Freeman, 98–103. New York: Oxford University Press.

Whiting, Robert. 1989. *You Gotta Have Wa*. New York: Vintage Books.

Whyte, Wiiliam F. 1956. *The Organizational Man*. New York: Simon and Schuster.

Wicks, Andrew C. 1990. "Norman Bowie and Richard Rorty on Multinationals: Does Business Ethics Need 'Metaphysical Comfort?'" *Journal of Business Ethics* 9, 191–200.

Williams, Bernard. 1973. *Problems of the Self*. Cambridge: Cambridge University Press.

———. 1985. *Ethics and the Limits of Philosophy*. Cambridge: Harvard University Press.

———. 1981. *Moral Luck*. New York: Cambridge University Press.

Wills, Garry. 1990. *Under God: Religion and American Politics*. New York: Simon and Schuster.

Winter, Sidney G. 1975. "Optimization and Evolution." In *Adaptive Economic Models*, ed. by R. H. Day and T. Groves, 73–118. New York: Academic Press.

———. 1971. "Satisficing, Selection, and the Innovative Remnant." *Quarterly Journal of Economics* 85, 237–261.

———. 1964. "Economic 'Natural Selection' and the Theory of the Firm. *Yale Economic Essays* 4, 225–272.

Wolfe, Alan. 1989. *Whose Keeper? Social Science and Moral Obligation*. Berkeley: University of California Press.

Yankelovich, Daniel and John Immerwahr. 1983. *Putting the Work Ethic to Work*. New York: Public Agenda Foundation.

Index

Abraham and Isaac, 21–22
Affirmative action, 49–51, 66n.35, 102, 110–11, 119n.63. *See also* Rawls: on justice: and affirmative action
Ajaye, Franklin, 31n.34
Allaire, Yvan, 149
Aristotle and Aristotelianism, 65n.32, 115n.31, 163n.10, 187–88n.22. *See also* Person, nature of: Aristotle on
on common sense, 109
on happiness
  character a matter of what makes one happy, 29n.24, 54, 135, 137
  difference between modern conception of happiness and Aristotle's, 27n.6
  good citizenship makes one happy, 27n.6
  and rationality, 167
  understanding happiness requires considering the good community, 167
  virtue a necessary condition of true happiness, 11–12
on human beings as rational and social, 30n.27, 38, 68, 85, 86n.1, 122, 145, 149, 160–61, 162, 180
on the incommensurability of goods, 41, 63n.6, 114n.24, 119n.60, 139n.9
influence on this book, 10, 31n.33, 64n.19
on politics as the culmination of ethics, 5, 7, 116n.41
on practical wisdom, 109, 188n.22
on the priority of the particular to the general, 116n.40, 117n.49, 119n.58
on things that are good in themselves, 15, 28n.17, 167
on virtue, 9, 186n.6
  and emotion, 29n.26, 159
entails being made happy by the right things, 9, 17, 27n.6, 29n.24, 54, 135
  a great *polis* necessary for, 167
  habituation as a means to, 135
  necessary condition of happiness, 11–12, 27n.6, 29n.26
  primacy of civic virtue, 149,161
Arrington, Robert L., 18, 26n.2, 29n.22, 31nn.33, 37, 115n.30
Asch, Solomon, 164n.12
Assurance problem, 77, 84, 88n.20, 157–58
Augustine, Saint, 140n.31
Autonomy, 64n.15, 107, 126, 121–42, 170, 185, 186nn.3,8, 187n.17. *See also* Community: effect on autonomy; Culture, corporate: effect on autonomy; Desires: first-order: and autonomy; Desires: second-order: and autonomy; Emotion: and autonomy; Good life: autonomy and; Libertarians and libertarianism: on autonomy; Person,nature of: persons as characteristically autonomous; Principles: and autonomy, and corporate culture; Rationality: autonomy and; Rawls: on autonomy; Values: autonomy and
and choosing one's conception of the good, 42, 61, 141n.30
and choosing one's desires, 142n.32, 178, 183
and the commons, 9, 78, 129, 133, 140n.19
definition of, 128–34
distinguishable from brainwashing, 143, 146
as essential to the person, 8, 124, 126
and organizations, 143, 146, 157, 162
and reflection, 127, 134, 148

Autonomy (*cont.*)
  and rights, 35, 39, 44, 62n.3, 93, 102,
    115n.37, 124, 128, 130, 132, 139n.14,
    143
  and second-order desires, 140n.21, 143
  supported by good community, 43,
    64n.22, 122, 135, 162, 167, 180, 184

Bamforth, K. W., 164n.16
Banks, W. Curtis, 147
Baumholtz, Frankie, 19
Belief
  first-order, 130, 153, 159, 163n.1, 164n.12
  affected by culture, 159
  relationship to second-order beliefs,
    140n.22
  vulnerability to social pressure, 149,
    164n.11, 164n.12
  higher-order, 148, 149
  and culture, 159
  second-order, 150, 157–58, 159, 163n.10,
    170
  affected by culture, 159, 174
  characteristically shared with others in
    community, 144
  commons supported by, 158
  created by loyalty, 174
  definition, 129–30
  effect of affection on, 136
  and meaning, 153
  relationship to first-order beliefs,
    140n.22
  vulnerability to social pressure, 149, 146,
    163n.10, 170, 173–74, 174
Bennett, William J., 53–54
Bentham, Jeremy and Benthamism, 35, 39,
    43, 61
Boesky, Ivan, 12, 57, 163n.6
Bork, Robert, 43–44, 65n.24
Bowie, Norman E., 27n.9, 114n.22
Brainwashing, 106, 129, 141n.26, 176, 180,
    185. *See also* Autonomy:
    distinguishable from brainwashing
  and second-order desires, 146, 162
  by social pressure, 8, 132, 145, 146, 158
Braybrooke, David, 65n.30, 88n.22, 139n.9
Brink, David O., 28nn.13,14, 32n.39, 62n.3
Browning, Robert, 63n.8
Buchanan, Allen, 62n.1, 77, 88n.20
Burke, James, 12, 94
Burr, Aaron, and Hamilton, Alexander, 22,
    98

Capitalism and capitalists, 66n.35, 111. *See
    also* Desert: capitalist notion of justice
    based on

productivity of, 32n.41, 39, 94
Carr, Albert Z., 91–93, 97, 112n.3, 119n.62,
    170, 185
Cartwright, Nancy, 65n.30, 139n.8
Chammah, Albert M., 80, 88n.18
Character, 23, 48, 80–83, 81, 92, 116n.40,
    145–46, 148. *See also* Aristotle: on
    happiness: character a matter of what
    makes one happy; Emotion: and
    character; Motivation: character and;
    Person, nature of: person closely
    identifiable with character
  choosing one's, 81, 123, 134, 136, 137
  and higher-order desires, 131, 140n.24
  not separable from the self, 123, 133, 134,
    160
  vs. principles as basic to ethics, 6, 48
  and second-order desires, 140n.24
  social influence on, 7, 8, 85, 145
Ciulla, Joanne B., 119n.58
Coleman, Jules L., 88n.22
Commons, 7, 65n.29, 74–78, 83, 87n.15,
    88n.19, 112n.6, 156, 167, 173, 183,
    185. *See also* Autonomy: and the
    commons; Community: commons
    and; Contracts and social contract
    theory: as a way to preserve the
    commons; Cooperation: and
    preserving the commons
  and being better off, 78–80, 127
  corporate culture may preserve, 9, 146,
    154, 156, 157–59, 162, 169, 170, 173
  loyalty may preserve, 169, 170, 172, 174
  may be undermined by rational
    maximizing, 69, 75–76, 78, 87n.13
  contracts may prevent this, 69
  the organization as a, 7, 76–79, 88n.17,
    93, 112
  preserving the, 76–84, 87n.16, 93,
    96, 106, 112, 127, 129, 136,
    165n.26, 168
  commons preservation as motivator, 77
  and self-fulfilling beliefs, 136, 154
  and utility, 80
Commons, John R., 113n.10
Communitarianism, 9–10
Community, 4, 46–50, 54, 68–89,
    120n.65, 163n.8. *See also* Aristotle: on
    happiness: understanding happiness
    requires considering the good
    community; Desires, higher-order:
    community's effect on; Desires,
    second-order: community's effect on;
    Principles: good community as origin
    of good principles; Rationality:
    socializing influence of the

community and; Values: communities
   and; Virtue: in a community
assessing communities, 8, 54, 58, 59,
   82–83, 100–101, 107, 166
as characteristically sharing beliefs,
   32n.44, 33n.46, 136, 144, 153–54, 181
as characteristically sharing language,
   32n.44, 144, 158, 181, 186n.1
commons and, 14, 74–78, 85, 146, 168
and constructivism, 4
corporate culture and, 161, 165n.24
determines one's desires, 58, 121, 131,
   137–38, 146, 149, 163n.4, 166, 169,
   176, 178
one's interests, 33n.46, 138, 156, 180,
   182, 184
one's view of the good life, 8, 32–33n.44,
   37–38, 51, 56, 88n.26, 100–101,
   163n.3, 166, 177; of being better off,
   58; of happiness, 36–38, 54, 57, 82–83;
   of morality, 23–25, 33n.45, 54, 101–2,
   107, 137, 163n.17, 166
differing moral principles developed in
   different communities, 54–55, 70,
   100–101, 104, 107, 137, 163n.17, 166,
   177
effect on autonomy, 61, 122, 124, 130–31,
   137, 138, 141n.30, 145–46, 168, 180
good community, conditions of, 17,
   83–86, 121, 182–85, 188n.22
exit, loyalty, and voice as, 169–82
nature of autonomy permitted by, 138,
   177–78
requires people of virtue, 9, 53–54
the good life as communal, 145, 159, 161,
   167
and interpretation, 22, 25, 57–59, 99,
   141n.27, 144, 181
moral significance of agreements in, 19,
   39, 69–74, 82, 87n.6, 97–98, 186n.2
organization as, 17, 25, 60, 71, 85–86,
   87n.5, 113n.21, 150, 152, 155,
   166–88
and personal identity, 122, 145, 169
as primary subject of ethics, 5, 7, 39,
   44, 60, 68, 82, 85, 138, 166, 168, 185
and rationality, 137, 138, 144–46, 163n.3,
   181
Rawls on, 61–62, 83–86, 108, 110–11,
   113n.21, 118nn.54,57, 124, 166, 168,
   172–73, 177, 186n.4
as supporting the good life, 8, 39
as supporting morality, 16–17, 25,
   30n.27, 44, 49, 68, 127, 138, 162,
   167–68
Compliance problem, 71–72, 79

Comprehensive moral theory, 108, 117n.51
Constructivism, 4, 5, 187n.17
Contracts and social contract theory, 5, 54,
   73, 83, 113nn.10,16, 133, 149,
   187n.13. See also Rawls: contractualism
applied ethics and, 92, 97–98
as the basis of business ethics, 7, 62,
   66n.40, 68, 69–75, 90, 92–98, 170
problems with contractual approach to
   business ethics, 73–74, 98
Friedman on employment contract,
   96–97, 106
good contract said to promote justice,
   97–98
how contracts can be assessed, 71, 73,
   79–80, 100
fairness as basis for assessment, 96,
   113n.15
hypernorms as basis for assessment, 71,
   97–98, 107, 113n.9, 114n.25, 116n.39,
   118n.56, 153–54, 170
utilitarianism as basis for assessment, 39,
   45, 48, 71, 77
how to ensure compliance with contracts,
   71–73
macrosocial contracts (Donaldson and
   Dunfee), 87n.6, 113n.18
problems with social contract theory,
   86nn.4,5, 87n.9, 107, 113n.20, 161,
   168, 171–74
Rawlsian contractualism, 7, 85, 87n.7,
   108, 111, 113–14, 118n.56
rights and, 70, 71, 79, 96, 97–98
as a way to preserve the commons, 77,
   79–80, 82, 112
Cooper, John, 27n.6
Cooperation, 32n.42, 49, 55, 67n.45, 70.
   See also Reciprocity: and cooperation
desire to be cooperative, 80, 110, 155, 176
effective managers create cooperation in
   organizations, 60, 113nn.12,14, 158,
   176, 180
exploitation of cooperators by noncooperators, 76, 82
good consequences of, 87n.16, 96
and loyalty, 169, 120n.65, 186n.4
and preserving the commons, 75, 79, 93,
   167
Rawls on, 83, 84, 186n.4
ways of ensuring cooperation, 55, 61, 71,
   78, 79, 80, 82
Corbit, John, 63n.12
Cox, Susan Jane Buck, 87n.15
Crosby, Fanny J., 164n.18
Culture, corporate, 13, 63n.11, 72, 88n.20,
   143–65. See also Commons:

Culture, corporate (*cont.*)
    corporate culture may preserve;
    Community: commons and; Desires:
    first-order: corporate culture affects;
    Desires: second-order: corporate
    culture affects; Emotion: and the
    commons; Japan, culture and
    management in; Principles: and
    corporate culture; Values: and
    organizations: corporate culture can
    affect people's values; Virtue: and
    organization: corporate culture
    creates and supports virtue; Virtue: as
    subject matter of ethics: culture of
    particular interest to virtue ethics
    affects employees' beliefs, 151, 153–54,
      173, 176
    affects employees' character, 81
    affects employees' conception of the
      good life, 166
    affects employees' desires, 87n.7,
      152–55, 159, 162, 173, 176, 178, 185
    affects employees' emotions, 135, 162
    affects employees' identity, 160–61
    affects employees' interests, 178
    affects employees' motivations, 117n.44,
      152, 153
    affects employees' preferences, 178
    affects employees' values, 37, 178
    affects employees' view of good life, 98
    affects what makes employees happy,
      152–53, 161–62
    definition, 146, 149
    different cultures appropriate for
      different kinds of organization, 72,
      156, 175, 179
    effect on autonomy, 9, 122, 138, 146, 157,
      159
    gives meaning to people, 66n.42, 153
    one's identity and, 113n.21
    and interpretation, 144, 151
    and language, 150, 151, 180
    may create loyalty, 174
    may support morality, 146, 182
    may undermine morality, 138, 146–50
    and organizational effectiveness, 151–54,
      177
    and thick concepts, 99, 105, 153

Darwall, Stephen, 28n.12
Davidson, Donald, 31n.35, 71
DeGeorge, Richard T., 27n.7
Dennett, Daniel C., 140n.15
Derry, Robbin, 27n.9, 114nn.22,23,
    116n.43, 188n.22

Descartes, Rene and Cartesianism, 10,
    29n.26
Desert, 45, 122
    capitalist notion of justice based on, 6–7,
      50, 56, 62n.5, 102, 103, 110–11,
      112n.7, 125
Desires,
    first-order, 140n.20, 143, 148, 163n.10,
      171
    and autonomy, 130–35, 159
    consistency among desires, 141–42n.31,
      170
    corporate culture affects, 152–53, 159
    definition of, 130–31
    effect of emotion on, 135–137
    and identity, 133
    managerial manipulation of, 157
    relationship to second-order desires,
      140n.22
    stability of, 134
    vulnerability to social pressure, 133, 149
    higher-order, 66n.43, 140n.23, 141n.30,
      146, 148, 149, 177. *See also* Person,
      nature of: person closely identifiable
      with higher-order desires; Values: and
      desires: values a special case of higher-
      order desires
    choosing the best possible ones, 182–84
    community's effect on, 141–42n.31, 166,
      168
    cultivation of, 134
    managerial manipulation of, 157
    part of one's character, 131
    lower-order, 135, 149
    second-order, 140n.20, 142n.32, 147,
      163n.10, 165n.22, 178. *See also*
      Motivation: and second-order
      desires
    and autonomy, 130–35, 140n.21, 143,
      148, 159
    choosing one's, 81
    community's effect on, 143, 181–82
    consistency among desires, 141–42n.31,
      170
    corporate culture effects, 152–53, 159,
      162
    cultivation of, 137, 159
    definition of, 130–31
    effect of emotion on, 135–37
    and identity, 141n.28
    loyalty creates, 173
    managerial manipulation, 157
    and meaning, 153
    relationship to first-order desires,
      140n.22

stability of, 134
and values, 131
vulnerability to social pressure, 149
DiMaggio, Joe, 19
discrimination, 46, 49–51
Dixit, Avinash, 88nn.18,23, 110, 184
Donaldson, Thomas J., 28n.10,
    113nn.16,19, 114n.21, 115n.31
  on hypernorms, 87n.6, 97, 98, 107,
    114nn.23,24,25, 116n.39, 118n.56
  on macrosocial contracts, 87n.6
  on moral free space, 107, 113n.18
Dostoevsky, Fyodor, 12
Drucker, Peter, 94, 97
Dunfee, Thomas W., 28n.10, 113n.16,19,
    114n.21, 115n.31
  contract theory as shedding light on
    business ethics, 71
  on hypernorms, 87n.6, 97, 98, 107,
    114n.23,24,25, 116n.39, 118n.56
  on macrosocial contracts, 87n.6
  on moral free space, 107, 113n.18
Duska, Ronald F., 118n.57
Durocher, Leo, 112n.5
Dworkin, Gerald, 29n.22, 139n.13
Dworkin, Ronald, 42–43, 44, 64n.22

Economics and economists, 11, 29n.24,
    46–47, 62, 62n.5. See also Psychological
    egoism: false assumption of: by
    economists
  compatibility with utilitarianism, 3, 16,
    36, 60, 62n.1, 64nn.14,23, 106, 121,
    140n.24, 155, 170
  use of false assumptions by, 36, 47,
    62nn.2,3,4, 65n.30, 105, 106, 126, 129,
    139n.8
  assumption of behaviorism, 62n.2,
    133
  assumption of rationality, 13–14, 34, 36,
    47, 110, 112, 125, 144, 187n.14
  assumption of stability of preferences,
    123, 134, 178, 180
Edel, Abraham, 64n.16, 66n.39, 113n.10,
    114n.27, 164nn.13,17
Elster, Jon, 56, 63n.12, 137, 139nn.6,7
    140nn.20,23
Emotion, 51, 53, 123, 135–38, 161, 169,
    179
  and autonomy, 135, 180
  and character, 136
  and the commons, 136, 162, 169, 183
  corporate culture and, 9, 135, 158, 159,
    173–74
  cultivating emotions, 145, 159, 182

as essential to humans, 122–23, 137,
    138n.5
  and loyalty, 173, 186n.11
  may support morality, 29n.26, 48, 54,
    142n.35, 137, 171
  relationship to reason, 9, 135, 157, 159,
    185, 137
  shared by people in communities, 52
  and virtue, 160, 185
Epstein, Richard, 113n.10
Equality, 102, 112n.7. See also Rawls: on
    equality; Rights: Rawls on: equality of
    rights
  as essential to morality, 44, 49, 65n.25,
    187n.16
  justice and, 6–7, 44, 49–50, 80, 110
  persons as free and equal, 44, 83, 84,
    187n.16
  presumption in favor of, 44–45, 104, 110
  in Rawls, 62, 108, 109, 119n.61
of respect for conceptions of the good life,
    42
Ethics, theoretical vs. applied, 90–120. See
    also Contracts and social contract
    theory: applied ethics and; Justice:
    problems with applying principles of
    justice to assess communities
  applied ethics
  prior to theoretical ethics, 108–11, 177,
    180–81
  supposed to show how the great princ-
    iples apply, 90
  business ethics as legitimate as theoretical
    ethics, 7, 85
  compare relationship between philoso-
    phy of science and epistemology, 104
  community standards not application of
    time-honored principles, 177
  problems with theoretical ethics, 46–47,
    103–5, 110–111
  unlike relationship between sociology
    and organizational behavior, 65n.31
  unlike relationship between theoretical
    and applied science, 46–47
Etzioni, Amitai, 29n.25
Exit, 168–71, 173, 174, 175, 178–79,
    186n.5, 187n.15

Fairness, 41, 49, 52, 53, 92, 152, 166. See
    also Contracts and social contract
    theory: how contracts can be assessed:
    fairness as basis for assessment;
    Desert; Rawls: on fairness; Utility and
    utilitarianism: relationship to other
    moral standards: overlap of utility

Fairness (*cont.*)
    with other standards: with fairness
  change in views of fairness over time,
    31n.38, 111
  community, description of fair, 60, 61–62,
    83, 176
  considerations of fairness motivate,
    55–57, 87n.7, 110, 113n.15, 136, 183
  entry and exit costs, fairness of, 172, 173
  libertarian view of, 66n.35, 93, 112n.7,
    117n.46
  Pareto optimality does not take into
    account, 62n.3
  Posner rejects, 117n.46
  reciprocity a form of, 45, 82
  test of fairness applied to contracts, 96,
    97, 107, 171
    difficulty of applying test, 102
Firsirotu, Mihaela E., 149
Fischer, Michael M. J., 99
Foot, Philippa, 30n.33
Ford, Henry, I, 19
Ford, Henry, II, 18–19
Foundations and foundationalism. *See also*
    Psychological egoism: as alleged foun-
    dation for morality; Rights: not
    foundational; Utility and utilitari-
    anism: not the foundation of
    morality
  Aristotle not entirely a foundationalist,
    119n.60
  foundational principles neither necessary
    nor helpful, 20, 162, 166, 167, 179
  Friedman considers freedom
    foundational, 93
  moral philosophy not a search for
    foundational principles of morality, 4,
    6, 7, 25–26, 29n.22, 67n.46, 110, 162,
    166, 167
  great principles of morality not
    foundational, 10, 38, 57, 104, 107
  moral realists not foundationalists,
    116n.40
  no foundational explanation of human
    action, 13–14
  self-interest not basis of all human
    action, 14
  no foundational principles of truth,
    4, 14
  epistemology not the foundation of
    philosophy of science, 103–4
  sense data not a foundation, 33n.46
  no foundational self, 132
  one's values not foundational, 66n.44
Rawls not a foundationalist, 108

Frank, Robert H.
  claim that demanding justice may lead to
    long-term goods, 56, 119n.62, 168,
    170, 172
  may preserve the commons, 136
  claim that justice is desired in itself,
    55–56, 88n.23, 113n.15
  vs. Posner, 117n.46
  claim that people act in others' interests,
    137, 142n.36
Frankfurt, Harry, 140n.20
Free will, 128, 142n.33. *See also* Autonomy
  Kant on, as opposed to autonomy, 186n.3
  part of the good life, 122
  relationship to political freedom, 140n.16
  relationship to rights, 141n.29
  Schopenhauer on second-order desires
    and, 140n.20
  utilitarianism as supporting exercise of,
    125
Freeman, R. Edward, 113nn.11,13, 130,
    140n.19
French, Peter A., 27n.8
Friedman, Milton. *See also* Libertarians and
    libertarianism; Rights: Friedman on
  does not discuss the commons
    extensively, 88n.19, 112n.6
  on fairness, 112n.7
  rejection of analogy of state and
    organization, 30n.27
  on the status of economic theories,
    139n.8, 170, 171
  view that capitalism is productive and
    respects rights, 39
  view that management's responsibility is
    profit, 26n.3, 105–6, 112n.8, 171
  differences between Friedman and
    other contractarians on this
    point, 97
  organization's consequent minimal
    obligations to employees, 93–96,
    105–6, 107, 118n.54, 168, 170
Fuchs, Judge Emil, 91
Fucini, Joseph J., 155–56
Fucini, Suzy, 155–56

Game theory, 32n.42. *See also* Prisoner's
    Dilemma
  accounts for unpredictability within social
    sciences, 142n.33
  facile use of, 47
  false assumptions in, 9, 80, 178
  situations in which players are
    concerned about one another, 136,
    137

Garvey, Steve, 30n.32
Gauthier, David, 88n.22. *See also*
   Rationality: Gauthier on morality and
   claim that human life is a commons,
   88n.17
   claim that human life is naturally
   communal, 70
   claim that moral action is rational, 14,
   27n.5, 87n.13, 142n.34
   conception of rationality, 28n.12, 84, 167
   claim that utility is a measure of
   preference,139n.9
   on self-management, 123
Geertz, Clifford, 22, 65n.34, 98–99
Gettier, Edmund, 140n.17
Gibbard, Allan, 28n.12
Gilbert, Daniel R. Jr., 113n.11, 140n.19,
   163n.5
Gilligan, Carol, 187–88n.22
Good life. *See also* Happiness
 affection as a part of, 15, 136
 autonomy and, 6, 8, 35, 39, 40, 44,
   122–124, 126, 138, 166
   importance of autonomy in defining
   the good life for oneself, 9, 40–41, 49,
   61, 88n.46, 124, 162, 168, 176–78,
   187n.18. *See also* Rawls: on autonomy,
   on the right to one's own conception
   of the good
 part of definition of autonomy, 102, 115,
   128, 131–32
 essential to morality, 5, 6, 8, 22–23, 38
 fairness protects, 56
 good community characteristically
   supports, 8, 17, 49, 70, 74, 83, 92,
   107, 121, 167, 179, 182–85
 may overlap with morality, 7, 8, 9, 16,
   30n.27, 80–81, 121, 127
   ancient philosophers on overlap,
   27n.6
   requires good community, 30n.27, 61
 not identical with fulfillment of desire, 8
 presupposes importance of individual
   person, 122
 promotion of, as essential to morality, 6,
   8, 27n.5
 requires satisfaction of preferences that
   are somehow rational, 36, 63nn.9,12
 respect as part of, 31n.33, 56–57
 and rights, 35, 39–44, 49
 utilitarianism as requiring a conception
   of, 34, 56, 101
 various forms and conceptions of, 5, 6,
   19, 26, 38, 60, 81, 121, 138n.1,
   188n.25

conceptions may change, 80, 102, 177,
   182. *See also* Moral progress
 limits on, 23–25, 26, 32n.44, 57–59,
   64n.20, 100, 150, 163n.3, 181. *See also*
   Interpretation: impossibility of
   interpreting an action except
   as making some sense to us
 community may influence one's
   conception of, 8, 32n.44, 52, 98–101,
   122, 166; influence may thereby
   threaten autonomy, 136, 138, 145
Gordon, George G., 156, 175
Green, Ronald M., 114n.23, 116n.43
Grich, Bobby, 30n.32
Griffin, James, 62n.3, 63n.9

Hammer, M. C., 37
Hamper, Ben, 187n.13
Hampshire, Stuart, 51–53, 66n.38,
   142n.35
Haney, Craig, 147
Happiness. *See also* Aristotle: on happiness;
   Culture, corporate: affects what
   makes employees happy; Good life
 bad community one in which the wrong
   things make one happy, 54
 deciding what one wants one's
   happiness to be, 66n.43, 80, 137, 183,
   184
 essential to morality, 18, 20, 23–24
 good life may encompass more than, 6
 good organization does not guarantee,
   185
 not identical with being better off, 26n.1
 question whether moral behavior makes
   the agent happy, 12, 16
   desirable for a manager to hire those
   whom moral behavior makes happy,
   17
 one might be made happy by another's
   happiness, 12, 84, 86n.3
 on whether a disposition to cooperate
   makes one happy, 7, 80
 socializability of one's notion of
   happiness, 32n.44, 37, 82
   depends on others' treatment of one,
   145
 a function of others' opinions, 37;
   Maslow on happiness, 37, 56,
 happiness therefore not adequate for
   evaluating communities, 54, 57
 limits to what can count as happiness, 59
 and utilitarianism
   desire fulfillment not the essence of
   happiness, 64n.14

Happiness: and utilitarianism (*cont.*)
    difficulty of interpersonal comparisons
        of happiness, 62n.5
    fairness as well as happiness a moral
        consideration, 40
    happiness cannot be measured or
        aggregated, 7, 35–36, 41
    inferior conceptions of happiness, 38,
        61
    no available account of happiness on
        which utilitarianism can be based,
        36–38, 54, 57, 60, 121
    question whether utilitarianism can
        identify true happiness, 121; difficulty
        of trying to describe true happiness,
        37–38, 162, 166–67
    rights as well as happiness a moral
        consideration, 44
    rule utilitarianism and happiness, 45
    some acts create happiness because they
        are right, 54, 55, 101
    undertaking to maximize one's
        happiness often unsuccessful, 63n.8
    utilitarian belief that a good community
        characteristically creates happiness,
        117n.51, 167
    utilitarian views of happiness and
        motivation, 125–26, 165n.22. *See also*
        Psychological egoism
    utilitarianism overrates happiness, 36,
        54
    variety of states that can make one
        happy, 127
Hardin, Garrett, 87n.14, 156, 168
Hare, R. M., 31n.33, 186n.10
Harman, Gilbert, 5–6
Hart, David K., 154–55
Hartman, Edwin, 5, 105, 106–7, 112n.9,
    115n.35, 142n.32
Heller, Joseph, 153
Herman, Stewart W., 113nn.9,14
Hirschman, Albert O., 96, 118n.54, 168,
    170, 172, 178–79, 186n.5
Hobbes, Thomas and Hobbesianism, 3, 14,
    27n5., 69, 84, 89n.28
Hollis, Martin, 65n.30
Hume, David and Humeanism, 8, 14,
    115n.37, 132, 162, 174
Huxley, Aldous, 36, 37, 38, 39, 63n.12

Immerwahr, John, 165n.23, 187n.14
Interpretation. *See also* Values: commu-
    nities with values different from ours
    assessing a practice requires interpretive
        skill, 101, 165n.24
    implies homogeneity of values in a
        community, 70, 181
    impossibility of interpreting an action
        except as making some sense to us,
        98–99, 150–51
    indicates the point of an institution or
        practice, 24
    and limits on what we can consider
        desirable, 144
    and limits on what we can consider
        intentional, 128
    and limits on what we can consider
        moral, 23, 57–59, 100
    and limits on what we can consider
        rational, 144
    and limits on what we can consider true,
        33n.47, 53, 100, 144
    may involve critical assessment, 101
    moral philosophy interprets the terms of
        social contracts, 92, 100
    of other corporate cultures, 152, 164n.15
    problems with interpreting and applying
        moral principles, 103, 105
    propagation of interpretive beliefs gives
        people meaning, 153, 158,

Japan, culture and management in, 58,
    155–57
Japanese traditions in baseball, 112n.5,
    115n.32, 165n.24
    lifetime employment in, 169, 175
    loyalty in, 173, 179
    management of second-order desires in,
        155–56
    moral assessment of, 157, 165n.25
    strength of corporate culture in,
        163n.8
    use of songs in, 164n.18
    workers' identification with the company
        in, 156, 165n.23, 187n.14. *See also*
        Loyalty
Johnson and Johnson, 12, 150, 152
Johnson, Lyndon B., 185
Justice. *See also* Affirmative action;
    Contracts and social contract theory:
        good contract said to promote justice;
    Desert; Equality: justice and; Fairness;
    Rawls: on justice; Utility and
    utilitarianism: rule utilitarianism:
    does not guarantee justice
    cannot be weighed against utility, 66n.36
    cannot serve as a foundation for morality,
        7
    characteristics of a just organization, 110,
        118n.53

different circumstances may legitimize different conceptions of, 64n.18, 107, 108, 111, 117n.51
difficulty of criticizing local practices from the point of view of, 52, 118n.56
possibility of doing so, 53
distributive justice, 67n.49, 110, 176
doubts about theories of, 4, 5, 115n.35
essential to morality, 65n.25, 100
Friedman on, 93–94
incommensurability of goods raises questions of, 42
injustice reduced by 1964 Civil Rights Act, 78. *See also* Commons: preserving the
just consent of the governed, 39, 94
just consent of the managed, 171
local agreements normally just, 79–80, 85
as motivator, 55–57, 117n.46. *See also* Frank, Robert H.
a theory of justice requires a view of human motivation, 110–11
problems with applying principles of justice to assess communities, 52, 101–2, 104, 177, 179, 180
reciprocity and, 45, 50, 88n.24, 110, 119n.62
relationship to the good life, 6
relativist views on, 12
requires that we develop supportive feelings, 53
structure of the community is essential to defining, 5, 49, 68, 168. *See also* Rawls: basic structure of the just community

Kahneman, Daniel, 55
Kant, Immanuel, and Kantianism. *See also* Free will: Kant on, as opposed to autonomy
Aristotelian vs. Kantian ethics, 187–88n.22
denial that making people better off is the most important characteristic of morality, 30n.29
on identifying the maxim of an act, 114n.27
practical form of the Categorical Imperative, 80
not acceptable to Kant, 88n.25, 119n.62
problems about choosing between Kantianism and some other ethical theory, 98, 114n.23
on treating people as ends and not only means, 15, 106, 117n.48, 129

view that morality is derivable from rationality, 26–27n.5, 45
view that a reason to act is a univeralizable reason, 28n.12
Keeley, Michael, 71, 97, 112–13n.9, 139n.14, 170, 186n.8
Keller, Evelyn Fox, 188n.22
Klein, Jonathan, 87n.8
Knetsch, Jack, 55
Kohlberg, Lawrence, 187–88n.22
Kraus, Jody S., 88n.22
Kravis, Henry, 37, 38
Kuhn, Thomas S., 19, 30n.31, 103, 116n.40

LaFollette, Hugh, 29n.25, 66n.41, 126
Levine, Dennis, 163n.6
Lewis, Michael, 32n.41, 163n.6
Libertarians and libertarianism. *See also* Fairness, libertarian views of; Friedman, Milton; Rationality: rational maximizers: libertarian view of
on autonomy, 102, 106, 129, 176
on limits to appropriate loyalty, 173
on organizations as markets, 171
questionable assumptions of, 47, 77, 125, 182
against regulation, 64n.23
reluctance to embrace implications of the commons, 77, 169
on rights
as essential to life, 67n.49
to discriminate, 66n.35
on importance of the right to exit, 169
negative rights, 43
Nozick on property rights, 64n.16
view of moral significance of contracts, 79, 106, 168
view of the purpose of the organization, 178
Likert, Rensis, 162
Lippke, Richard L., 115n.35
Locke, John, 70
Loyalty, 5, 66n.42, 100, 186n.5. *See also* Belief, second-order: created by loyalty; Commons: loyalty may preserve; Community: good community, conditions of: exit, loyalty, and voice as; Cooperation: and loyalty; Culture, corporate: may create loyalty; Desires: second-order: loyalty creates; Emotion: and loyalty; Libertarians and libertarianism: on limits to appropriate loyalty; Moral progress: exit, voice, and loyalty support; Motivation: self-interest not the only motivator:

Loyalty (*cont.*)
  loyalty as motivator; Rationality: and
  loyalty; Reciprocity: and loyalty
characterizes a good organization, 54,
  101, 168–70, 171–75, 178–79, 181–84,
  186n.1
as a civic virtue, 171, 175
difficult to determine the appropriate
  level of, 173, 179, 181, 184
communities differ as to the
  appropriate level of, 111, 172, 178;
  varies with difficulty of entry, 172
excess is possible, 54, 118n.54, 174
may be based on caring about others'
  interests, 98, 173
may bind people where rules cannot,
  50–51, 171
Lyons, David, 46

Machiavelli, Niccolo and
  Machiavellianism, 92
MacIntyre, Alasdair, 116n.41, 117n.47,
  118n.54, 157, 162
Maitland, Ian, 154
March, James G., 162
Marcus, George E., 99
Martin, Joanne, 149
Maslow, Abraham, 37, 54, 56, 115n.33, 145
Mays, Willie, 19
McClintock, Barbara, 188n.22
McCloskey, Donald, 183
McGregor, Douglas, 154–56, 164n.16
Mendola, Joseph, 88n.22
Milgram, Stanley, 147, 149, 157
Milken, Michael, 37, 163n.6
Mill, John Stuart, 43
Mintzberg, Henry, 112n.9
Moral progress, 4, 5, 180, 184. *See also*
  Foundations and foundationalism
discussion of moral issues and, 58, 176–77
  esp. consideration of an alien culture,
  151
  esp. disagreement on moral issues,
  117n.46, 178, 181
  esp. discussion of the good life, 177, 182
exit, voice, and loyalty support, 169, 179
good community characteristically
  supports, 107, 111, 162, 178, 185
made by testing intuitions and principles
  against each other, 105
may coincide with vocabulary change, 19,
  151
not a matter of finding a foundation for
  ethics, 57, 162, 170

requires a combination of conservatism
  and reconsideration, 182
technological progress may lead to,
  116n.38
there has been, 19, 31n.38, 43, 103
  cf. scientific progress, 19, 103, 177
Morgan, Gareth, 112n.9
Motivation, 33n.45, 162, 163n.6. *See also*
  Autonomy; Commons: preserving the:
  commons preservation as
  motivator; Culture, corporate: affects
  employees' motivations; Fairness:
  considerations of fairness motivate;
  Happiness: and utilitarianism: views of
  happiness and motivation;
  Psychological egoism; Rationality:
  compatible with motivation by
  emotion, compatible with motivation
  by fairness
assumption that all moral behavior is
  motivated by altruistic motives,
  30n.28
assumption that self–interest and interest
  in others must be separate motives,
  30n.28, 165n.21
character and, 53–54, 80–83
differs from belief that some act is right,
  30n.28
differs from reason for action, 14, 15
differs from valuation, 141n.31
and ideology, 102
limits on morally good motivation,
  120n.65
limits on possible motivation, 120n.64
moral views rest on assumptions about
  motivation, 20, 89n.27
motivating people to do the right thing a
  significant managerial task, 79
and second-order desires, 125–26, 143,
  131, 134, 148, 173
self-interest not the only motivator, 10,
  14, 15, 29n.26, 125, 139n.10
desire to find agreeable principles as
  motivator, 61–62, 28n.20, 55–56,
  61–62, 80, 137, 187n.21
loyalty as motivator, 173
self-respect as motivator, 56
Theory X and Theory Y on, 154–55,
  165n.22
Theory Z on, 155
Mozart, W. A., 37, 38, 63n.12

Nagel, Thomas, 28n.12, 122, 135n.5
Nalebuff, Barry, 88nn.18,23, 110, 184

Nell, Edward, 65n.30
Nozick, Robert, 64n.16, 67n.49
Nussbaum, Martha Craven, 28n.17, 63n.6,
    66n.41, 114n.24, 115n.31, 119n.58

Ouchi, William G., 155

Paine, Lynn Sharp, 119n.58
Parfit, Derek, 28n.12, 63n.8, 66n.44,
    115n.31, 122, 138n.4
Pastin, Mark, 88n.17
Paul, Saint, 164n.19
Person, nature of. *See also* Community: and
    personal identity; Principles: personal
    identity and; Utility and
    utilitarianism: persons, utilitarian
    assumptions about; Values: and
    personal identity
  Aristotle on
    as rational and civilized, 122, 185
    as reflective and intentional, 86n.1
  person as characteristically
    autonomous, 8, 39
    communal, 134, 145
    rational and political, 111
    rational and reflective, 123–24
  person closely identifiable with
    character, 134
    higher-order desires, 133, 153
    political and familial associations, 172
    roles, 160–61
  personal identity, 122–23
    criteria of, 138nn.4,5
    and stability of preferences, 134
Pfeffer, Jeffrey, 106, 139n.12, 140n.18
Phillips, Nelson, 114n.25
Plato and Platonism. *See also* Rights: Plato
    on; Virtue: Plato on well-being and
  author not a Platonist, 4
  on piety as a moral category, 22
  view that ethics is concerned with ra-
    tional and omniscient maximizers, 46
Pluralism, 5, 8
Poe, Edgar Allan, 12
Posner, Richard, 62n.1, 117n.46
Postmodernism, 10
Pragmatism, 4, 63n.7, 118n.57, 139n.8,
    163n.3
Principles, 8, 32n.39, 42, 44, 118n.56,
    119n.58, 162n.1, 169, 176. *See also*
    Community: differing moral princi-
    ples developed in different commu-
    nities; Ethics, theoretical vs. applied;
    Foundations and foundationalism:

moral philosophy not a search for
    foundational principles of morality;
    Motivation: self-interest not the only
    motivator: desire to find agreeable
    principles as motivator; Rawls: limits
    on the Rawlsian view: public princi-
    ples must change over time; Rawls: on
    principles; Utility and utilitarianism:
    rule utilitarianism: good principles
    obligate even in the absence of
    utilitarian consequences; Virtue: as
    subject matter of ethics; cf. principles-
    based ethics
  and autonomy
    autonomy involves consistency of
      principles, 135
    autonomy may involve binding oneself
      to principles, 124, 133
    autonomy related to the extent to which
      one acts in character, 133
    considering what principles shall guide
      one's life, 134
    cultivating adherence to principles, 134
    emotion may or may not strengthen
      adherence to principles, 135
    persuasion by reference to principles
      rather than manipulation respects
      autonomy, 157
  conflicting principles, 27n.7, 147
    difficulties for business ethicists of
      competing principles, 115n.35
    hard to settle arguments where
      principles compete, 66n.37
    a morally good person can prioritize,
      65n.32, 92; by practical wisdom,
      164n.10
  and corporate culture
    corporate culture a vehicle for
      imparting principles, 146, 150
    different industries may call forth differ-
      ent cultures, hence principles, 156
    difficulty of assessing cross-cultural
      principles, 59, 100, 105
    difficulties with assessing thick concepts
      by reference to moral principles, 23
    difficulties with evaluating local
      principles by universal ones, 101–3;
      local rules clearer, 51; language as
      analogous relationship, 52
    difficulty of criticizing business practices
      by reference to ethical principles, 92,
      94
    difficulty of criticizing principles of one's
      community, 151, 166

Principles(*cont.*)
few principles natural rather than social,
145
one's values as corporate creations,
153
good community as origin of good
principles
principles and applications evolve
through activity in a community; cf.
scientific principles, 177, 179
principles come from consensus in a
good community, 185
principles insufficiently consistent with
our own moral principles are not
moral principles, 53
we arrive at good principles by seeing
what a good community requires, 9,
49, 85, 162
the inadequacy of principles to morality,
10
ephemeral nature of principles, 111
good life cannot be characterized just by
the use of principles, 6
importance of being the kind of person
who follows utilitarian principles, 48
knowledge of moral principles does not
guarantee moral action, 173
principles insufficient to create good
community, 176
virtue vs. principles-based ethics. *See*
Virtue: as subject matter of ethics: cf.
principles-based ethics
and intimate matters
in intimate matters abiding by
principles creates happiness because
it is right, 101
utilitarian principles least adequate
where people care most, 51
Williams vs. principles-based morality as
applied to intimate matters, 53
without intimate experience we would
not take principles seriously, 53–54
personal identity and
principles as part of personal identity,
123, 153
vs. personal values, 141n.25
practical issues affecting principles,
115n.30, 119n.59
advantage of simple principles, 48
characteristics of best principles, 49
difficult to find principles that would
permit rational decisions, 41
important to see where certain
principles do not work, 4
managers must attend to consequences
of principles, 35

principles that business ethics should
not apply; those that cannot be
publicly agreed to, 47–48; those that
damage people in practice, 46–47;
those that make false assumptions, 47
problems about consistency, 114n.24
why good principles obligate even in the
absence of utilitarian consequences,
48
priority of, 114n.24
neither principles nor intuitions prior,
116n.43
principles are in reflective equilibrium
with intuitions, 119n.58
principles are not known a priori, 52
similarity of moral principles to
principles of scientific inquiry, 103–4,
116n.39; moral realists on the status of
principles, 32n.39
Prinzip, Gavrilo, 114nn.27,28
Prisoner's Dilemma, 24, 112n.6
and commons, 76, 88n.17
description of the problem, 32n.42, 75
patient reciprocal strategy appropriate
for success in solving, 80, 88n.19,
187n.12
questionable standard assumptions of, 7,
10, 76
Profit, 12, 22, 35, 41
as alleged purpose of the firm, 35, 93–95,
105, 112n.8
managerial obligation to give priority
to, 40, 66n.35
as a criterion of management quality,
18–19
difficulty of defining, 19, 30n.30, 62n.5
focusing on maximizing profit may
reduce profit, 35–36, 63n.8
and organizational effectiveness
as a criterion of, 76
as a necessary condition of, 113n.11
Property, right of, 31n.38, 39–40, 77, 93,
95, 96, 113n.10. *See also* Rights:
property rights
Psychological egoism
as alleged foundation for morality, 33n.46
arguments for, 126–27, 139n.10
arguments against, 41, 49, 83, 126–27,
139n.10
Bowie and Derry on, 27n.9
Etzioni on, 29n.25
false assumption of
by economists, 9, 13–14, 106
by traditional notion of rationality,
125–27
false presuppositions of, 16–17

LaFollette on, 29n.25, 126
Theory Y compatible with, 154–56,
    165n.22

Quine, W. V. O., 19, 30n.31, 31n.35, 103,
    114n.26, 115n.36, 116n.41

Railton, Peter, 28n.12
Rapoport, Anatol, 80, 88n.18, 184
Rationality, 121, 162n.1, 180, 183–84. *See
    also* Aristotle: on human beings as
    rational and social; Community: and
    rationality; Economics and econo-
    mists: use of false assumptions by:
    assumption of rationality; Good life:
    requires satisfaction of preferences
    that are somehow rational; Kant: view
    that morality is derivable from
    rationality; Psychological egoism;
    Rawls: on rationality
  attributing intention entails attributing
    rationality, 59, 63n.12, 124, 162–63n.2
  attribution not subjective, 10
  attributing rationality presupposes some
    commonality of beliefs and desires,
    144–146
  difficulty of attributing rationality,
    163n.3
  view in organizational behavior that
    attributing rationality is impossible,
    139n.12, 157
  autonomy and, 28n.16, 39, 59, 63n.9,
    67n.47, 102, 106, 115n.37, 122,
    128–29. 132, 134, 137–38, 140n.17,
    141nn.27,29, 143–45, 168, 180
  compatible with motivation by emotion,
    135–36
  compatible with motivation by fairness,
    113n.15
  Gauthier on morality and, 14, 28n.12, 84,
    88n.17, 142n.34 167
  limits on rationality, 136
  Donaldson and Dunfee on, 118n.56
  and loyalty
    possible excess of, 174
    rationality of, 155, 174; among Japanese,
    175, 187n.14
  a matter of the appropriateness of means
    to ends, according to Hume and
    Weber, 14, 162
  not necessarily a matter of self-interest
    alone, 14
  not necessarily rational to be a free rider,
    82
  rational maximizers
    ethics is not about, 46–47, 49

a good community benefits person who
    is not, 84
libertarian view of; a fair agreement is
    one made by, 107; individuals are, 77
problems and advantages in the
    assumption that all people are,
    105–6
whether people are is a psychological
    issue, 110
self-binding and, 124, 127, 139n.6,
    142n.33, 140n.20
socializing influence of the community
    and, 185
desirable community for the rational
    person, 183
may support or undermine rationality,
    135, 137–38, 168
Rawls, John, and Rawlsianism, 7, 10, 41, 62,
    140n.19, 168, 186n.4, 187n.17. *See also*
    Community: Rawls on; Contracts and
    social contract theory: Rawlsian
    contractualism; Cooperation: Rawls
    on; Equality: in Rawls; Foundations:
    Rawls not a foundationalist; Rights:
    Rawls on; Utility and utilitarianism: as
    a Rawlsian comprehensive doctrine
  applicability of Rawlsian system to states
    but not organizations, 85–86, 89n.29,
    165n.27, 178
  claim that one's community is involved
    in one's identity, 113n.21
  exit an option for employees but not
    citizens, 168, 170, 172–73, 175
  Friedman agrees with Rawls, 95–96,
    107–11
  Rawls considers state independent of
    rest of world, 118n.53
  Rawlsian approach permits experimen-
    tation, 118n.54
  rights based on contributions in
    organizations but not in states,
    119n.61
  on autonomy
    autonomous people can choose their
    own ends, 141n.30
    autonomous people can choose their
    interests, 142n.32
    founders can choose their higher-order
    desires, 188n.24
  on basic goods, 67n.48
  on the state's obligation to protect,
    117n.52
  on whether the organization is obligated
    to protect, 117n.52
  basic structure of the just community, 7,
    83–85, 109

Rawls: on autonomy (*cont.*)
  as applied to organizations, 9, 109, 166,
    185, 189
  impartiality of Rawlsian founders, 184
  as primary subject of justice, 61, 68,
    82–83, 86n.2
contractualism, 7, 85, 87n.7, 108, 111,
    113–14, 118n.56
  exempt from Schmidtz's criticisms of
    social contract theories, 86n.4
  not a standard social contract theory,
    89n.28
  Rawls does not focus on local social
    contracts, 87n.7
on equality, 62, 108, 109, 119n.61
  free and equal person central to
    morality, 44
  only those rights can be granted to any
    citizen that can be granted to all, 44
  principle of fair and equal opportunity,
    111
  various conceptions of the good deserve
    equal respect, 42, 178
on fairness, 83, 84, 110–11, 119n.63
on justice
  and affirmative action 111
  defined by original position, 175
  distributive justice, 110
  good community does not impose a
    rigid notion of justice, 108
  impartiality as just, 89n.28
  political not metaphysical, 6, 118n.55,
    179
  procedure models equality and justice,
    108
  reward and punishment in Rawlsian
    organization, 110
views of justice should change over time,
    111
limits on the Rawlsian view
  can adjust to changing circumstances,
    118n.55
  consensus is sometimes the best we can
    do, 187n.20
  different circumstances may call for
    different conceptions of rights and
    justice, 64n.18, 117n.51
  no argument against those who do not
    take freedom and equality seriously,
    65n.25
  no independent basis for judging
    whether procedure is fair, 111,
    118nn.56,57, 119n.63
  no universality claimed for procedure,
    187n.16

not a foundationalist view, 108
  public principles must change over
    time, 109, 177
  political rather than metaphysical
    basis for justice, 6, 118n.55, 179
on principles
  a Rawlsian community achieves
    consensus on, 177
  Rawlsian impartial principles, 84
  a Rawlsian way of developing moral
    principles for business, 107–10
on rationality
  founders are impartial and rational, 173
  founders are not rational maximizers,
    110
  rational conceptions of the good may
    differ, 115n.34; just community
    seeks accommodation among them,
    118n.57
  rational vs. reasonable, 187n.21
  reflective equilibrium, 6, 116n.43,
    119n.58
  against relativism, 5–6
  on the right to one's own conception of
    the good, 115n.34
  multiple moral views are reasonable,
    117n.50
  must be compatible with others having
    the same right, 41–42, 61
  not all conceptions are equally good, 61
  state must not force a view of justice
    or utility on anyone, 42, 108, 124,
    157, 162, 178; diversity of views
    coincides with a consensus on
    public principles, 177
Rayburn, Sam, 185
Realism and realists, ethical or moral, 6,
    105, 116n.40, 162, 167
Reciprocity, 55, 89n.27, 137, 184, 185. *See
    also* Fairness: reciprocity a form of;
    Justice: reciprocity and
  and cooperation, 55, 93, 95–96, 110,
    186n.7
  and loyalty, 179, 184, 186n.4
Reflective equilibrium. *See* Rawls: reflective
    equilibrium
Relativism, 4, 26. *See also* Foundation
    and foundationalism; Interpretation
  Arrington on, 26n.2
  contrary to relativism, there are limits to
    any possible morality, 5, 6, 18–20,
    100–101
  differs from constructivism and realism,
    5–6
  differs from pluralism, 8

Edel et al. against, 66n.39
not implied by anti-foundationalism, 10,
    57
not implied by diversity of community
    standards, 69, 107
not implied by diversity of ways of dealing
    with intimate matters, 52
not implied by issues of interpretation,
    57–59
Respect, 6, 26n2, 31n.33, 40, 42, 45, 50, 52,
    55–57, 155, 161, 165n.25, 173–74, 183
Rights, 4, 49, 151, 181. *See also* Autonomy:
    and rights; Contracts and social
    contract theory: rights and;
    Libertarians and libertarianism: on
    rights; Rawls: on equality: only those
    rights can be granted to any citizen
    that can be granted to all
of animals, 86n.1
Bentham on, 39
Bork on, 43–44, 65n.24
community understandings about rights,
    166, 186n.2
of corporations, 64n.23
of distribution, 173
Donaldson and Dunfee on status of
    personal rights, 114n.24
Drucker does not take account of, 94
Dworkin on, 42, 46
of employees, 40, 42–43, 64n.17
of entry, 172
as essential to life, 59, 67n.49
as essential to morality, 31n.33, 65n.25,
    100
exit as a support of rights, 168, 169,
    187n.15
    inadequate, 171
Friedman on, 39, 93, 94, 96
of governments, 87n.9
Keeley on, 111–12n.9, 139n.14
limitations on rights as a moral criterion
    cannot be neutral arbiters among com-
        munities, 101–2, 107, 118n.56, 177
different circumstances may call for
    different conceptions of rights and
    justice, 64n.18, 117n.51
of limited use in intimate matters, 52
management and rights
    good organization protects, 42
    issues of rights cannot arise for certain
        organization theorists, 107
    negative rights, 43
    not all management directives violate,
        113n.14, 133
    not foundational, 7, 57

Nozick on, 64n.16, 67n.49
Plato on, 39, 41–42, 61
property rights, 40
    in organizations, 95
    problems about, 64nn.16,17, 113n.10
Rawls on, 109, 110–11
    equality of rights, 41–42, 44, 61
    rights in a Rawlsian organization,
        186n.9, 119n.61
    right to one's own conception of the
        good, 115n.34
    right of managers to discriminate, 66n.35
as a thick concept, 22, 25
and utility
    as a basis for rights, 6, 35, 38, 39–44, 49,
        65n.27, 175–76
    does not take adequate account of
        rights, 5, 44, 46, 60, 64n.14; Pareto
        optimality does not take adequate
        account of, 62n.3; utility and rights
        not commensurable, 63–64n.6
voice and the rights it supports, 169, 170,
    174
Rochefoucauld, Duc de la, 24, 38, 57
Role, 137, 146, 148–49, 150, 160–61,
    164n.13
Rorty, Richard, 10, 30n.31, 31n.35, 103,
    115n.30, 118n.57, 170, 174, 179
Rousseau, Jean-Jacques, 141n.27

Sartre, Jean-Paul, 115n.33
Sathe, Vijay, 149, 164n.14
Satisficing, 5
Sayre-McCord, Geoffrey, 30n.31
Scanlon, T. M., 28n.20, 49, 56, 62, 63n.7,
    80, 84, 115n.31, 137, 142n.35
Schein, Edgar H., 149
Schelling, Thomas, 62n.1, 63n.8,
    139n.6
Schmidtz, David, 55, 86n.4, 88nn.20,24,
    93, 119n.62, 168, 184
Schopenhauer, Arthur, 140n.20
Science and ethics, 3–5, 19, 30n.31, 102–4,
    107, 108, 109, 116nn.39,40,41, 162,
    177, 179. *See also* Realism and realists,
    moral and ethical
Sen, Amartya K., 29n.24, 30n.28, 54,
    62nn.3,5, 63n.10, 87n.16, 114n.22,
    125, 165n.21
Shakespeare, William, 136
Simon, Herbert A., 5, 112n.9, 162
Smith, Adam, 12, 29n.24, 74, 76, 126, 137,
    168
Socialist and socialism, 50, 102, 103, 110,
    185

Socialization, 8, 34, 36, 61, 146–49, 152, 153, 162, 167
Socrates, 186n.10, 187n.18
Solomon, Richard, 63n.12, 113n.19
Solomon, Robert C., 87n.5, 118n.57, 140n.23, 183, 186n.7
Stakeholders, 43, 85, 90, 95–96, 109, 113n.13, 118n.53, 130, 156, 158, 186nn.7,9
Stark, Andrew, 27n.7, 30n.28
Stewart, James B., 37, 163n.6
Sturgeon, Nicholas L., 116n.40

Taylor, Charles, 140n.24
Thaler, Richard, 55
Thick concepts, 22, 23, 65n.33, 98, 100, 103, 105, 144, 153. *See also* Rights: as a thick concept; Virtue: as a thick moral concept
Thoreau, Henry David, 37
Thurow, Lester, 175, 187n.14
Trist, E. L., 164n.16
Turnbull, Colin M., 32n.40, 33n.44

Ullian, Joseph S., 103
Utility and utilitarianism, 3, 15, 62n.3, 64n.23, 93–94, 95, 112n.7, 179. *See also* Commons: and utility; Contracts and social contract theory: how contracts can be assessed: utilitarianism as basis for assessment; Economics and economists: compatibility with utilitarianism; Free will: utilitarianism as supporting exercise of; Gauthier, David: claim that utility is a measure of preference; Good life: utility as requiring a conception of; Happiness: and utilitarianism; Justice: cannot be weighed against utility; Principles: the inadequacy of principles to morality: importance of being the kind of person who follows utilitarian principles; Principles: and intimate matters: utilitarian principles least adequate where people care most; Rawls: on the right to one's own conception of the good: state must not force a view of justice or utility on anyone; Rights: and utility; Virtue: and utility
as a basis for assessing communities
difficulties of evaluating communities on a utilitarian basis, 60; Rawls on, 108, 118n.56

utilitarian belief that a good community characteristically creates happiness 117n.51, 167
utilitarianism does not provide a neutral basis for evaluating cultures, 156, 165nn.24,25
commons and utility, 80
commons considerations may create obligation to do something futile, 77–78
contracts and utility
a contract cannot be breached merely on utilitarian grounds, 71
the utilitarian basis of social contracts, 71, 79, 97–98
difficulties in defining utility
diversity of and incommensurability among goods, 6, 7, 35, 41–42, 49, 60–61, 62–63n.6, 112n.9, 114n.24, 119n.60, 139n.9
not the foundation of morality, 33n.46, 55, 57, 60, 67n.46
notion of being better off seems to lead to, 16, 34, 60
persons, utilitarian assumptions about, 125–27
as individual utility maximizers, 82, 106, 140n.24; early utilitarians did not accept, 12; McGregor accepts, 155
practical problems in using
moral deliberation cannot be utilitarian, 35–36, 60, 63nn.7,8,9, 65n.29
problems with deliberating about how one wants to be happy, 66n.43
problems with interpersonal comparisons of utility, 62n.5
unsuitable for important personal issues, 51–55, 58, 115n.31, 137; family life as basis of rather than subject to utilitarian evaluation, 101
utilitarian intention does not usually have utilitarian result, 72, 82, 86, 91–92
as a Rawlsian comprehensive doctrine, 117n.51
relationship to other moral standards
difficulty of combining with other moral considerations, 5, 98, 114n.23, 115n.35
does not encompass autonomy, 64n.16
does not encompass justice and rights, 5, 38, 60, 64n.14
justice cannot be weighed against utility, 66n.36

overlap of utility with other standards:
with autonomy, 59, 125; with fairness,
50–51, 56, 57, 111; with justice, 49–51,
55–57; with promise-keeping, 99; with
Rawlsian considerations, 84; with
reciprocity, 88n.24; with rights,
65n.27, 67n.49; with virtues, 81
rule utilitarianism, 44–49, 65n.25, 77–78,
80, 112n.7
does not guarantee justice, 44–47
good principles obligate even in the
absence of utilitarian consequences,
48, 102–3, 145

Valachi, Joseph, 98
Values, 8, 42, 81, 135, 141n.25, 163nn.5,6,
164n.15
autonomy and
autonomous people act on their own
values, 39, 132
autonomous people choose their values,
131, 134
autonomous people have values based
on a coherent conception of the good
life, 128, 132, 135
stupidity, incoherence, untruth in value
systems undermine autonomy, 133
very rational people bind themselves to
values, 124, 132
communities and
community as origin of many of one's
values, 85, 108, 145, 146
community solidarity as a basis for
choosing values, 159
explanation of individual behavior by
reference to community values,
32n.44
technological change may change a
community's values, 116n.38
values come out of our social
experience, 177
whether one's values are affected by
one's community has no bearing on
autonomy, 132; good communities
promote values in a way that respects
autonomy, 146; problem of
distinguishing appropriate from
inappropriate community
determination of values, 162, 166, 168
communities with values different from
ours, 19
impossibility of imagining people having
values radically different from ours,
21; interpretation of an alien culture

involves identifying some values that
make some sense to us, 98
understanding thick concepts and
associated values, 22
values of the Ik, 23
and desires
mature people can decide what to value,
40
possible to desire what one does not
value, 131
values a special case of higher-order
desires, 131
values differ from immediate desires,
125
values give one reason for action but not
all desires do, 131
and interests
one cannot know what one's interests
will be until one knows what values
one will develop, 142n.32
not the case that what we value by
definition does us good, 139n.10
values need not be narrowly selfish, 121,
137
and language
no value-neutral language in which we
can discuss our culture, 151
most important values are least open to
discussion, 58
in a good organization explicit
discussion is part of the process of
developing shared values, 185
and organizations
corporate culture can affect people's
values, 138, 146, 149, 150, 152, 153,
155
managers can affect people's values, 48,
152
some agreement on values in an
organization is appropriate, 41
values develop in organizations, 178,
180; a good organization is hospitable
to the autonomous search for values,
43
and personal identity
changes in values compatible with
personal identity, 76, 122, 123, 124
changing values a difficult process, 103;
close relationship of self and values,
66n.44, 123, 153, 160
van Inwagen, Peter, 140n.15
Virtue, 6, 50, 83, 163n.6. *See also* Aristotle:
on virtue; Emotion: and virtue;
Loyalty: as a civic virtue

Virtue (*cont.*)
  bourgeois virtue, 120n.65, 183
  in a community
    civic virtue, 10, 43–44, 184
    enforcing virtue: conservatives favor, 43;
      Dworkin opposes, 42
    a good community encourages
      appropriate virtues, 81, 85, 88n.26
    structure supports virtue, 83
  criticizing virtue, 135, 150, 161
  developing virtues through experience,
    104
  the virtues of practical wisdom, 109,
    119n.58
  and organization
    corporate culture creates and supports
      virtue, 117n.44, 164n.17, 182
    the good organization makes virtue and
      good life coincide, 9
    managers create virtues, 35
    rewards and punishment support virtue,
      18
  Plato on well-being and, 11, 16, 27n.6
  as playing a role, 149, 160–61
  as subject matter of ethics; cf. principles-
    based ethics, 51, 60, 116n.40, 138n.3,
    164n.17, 179, 186n.6
  culture of particular interest to virtue
    ethics, 117n.44, 164n.17
  as a thick moral concept, 22, 98
  and utility, 27n.6, 81, 101

Vogel, David, 28n.11
Voice, 168–70, 174–82, 186n.5. *See also*
  Rights: voice and the rights it
  supports
Waters, James, 87n.8
Watson, Gary, 140n.15, 141n.25
Watson, Thomas, Jr., 18
Watson, Thomas, Sr., 19
Weber, Max, 14, 162
Weick, Karl E., 165n.20
Werhane, Patricia, 76, 87n.10, 118n.54
Whiting, Robert, 112n.5, 115n.32,
  165n.24
Why should I be moral?, 9, 11–13, 25,
  29n.22
Whyte, William F., 184
Williams, Bernard, 26n.3, 27n.6, 28n.14,
  53, 62n.3, 64n.22, 74, 100, 105,
  114n.24, 115n.31, 116n.40,
  140n.24
Wills, Garry, 175
Winter, Sidney, 5
Wittgenstein, Ludwig and
  Wittgensteinianism, 117n.45
Wolfe, Alan, 172, 173, 178, 186n.5,
  187n.17
Wolff, Robert Paul, 87n.9

Yankelovich, Daniel, 165n.23, 187n.14

Zimbardo, Philip, 147–48, 149, 157, 160